MELTING POTS & RAINBOW NATIONS

Jacklyn Cock and

Alison Bernstein

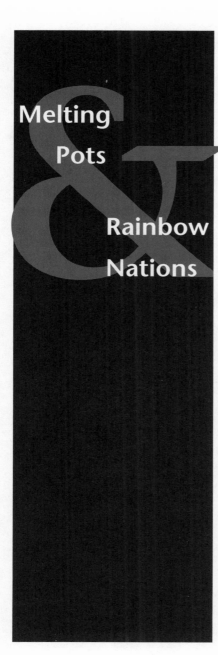

Melting
   Pots

        Rainbow
        Nations

Conversations

about

Difference

in the

United States

and

South Africa

UNIVERSITY OF
ILLINOIS PRESS
URBANA AND CHICAGO

Library of Congress
Cataloging-in-Publication Data

Cock, Jacklyn.
Melting pots and rainbow nations :
conversations about difference in the
United States and South Africa /
Jacklyn Cock and Alison Bernstein.
p.   cm.
Includes bibliographical references
and index.
ISBN 0-252-02715-9 (cloth : alk. paper)
ISBN 0-252-07027-5 (paper : alk. paper)
1. Pluralism (Social sciences)—United
States. 2. Pluralism (Social sciences)—
South Africa. 3. United States—Race
relations. 4. South Africa—Race relations.
5. Minorities—United States.
6. Minorities—South Africa. 7. Difference
(Psychology) 8. Equality. 9. Biological
diversity—United States. 10. Biological
diversity—South Africa. I. Bernstein,
Alison R., 1947– . II. Title.
E184.A1C63   2002
305.8'00973—dc21   2001002658

For Emma and Julia

Contents

Acknowledgments

This book is the product of a decade-long conversation during which we benefited greatly from the ideas and analysis of many friends and colleagues. In this regard, we would like especially to thank Susan Berresford, Blanche W. Cook, Claire Coss, Cynthia Enloe, Susan Heath, Melvin Oliver, Joan W. Scott, and Margaret Wilkerson for their sound advice and helpful critiques.

In addition, several individuals provided crucial assistance in bringing our divergent worlds together, making our "virtual" conversations possible. We are grateful to Alsie Falconer and Will Miller for their patience and professionalism in helping us to bridge our own digital divides. Brandi Brimmer helped with the final edits. Also, we wish to thank Joan Catapano, our editor, whose support, as she made her transition from Bloomington to Urbana, was unwavering.

Lastly, we wish to acknowledge the inspiration we have drawn from the many women in South Africa and the United States who continue to struggle for social justice and equality. We hope our effort has, in some way, helped to amplify their voices.

Introduction

Paddling a canoe in opposite directions is exhausting. If the alligators sunning themselves in the Everglades had been watching us, they would have observed a ridiculous scene. The two women canoeists clearly had different agendas: one was agitated, paddling away from the bank and trying to put as much distance between the canoe and an eight-foot-long alligator as possible. The other was trying to get closer and talking excitedly about alligator behavior, how they engage in foreplay for three days before finally mating, their delicate eating habits, and so on.

That was us on a summer's day in 1991. We had rented a canoe, named it *Harpies Bizarre,* and set out to explore the dark waters of the Everglades for a few days. We wanted to feel its wildness, see its creatures—turtles, manatees, crabs, and alligators—and smell the mud of the mangrove swamps. It was also the start of a partnership that has involved intense debate and discussion over the last ten years.

This book is a record of an improbable conversation between two middle-aged women who live eight thousand miles apart begun when one had turned fifty and the other forty-four. We are an unlikely couple—one, a New York Jewish intellectual and mother of twins whose idea of nature used to be "a walk through Central Park," and the other, a spoiled white middle-class South African academic who loves birds as much as books and initially had no interest in children. We have to work hard at bridging the separations of space and time. So this is also a book about how the two of us have tried to connect our contrasting identities and contexts in a relationship in which being equal does not mean being the same.

The idea of putting this book together came to us in the middle of the night in March 1997 during a nightmarish bus journey to the small Brazilian town of Ouro Preto to see Elizabeth Bishop's home. Born in Nova Scotia, Bishop was an American poet who traveled most of her life in search of a place to belong and spent her happiest years—sixteen of them—in Brazil with Lota Soares, her lover. She is one of the many women we refer to in this book who chose to ignore the life script prescribed for women of her class and time.

To gain inspiration in the middle of the night is fitting, since the night serves as one marker of our dissimilarities. One of us lives in Johannesburg, South Africa, which is seven hours ahead of New York, where the other resides. Thus one of us is often asleep while the other is rushing from one meeting to another.

Despite these differences in time and space, we have been engaged for the last few years in a conversation to try to understand the relationship between "difference" and "disadvantage" in our respective societies during the last decade of the twentieth century. This book records the products of this conversation, which has taken place in settings around the world, and it describes some of the people, places, and ideas we have encountered along the way.

The bulk of the conversation is communicated in six essays in which we compare and contrast difference and disadvantage with regard to various aspects of culture, gender, race, sexual orientation, and biology. We have focused on differences assumed to be biologically based and have demonstrated how they play out in the almost opposing contexts of the United States and South Africa. For example, in chapter 1 we compare the South African notion of nonracialism to the American notion of multiracialism and show how the two societies are moving in opposite directions as regards certain policies, such as Affirmative Action. In chapter 3 we compare the San with southwestern American Indian cultures. In chapter 5 we analyze the dramatically disparate forms gender politics have taken in the United States and South Africa as illustrated by two women's organizational initiatives, the National Organization for Women and the Women's National Coalition. As we proceed, we try to make the book more colorful and readable by illustrating through excerpts from letters and diary entries some of our own experiences that relate to these issues. The outcome is a discussion of difference on three levels—personal or experiential, contextual, and conceptual or theoretical.

Currently, difference and diversity are framed in opposing ways in our respective countries. The United States, a society that has historically claimed to value diversity and has created a melting pot of cultures, seems to be moving toward closed borders and a heightened intolerance and repression of difference. At the same time, apartheid South Africa, a society that has historically come to be synonymous with racism and the denial of human dignity, is struggling to create a rainbow nation that celebrates difference.

While our focus is the relationship between difference and disadvantage, it must be stressed that we are both products of privilege—one of us from the very best of American education at Vassar and Columbia University and the other from the benefits that the apartheid system conferred upon whites. This book also reflects the privileges we currently enjoy—one through her work at a large philanthropic organization in the United States and the other through work with small nongovernment organizations and at an elite South African university.

The foundation world and the academy provide divergent platforms for social engagement that could perhaps be contrasted as critique and coalition. The academic project is about critique, and the resulting research is often not made accessible to a wider audience or translated into policy proposals and problem solving. Frequently academic work is reduced to building individual reputations through criticizing other people's work. Academics are not trained to be appreciative and supportive of one another. By contrast, modern philanthropy is about building coalitions—about enabling other people to do things. We try to connect the two projects through one's aspiration to be an "activist-academic," which means linking academic teaching and research to political struggles, and through the other's commitment to intellectual work, which she uses to ground her philanthropic interventions in sound analysis. In various ways, much of our work in these institutions is concerned with studying and protecting diversity so that it is not interpreted as deficiency or disadvantage.

The beginning of a new century is a good time to be writing about difference because we have entered an era of globalization that is deepening inequalities and divisions both between developed and nondeveloped countries and between the marginalized and the rich within nations. The gap between the rich and the poor both within and between nations is growing. However, the very changes in technology that are contributing to these disparities—the rise of e-mail and the Internet and cheap international air travel—have made this relationship and our conversations about difference and disadvantage possible. Apart from our unconventional status as middle-aged women writers, our unique perspectives and some of our experiences as an American and as a South African could be relevant to people trying to understand these changes.

We engage in this conversation as lesbians and feminists. This process includes personal disclosures and an acknowledgment of a few of the extraordinary women we have been privileged to encounter, directly or indirectly, who have influenced us. Our main concern is how these women have dealt with difference in their lives. This includes women such as Wilma Mankiller, the first woman principal chief of the Cherokee Nation, the second largest tribe in the United States, and Thenjiwe Mtintso, who was transformed from a guerrilla fighter to a parliamentarian in South Africa's negotiated revolution from apartheid to democracy. We refer to Frene Ginwala, who became the speaker of South Africa's first democratically elected Parliament, Audre Lorde, the first black lesbian to be named a poet laureate in the United States, and Ruth First, who was assassinated by agents of the apartheid state in 1982.

We talk of the struggles of some of our feminist forebears who believed that the differences between men and women should not be the grounds of women's exclusion and disadvantage. We comment on American women such as Eleanor Roosevelt and our experience of visiting her home at Val-Kill in New York as well as pioneering

South African feminists such as Olive Schreiner, whose presence we felt in her desert home in Craddock, South Africa.

We speak of other women who have challenged the conventional understandings of sexuality. They tried to—and did—live differently. We focus on women such as Gertrude Stein and Alice B. Toklas, whose apartment we tracked down in Paris, and of our visit to Wales to see where "the Ladies of Llangollen" lived.

We write of women we have encountered such as Jane Goodall, whose struggles to preserve biodiversity have impressed us, and about Mamphela Ramphele, whose inauguration as the first black woman vice chancellor of the University of Cape Town we were privileged to attend. All these women were following scripts that were radically different from those prescribed for women of their class, race, and time, but Elizabeth Bishop was perhaps the most innovative of them. Along with Marion North and Alexander David-Neel, Bishop has been a guide in our travels.

At this time of doubt and threat, when feminism seems to have lost much of its revolutionary potential, it is important to reassert these themes of independence, solidarity, and support among women. The essence of feminism is a redefinition of women's identity and we need models and examples of strong, feminist identities. The scholar Carolyn G. Heilbrun emphasizes that "women catch courage from the women whose lives and writings they read."[1] But finding stories of both solidarity and independence among women is not easy. Trying to do so is vital as we attempt to strengthen and widen networks of support and sharing among women and supportive men.

For us, feminism has analytical, political, and personal aspects. Analytically, it means that we recognize that all experience is shaped by gender relations, which operate in diverse systemic ways and contexts to privilege men and subordinate women. This implies a broader focus than that involved in the notion of "women's issues" because it acknowledges that all experience is gendered. Politically, feminism means a commitment to struggling to end these unequal relations—in global terms it is women of color, rural women, and poor women who are most seriously disadvantaged. We identify with an independent women's movement—a strong, collective women's voice rooted in civil society and thus independent from the state. Personally, feminism for us means trying to realize the principles of autonomy and solidarity with other women. It also means honoring the women from whom we have learned.

These characteristics underline the complexities we have struggled with while working out how to be feminists in our own way. We have not asserted a monolithic conception of Western feminism. On the contrary, we have applied a feminist lens to specific historical moments and particular localities and have used it to reveal oppression, subordination, resistance, and possibility. We have, however, tried to learn from other women—both historical and contemporary individuals—who have grappled with and lived "different" lives and thereby exemplified some of the transformative potential feminism contains.

Our book illustrates this potential in a variety of ways. We use it to explain how understanding difference and disadvantage can illuminate struggles for justice. We have pointed to the lives and experiences of little-known women, not all of whom would claim the identity of feminist, but who confronted difference in path-breaking ways.

This power of feminism is especially important to assert at this moment in history. Women's movements around the world have affected institutions, thinking, and the material lives of women, but their very existence has resulted in a paradox. Globally, both poverty and power have been feminized. At the same time that increasing numbers of women have access to political power, increasing numbers of women are living in poverty.

Carolyn G. Heilbrun has observed, "I have read many moving lives of women, but they are painful, the price is high, the anxiety is intense, because there is no script to follow, no story portraying how one is to act, let alone any alternative stories."[2] This book comes out of our search for such scripts and alternative stories in the broader project of trying to understand the relationship between difference and disadvantage. As a result, this book is more than an intellectual exploration, more than a collection of essays about differences of gender, race, sexual orientation, culture, and biology, more than glimpses of interesting women. In the letters and diary entries we try to describe some of our experiences, such as our feelings as we tracked lemurs in Madagascar, tried to decipher rock paintings done by San people in a remote area of the Drakensberg Mountains in South Africa, went to the Old Jewish Cemetery in Prague, and visited Theresienstadt, the transit post to Auschwitz during the Holocaust. The result is probably a mixture of awe and what the American sociologist Manuel Castells has described as "informed bewilderment"[3] as we continue to try to make sense of the relationship between difference and disadvantage in this increasingly complex and crisis-ridden world.

Genocide represents the ultimate in the continuum that begins with difference and can lead to discrimination and disadvantage. We talked a lot about the Holocaust when we visited Prague. In particular we discussed Hannah Arendt's view that the Jerusalem court should have refused to sentence Adolph Eichmann because he was guilty, not of a crime against the Jewish people alone, but against the whole of humanity. Arendt claimed that the monstrousness of the Holocaust is "minimized" by a tribunal that represents just one nation. Genocide, she stressed, is an attack upon human diversity— that is, upon a characteristic of the human status.

Talking about these issues in Prague gave them a special depth and intensity. It's a wonderful city of old stone, water, and bridges. We were moved by the historic Jewish quarter, one of the oldest ghettos in Europe, dating back at least to the tenth century. We spent most of our time in the Old Jewish Cemetery. Because space was restricted, more than twelve thousand graves were superimposed on one another in a dozen layers, so that the crammed, ancient tombstones lean against

each other. We also saw the dark interior of the thirteenth-century synagogue with its cave-like vestibules for women to observe the services. Most touching of all was a collection of drawings and paintings by children from Theresienstadt, the transit concentration camp, which made us decide to hire a car and driver and see it for ourselves. Less than thirty miles away, it took us a brief journey to reach, but when we got there, it seemed like a world apart and very disturbing.

The small fortress is a depressing complex of stone buildings. According to Hannah Arendt it was designed to serve as a ghetto for certain privileged categories of Jews—functionaries, prominent people, and German Jews over sixty-five years of age. However, it soon came to play the role of a transit camp for Jews and others being sent to the extermination camps like Auschwitz, which were situated primarily in Poland. These victims were mainly Czechs, including Jews and people arrested for various forms of protest against the Nazi system. Altogether thirty-five thousand people died in Theresienstadt from malnutrition and disease.

The whole place is a powerful reminder of the connection between exclusion and extermination and of the human capacity for both cruelty and creativity. The inmates organized literary evenings, delivered lectures, gave concerts, and staged theatrical performances. We argued a lot about the accuracy of Arendt's analysis of Jewish collaboration with the Nazi extermination machine. It's painful stuff for Alison, whose great-grandparents came to the United States as penniless Jewish immigrants in the 1890s.

What I remember most vividly about the whole visit is a tiny detail—a stone carving of an owl above the crematorium. It jarred horribly with its green, leafy, tranquil setting. Of course one thinks of owls as symbols of wisdom, but the Nazis used them to reinforce a sinister image of the Jews.

1

Race, Difference, and Disadvantage: The Politics of Nonracialism and Multiracialism

On a mild May 1 night in 1992, we attended a party in Princeton to celebrate the publication of Gail Pemberton's book *The Hottest Water in Chicago: On Family, Race, Time, and American Culture.* We had some disappointments—Jackie had hoped to meet two of Princeton's superstars, Cornel West and Toni Morrison, but neither showed. However, there was lots of whiskey, fried chicken, cornbread, and great dancing to the music of the Pointer Sisters. Everyone was on the dance floor—men with women, women with women, blacks with whites, students with teachers. Jackie wondered whether this behavior was at all typical of Princeton parties. I said it was a highly unusual case of nonracialism in action and confirmed Nadine Gordimer's claim that there was more socializing between black and white people in apartheid South Africa than in the United States. Sadly, we have not been to such a party since, but it remains a hopeful memory and got us talking about the disparate politics of race in our two societies.

Race as a Social and Historical Construct

In 1903, the eminent African American civil rights leader and Harvard-trained philosopher W. E. B. Du Bois wrote, "The problem of the Twentieth Century is the problem of the color-line."[1] No single statement has been more prophetic regarding the last one hundred years of U.S. and South African history. Racism has been the most explosive issue in both societies, triggering its worst disturbances. Apartheid was one of the most offensive and systematized forms of racial oppression in the whole of human history. Many believed that this oppression would end in a bloodbath in which white South Africans—who constituted less than 20 percent of the population—would perish. Instead, in 1994, after a long struggle, South Africa repudiated apartheid and proclaimed itself a nonracial democracy.

In the United States, despite over five decades of legislation outlawing racial discrimination, race is still the "American dilemma," as Gunnar Myrdal noted in his book of that title in 1944. In 1997 it led Bill Clinton to create a special presidential advisory committee that he hoped would address "the unfinished work of our times to lift the burden of race and redeem the promise of America."[2] Nearly one hundred years after Du Bois's proclamation, another Harvard philosopher, Cornel West, remarked, "Race is the most explosive issue in American life precisely because it forces us to confront the tragic facts of poverty and paranoia, despair and distrust."[3] Ironically, in South Africa today, where poverty is surely more widespread and where the legacy of apartheid has left behind deep levels of distrust, reconciliation has replaced paranoia and hope has replaced despair.

While South Africa and the United States have similar problems with racism, their constructions of "race" as a category are almost diametrically opposed. In the post-apartheid era, the fundamental social ideology of South Africa is *nonracialism,* which contrasts with the emerging American concept of a *multiracial* society. But before we examine how difference is understood in racial terms in the world's oldest democracy and in one of its youngest, it is important first to understand what is meant by the term *race.*

Deeply held convictions on all sides of the political spectrum to the contrary, no intrinsic biological basis exists for this concept. Scientists in the late twentieth century have finally concluded that "race" is a cultural construct, not a biological category. As the Columbia University biologist Robert Pollack has explained, "Molecular-historical biology has told us something important about our species: despite our tendency to live or die by the dream that it might be so, none of us has come from a pure ethnic or racial stock. . . . We now know that the genes of today's so-called 'white' Europeans are a hybrid intermediate between Asian and African ancestors."[4] But more important, the African and Asian ancestors did not emerge from specific racial gene pools, but were hybrids themselves.

Where did this categorization by race come from if it has no firm biological basis? Most historians trace the history of racist thinking to the fifteenth century, which has come to be known in the West as the "age of exploration," though many of the peoples the Europeans encountered during this time would surely call it the "age of exploitation." Following the lead of European colonizers, Western science tried and failed to find a biological basis for human differences. First, scientists relied on definitions of individuals' physical characteristics: skin color, hair type, and physique. Up through the first half of the twentieth century, scientists, joined by anthropologists, argued that there were three relatively distinct groups of people, namely, the Caucasoid, the Mongoloid, and the Negroid. As late as 1962, many scientists were convinced five human racial subspecies existed: the Australoid, the Mongoloid, the Caucasoid, the Congoid, and the Capoid (the last two corresponding with the main black African populations and the San of southern Africa, respectively). Even though researchers have demonstrated that the concept of race has no scientific validity and, in fact, that there is more genetic variation within one human so-called race than there is between that so-called race and another, such outmoded terminology has not declined.

Interestingly, the continued persistence of the belief that race constitutes a separate biological category can be contrasted and compared with the categories of sex and gender. As the historian of women Joan W. Scott has pointed out, the term *gender* was coined to resist the reduction of social relations to physical sexual differences. The sex/gender distinction would analytically separate the physical body from the social body. Thus, she writes, "it would then no longer be conceivable that anatomy was destiny."[5] Unfortunately, a similar distinction has not been drawn between the physical characteristics of "race" and its social construction.

While race is not a verifiable biological condition, the concept nevertheless has deep social and historical significance in the United States and South Africa and has been used in both societies to exclude and discriminate. The modern construction of race began when Europeans conquered and colonized these parts of the world. Racism, defined as dominance or hostility to those with racial characteristics, origins, and identity that are assumed to be different and inferior, began as a hierarchy in which physical appearance was the first marker. For example, Thomas Jefferson, writing in 1789, the year the American constitution was drafted, argued, "The first difference that strikes us is that of color. . . . And is the difference of no importance? Is it not the foundation of a greater or less share of beauty in the two races? Are not the fine mixtures of red and white . . . in the one preferable . . . to that immovable veil of black . . . in the other race? . . . The circumstance of superior beauty is thought worthy of attention in the propagation of our horses, dogs and other domestic animals; why not in that of man?"[6] Racism in the United States began with this kind of denigration of black physical features and quickly moved from external physical attributes like skin color to a consideration of whether people who looked different were actually not of the same species.

The comparison of blacks to animals has always been a common theme in racist discourse in South Africa and in the United States. Defining certain people as animals is a means of distancing members of other so-called racial groups; it is used to strip them of rights, to locate them outside the boundaries of human/humane treatment. In apartheid South Africa, the implication of this rhetoric was that black Africans did not have the same needs and feelings as whites. As a result, they could not be citizens, but they could be paid lower wages and be forced to work excessively long hours under bad conditions, particularly as farm and domestic workers. In this way racism became linked to the power of one group to exploit the labor of another. In the United States, slavery provided a powerful pretext for viewing blacks as something other than fully human. Blacks' physical characteristics set them apart in white's eyes, and therefore it was easy to treat them as animals and use them for hard physical work. Once they were assigned to this subordinate role, it was much easier to continue to view them as inferior. This racism was even codified in law. According to the U.S. Constitution, a freed black was legally

Alison,

Horrifying stuff from the Truth and Reconciliation Commission about how agents of the apartheid regime viewed opponents as outside the boundaries of human identity. For example, a young activist, Stanza Bopape, was murdered through torture by electric shock that induced a heart attack; then his body was thrown into a crocodile-infested river. What gives the horror a special edge is that the policemen testifying about this in their amnesty applications are free at present—as are the people who ordered the assassination of my former colleague David Webster. So the long prison sentence given this week to the man who pulled the trigger—a particularly unsavory character called Ferdi Barnard—is deeply unsatisfying. The people who gave the orders and who created the climate that allowed this pattern of torture and abuse are living soft and comfortable lives.

Then even more horrifying stuff about the demonization of apartheid's opponents is emerging from the commission about the regime's chemical and biological weapons program. We knew some of what was happening at one of the South African Defense Force front companies, Roodeplaat Research Laboratories, but we did not know how extensive and diabolical the program was. It manufactured lethal poisons and biological agents for use against the apartheid government's enemies, as well as lethal bacteria capable of decimating entire populations, specifically "pigmented people." The commission was told about cigarettes laced with anthrax, chocolates with botulism, whiskey with weed killer, vaccines to reduce the fertility of black women, tons of ecstasy and mandrax for "riot control," salmonella put into the sugar at an ANC conference.

One plan was to induce brain damage, through slow chemical poisoning, in Mandela after his release. The anti-apartheid activist Frank Chikane became ill while visiting the United States in 1989 and a highly toxic paraoxane was found to have been dabbed onto five pairs of his underpants. One person giving evidence to the commission said that it would have been lethal if it had come into contact with a larger area of his body. Clearly there is much we will never know, and it's possible that many deaths that seemed natural were the result of poisoning. A Pan-African Congress political detainee, Jeff Masemola, died inexplicably immediately after being released, and the ANC's Harry Gwala ended up paralyzed after his detention. The commission also heard evidence of a chemical attack on Frelimo troops in Mozambique as late as 1992, and it's been suggested that drugs were fed into politically active communities to destabilize them. It could be that the present gang warfare in the Cape, for instance, is the legacy. All this involved hideously cruel experiments on dogs, baboons, and even a chimpanzee—experiments such as blowtorching animals to test heat-resistant uniforms.

Allegedly this was all done on the instructions of a Dr. Wouter Basson of the SADF. He was shown on television the other night and presented the face of evil—a bland, unfeeling, psychopath, nothing of the banal about him at all. Earlier this year I suggested (half-jokingly) to Ronnie Kasrils, the deputy minister of defense, that he should be assassinated. But Ronnie laughed and said, "We don't do things that way." I suppose we should be grateful that this information is surfacing now. But it feels like the tip of the iceberg—most perpetrators of human rights violations have not come forward. The commission has received twenty thousand submissions from victims and only seventy-five hundred amnesty applications from perpetrators. In only a handful of cases have political leaders been directly implicated. Also the promotion of the National Unity and Reconciliation Act that established the commission has a very narrow definition of what a human rights violation is. It doesn't include the 3.5 million people dispossessed of their land and homes. For these millions of "surplus people" who were resettled in remote, desolate areas, this was a genocidal policy.

considered to be the equivalent of three-fifths of a white man. Southern white slaveholders took racism beyond denigrating physical characteristics to assign behavioral traits deemed inferior—such as lazy, slow-witted, and childlike—to black slaves.

In colonial times, then, racism in the form of prejudice against those with physical characteristics that were assumed to be inferior became the chief justification for enslaving Africans; this made their labor free and available as a form of property. But owning humans was difficult to justify unless those humans were stripped of their humanity and put in a different category. What makes racism especially venal and morally repugnant is that it is connected to the power to operationalize prejudice. Racism is racial prejudice linked to power that isolates, separates, or exploits others. It is much more than a negative attitude toward someone or a group based on a belief in another group's superior racial origin. Racism is often institutionalized in discriminatory legal and social systems.

Over time the meaning of *race* has shifted from denoting a group of people sharing distinct physical characteristics to, as the legal scholar Patricia Foster has written, "connoting power relations between groups. . . . Race is now a social construction, rooted in the structures of exploitation, power and privilege that was imposed on subordinated groups of people five centuries ago and continues to affect the social standing of groups today."[7]

Indeed, while many people now acknowledge that race has no biological basis and that therefore racism is irrational, they believe this hatred is functional. Racism persists because it serves a purpose and confers benefits on one group while denying those benefits to another. As the American historian Gerda Lerner has pointed out, the social construct of race exists on three different levels of reality: (1) "as a tool for dominance which has become institutionalized in the United States and in some other countries (institutionalized racism); (2) as a historic experience, a force shaping the lives of the designated group (experiential racism); and (3) as a distinguishing marker for the oppressed group transformed into a mark of pride, resistance, and a tool for liberation (resistance formation)."[8] In both the United States and South Africa, this reclaiming of race has been a powerful weapon in the civil rights movement and the anti-apartheid struggle.

In Lerner's approach, race is a process: "Gender, race, ethnicity and class are processes through which hierarchical relations are created and maintained in such a way as to give some men power and privilege over other men and over women by their control of material resources, sexual and reproductive services, education and knowledge."[9] All are systems of domination and all are interconnected and interlocking. This nexus of power has important implications for political organizing. Further, Lerner has written that, of all these processes, the subordination of women occurred first in human history, and it set the example for discrimination based on race, ethnicity, and class. The differentiation of peoples by sex, Lerner asserts, lies at the foundation of all discriminatory processes. While it is not possible to confirm or deny her claim, the presence of patriarchy in virtually all societies suggests the power of sex-based distinction and subordination.

While race has physical referents in the sense that a racial group comprises people who share certain broad physical characteristics, such as skin color, an ethnic group comprises people who share a sense of belonging on the basis of cultural criteria, such as language, religion, and custom. It is arguable that ethnicity is replacing race as the central marker of identity in both South Africa and the United States. While the boundaries of these identities are not sharp or static, the sociologist Manuel Castells has warned that the global future may see "a tribalization of society in communities built around primary identities."[10]

Like racial identities, ethnic groups are "invented" or "imagined" social constructs that are constantly shaped and reshaped. Neither type of identity is primordial or essential: racial identity is not located in a biological essence and ethnic identities are not anchored in social or cultural institutions. Nor are these identities inherently antagonistic or irreconcilable with a national identity—a group of people with political sovereignty over a common territory. Ethnicity, however, is an increasingly powerful and divisive force in the world as it is mobilized and manipulated for political ends. That political and ethnic borders do not correspond means that ethnonationalist movements will increasingly challenge existing nation-states.

An example of such a challenge in South Africa would include political groupings such as the Afrikaner separatist movement and the Inkatha Freedom party (IFP) of Gatsha Buthelezi, who has attempted to mobilize a militant Zulu nationalism for political purposes. But this ethnic emphasis is reminiscent of the apartheid government's use of tribalism and ethnicity to maintain white domination. Ironically, the IFP has attracted a number of white members, several of whom are prominent Buthelezi advisers. These whites were drawn to his rejection of economic sanctions as a means of exerting pressure on the apartheid regime and his glorification of free enterprise.

The Politics of Racial Difference: Comparing the United States and South Africa

When Nelson Mandela called for the creation of a "rainbow nation" in his May 10, 1994, inauguration speech as president of South Africa, he echoed Jesse Jackson's appeal for a "rainbow coalition" in his unsuccessful 1988 bid for the U.S. presidency. Despite the metaphorical resonances, however, race—the subtext of these rainbow images—is understood very differently in these countries' politics. Under apartheid South Africa, the dominant discourses of both liberation and subordination centered on race. In the United States, the race question, as the Nobel Prize–winning author Toni Morrison has warned us, is hidden and covert. More than fifty years after Gunnar Myrdal's ground-breaking study, *An American Dilemma,* Americans still have enormous difficulty confronting and finding a common ground on which to move beyond the politics of race. During the nineties, race politics were everywhere—in the O. J. Simpson trial, in the Los Angeles riots, in the Million Man March on Washington, and in the Amadou Diallo shooting in New York City—and yet it is nowhere in the formal political system. This political subtext is often barely audible even four decades since the civil rights struggles of the sixties. For example, no comparable study of race relations has been completed since *An American Dilemma* and it is not even clear whether anyone, white or black, would undertake such an impossible task today. As Lani Guinier, a public victim of America's confusion about racial issues, lamented, "What is missing from public discourse is a vision of the future in which society commits itself to working through, rather than running from, our racial history and racial present."[11]

In short, in the United States race is not talked about enough nor are racist practices always confronted, and yet the issue still divides the population as bitterly now as it ever has. An ominous finding of a 1997 Gallup poll was that a majority of Americans—58 percent of blacks and 54 percent of whites—agree that relations between blacks and whites will always be a problem. Sadly, the most despairing among those polled were young, college-educated blacks. A similar study conducted by the Joint Center for Political Studies in Washington, D.C., a distinguished black-led think tank, came to roughly the same conclusions. And, in July 2000, a nationwide *New York Times* poll found that, on many questions, particularly those related to whether blacks are treated equitably and whether race plays too large a role in the national discourse, blacks and whites seemed to be living on different planets. Blacks were four times more likely than whites to say blacks were treated less fairly in the workplace.

Clearly, the public evidences considerable pessimism about progress in race relations. Both the general population and blacks as a subgroup in 1997 showed widespread concern about the state of race relations in the nation as a whole—87 percent of blacks and 80 percent of the general population felt that race relations in the United States were poor or only fair. Another sign of the intractability of racial politics has been the differing reactions of blacks and whites to a piece of bipartisan legislation calling upon Congress to apologize to blacks for slavery—61 percent of nonwhites supported it and 60 percent of whites opposed it.[12]

Hugh Price, president of the Urban League, reported in 1995 that a "hardening of racial attitudes is happening on all sides, not just among whites."[13] For instance, the black Muslim leader Louis Farrakhan is frequently alleged to say that murder and lying come easy for white people. Analogously, a negative stereotype of whites in South Africa is hardening around qualities such as selfishness, materialism, greed, and cruelty. The politics of race in South Africa, however, contrast sharply with those in the United States.

The metaphor of South Africa as a "rainbow nation" is firmly anchored in the broader concept of nonracialism that serves as the prevailing ideology of the African National Congress (ANC), which led South Africa's struggle and is now the majority party. In South Africa,

MELTING POTS & RAINBOW NATIONS

the rainbow is an ambiguous and paradoxical metaphor given the ANC's commitment to nonracialism. The ANC has an inclusive style and its emphasis on nonracialism and reconciliation are important building blocks in creating a national identity. The discourse of non-racialism does have the potential to ignore or erode particular ethnic identities. Two such identities—those of Zulus and Afrikaners—are potentially divisive, as they have strong separatist tendencies. Importantly, this ideological position does not involve a denial of racial inequalities; indeed, the liberation struggle was directed precisely against such inequalities and the coercion that maintained them. The ANC worked to combat the institutionalized racial exclusions of apartheid, which governed where blacks lived, what work they could do, where they went to school, and whom they could marry. Nonracialism, however, does mean the denial of race as an operative category in the political process and public life and calls for nationalistic solidarity and a common South African citizenship, irrespective of race or ethnicity.

This inclusive ANC nationalism has always been linked to its notion of democracy, which was similarly broadly defined to include the democratization of both the state and of civil society. The commitment was, and is, to the creation of a nonracial democracy, a vision in which the coupling of nationalism and democracy is pivotal. Many of the ANC's ideas were inspired by the role of progressive whites in student politics, the trade unions, the South African Communist party, and the ANC itself. But some of them came directly out of the American civil rights movement, and it is not surprising that much of Mandela's imagery is reminiscent of the soaring, spiritual legacy of Martin Luther King Jr.

South Africa's commitment to nonracialism has recently and increasingly been put to the test. Nelson Mandela made a strong appeal to blacks and whites in 1993 in the aftermath of the assassination of the highly popular black leader Chris Hani. Because he feared a bloodbath, Mandela went on national television and appealed to whites and blacks to stand together. "A white man, full of prejudice and hate, came to our country and committed a deed so foul that our whole nation now teeters on the brink of disaster," he said. "But a white woman, of Afrikaner origin, risked her life so that we may know and bring to justice the assassin."[14]

Alison,

This week the students marched peacefully on the ANC national headquarters to protest against Mandela's call to white university administrators to clamp down strongly on disruptive black students. I'm wondering where the new deputy vice chancellor, William Makgoba, stands in all this. It worries me that he's been out of the country for so long and wasn't part of the 1980s struggles in which the ideology of nonracialism was really practiced. I suspect he might subscribe to a different ideology—he was interviewed recently and talked about how Witwatersrand must become an African university, meaning not only that the student and academic populations should be more racially representative but also that the system of governance should be more broadly consultative.

These are sentiments I agree with totally but then he is quoted as saying, "Whites are used to an autocratic, top-down system which traditionally is not Africa's way." This kind of racial essentialism is really dangerous and threatens the ANC's tradition of nonracialism. It makes me feel lonely and hopelessly middle-aged and white and middle class. Also, how does one distinguish between this glorification of African culture and views like that of the vice chancellor of Zimbabwe University, who believes in witches and defends "traditional" methods of identifying them.

It's a strange time and our gains feel fragile.

Nonracialism is not just rhetoric. The ANC has put this ideology into practice. Both whites and blacks have played key roles in the ANC leadership. In the first post-apartheid government, several cabinet posts were held by these same nonblack Africans, among them speaker of the parliament, minister of justice, and minister for land reform. This kind of integration has disappeared since the late sixties in the United States. Indeed, it is difficult to imagine a successful grass-roots nonracial movement in the United States today. Although labor unions, environmentalists, and feminists aspire to build coalitions across different racial and ethnic groups, and civil rights organizations like the Urban League are rebuilding their power bases among whites as well as blacks, all too frequently this multiracial goal breaks down in the selection of largely white or black leadership and in the choice of focus issues. Abortion rights or protecting endangered species are seen by a majority of blacks as irrelevant, while many whites cannot see the urgency of correcting persistent poverty and economic inequality.

Beyond ideology and beyond the "rainbow," several demographic and economic factors make nonracialism more possible and more palatable in South Africa than in the United States. First, people of color, and in particular, black Africans, will always be the majority in South Africa, and the new democratic system cannot easily subordinate the will of the majority in the way that the U.S. government has been able to subordinate the black minority for more than two centuries. Second, the ANC can rely on a sense of place and a sense of history to unite the people of South Africa. As Nadine Gordimer wrote about black South Africans in the *New York Times* in 1997, "Despite neglect in official education, their *languages have remained intact as mother tongues. Their names are their own ancestral names.* Nothing—neither cruel apartheid denigration nor liberal paternalism—has destroyed their identity. They know who they are."[15] In this knowledge of place, black Africans have more in common with American Indians than they do with African Americans. It is estimated that some 75 million Africans were uprooted, sold into slavery, and brought to the United States. Clearly, blacks and whites share a three-hundred-year history on American soil, but the circumstances that gave rise to this relationship make simple appeals to a common nationhood problematic. Third, South Africa cannot survive, let alone prosper, without the labor of black Africans. Many white South Africans rightly conclude from this economic reality that blacks and whites are inextricably linked in striving for the society's future. No such economic imperative guides the United States.

The politics of race can be hidden and ignored in the United States precisely because there race is synonymous with the subordination of a minority group, not the majority. Perhaps this is why other progressive politicians, not just Jesse Jackson, cling to a vision of a rainbow— a metaphor for a multiracial, as opposed to a nonracial, society. In South Africa, where the majority are people of color, the rainbow speaks powerfully of unity; in the United States, the multicolored rainbow hints at how the society's minorities need to be recognized, not ignored. Clearly, the rainbow metaphor is being used in contradictory ways in these societies. In appealing to and acknowledging multiple racial and ethnic group identities, politicians from both countries recognize strength in numbers. That demographic fact was something the ANC could bank on, but the American civil rights movement could not. By the nineties, multiracialism seemed to have become the new ideology of race relations in the United States. Paradoxically, in the most superficial sense, it managed to acknowledge racial difference without ever confronting the historic disadvantage and subordination of African Americans. Proclaiming itself a multiracial democracy enables the United States to deny again its particular forms of racism in ways that South Africa cannot. In the guise of fairness, American pundits and policy analysts were eager to proclaim the advent of a multiracial society, which in fact treats all people equally and thereby uses difference to obscure and subordinate disadvantage.

One peculiar variant on this multiracial ideology that has gained some media attention in the United States is the argument of neoliberals like Jim Sleeper. He maintains in his provocative book, *Liberal Racism,* that given the multitude of races, the best thing whites and blacks can do is surrender their own race consciousness. "Give it up" is the advice of this intellectual journalist, as if blacks and whites can take a pill and wipe out past and current discriminatory practices, whether legally endorsed or not. Sleeper's solution turns multiracialism into racial amnesia.

Dear Jackie,

I think I am about to close the deal on one of the most exciting things I've done since I joined Ford. Do you recall meeting Anna Deavere Smith with me in Johannesburg about a year ago? She was doing some work with the Market Theatre and we had a rushed drink at a hotel bar. Anyway, Anna is one of the most interesting younger (anyone under fifty these days!!!) theater artists in America. And her concerns focus directly on racism in America. A black woman who refuses to be typecast as only focused on black theater or women's theater, she's a boundary crosser not to mention a gender-bender! But I am running ahead of myself. I first got to know Anna in the fall of 1992. She had just finished writing and performing in a one-woman play, *Fires in the Mirror,* in which she depicted and interpreted a tragic incident that took place in 1989 in Crown Heights, Brooklyn, involving the death of a seven-year-old black child, Gavin Cato. Cato was accidentally run over by a car that was part of a Hasidic Jewish funeral procession. In revenge for what the black members of the community thought was the thoughtless racism of the Hasi-

dim—apparently the religiously sponsored ambulance that arrived refused to take Cato to the hospital—some blacks took to the streets and rioted. In the ensuing chaos a young rabbinic student from Australia, Yankel Rosenbaum, who sadly was in the wrong place at the wrong time, was stabbed to death. (His assailants have to this day not been convicted.) The Crown Heights incident, as it's been called ever since, was one of the most racially explosive events in recent memory. What Anna Deavere Smith did was go to Crown Heights and interview as many of the victims on all sides as possible and then wrote a remarkably honest and poignant play about what happened there. It was produced on Broadway with Anna playing all the parts—whites, blacks, women, men, rabbis, ministers, political figures, you name it. It was nominated for the Pulitzer Prize and it catapulted Anna into the ranks of the near-famous. Anna had come to Ford in 1992 to see if we were willing to help support her translation of *Fires* from a theater piece into a film to be broadcast on public television. Our unit gave her modest funds (as did many other philanthropies) and the video produced was shown several times on television and is still being used in college classrooms. A little while later, Anna took the same theatrical methodology—careful interviews of all involved parties—and created a second award-winning piece entitled *Twilight: Los Angeles,* which is a consideration of the events leading up to, including, and following the Los Angeles riots set off by the acquittal of the police officers accused of beating Rodney King. The text of the play is based on the words of forty-six people—this time not only blacks and whites but also Hispanics and Asian Americans who in one way or another were affected by the rioting. *Twilight* confirmed that Anna Deavere Smith is a gifted artist and more. She combines a journalist's knack for getting the scoop, an anthropologist's meticulousness about understanding and getting into the head of her informants, and a professor's ability to teach the material in powerful and provocative ways. I am going on so long about her because I have just negotiated with Anna for her to become Ford's first-ever Artist in Residence beginning January 1996.

In the midnineties a movement to add a "multiracial" category to U.S. Census forms began. The racial classifications were limited to the categories "white," "black," "American Indian or Alaskan Native," "Asian or Pacific Islander," and "Hispanic." Supporters of the multiracial category argued that it is inaccurate and unfair to ask millions of children born to parents of different races to choose between them. In the summer of 1997, a federal commission looking into the question recommended that the categories remain the same, even though the multiracial designation seemed to curry favor with right-of-center politicians who see multiracialism as a means of undercutting race- and identity-based politics. As the *New Republic* noted sadly, the majority of Americans preferred the old categories: "Alas, surveys indicate few Americans would choose to identify themselves as multiracial if offered the choice."[16]

In reviewing this debate over census classifications, the most important point is not whether there is a box that matches an individual's complex so-called racial makeup, but whether, as the journalist Ellis Cose posits in his book *Colorblind,* "it is possible to divorce any system of racial classification from the practice of discrimination, whether a nation splintered along racial lines is capable of changing that propensity."[17] In November 1997, the Federal Office of Management and Budget issued new rules for reporting racial and ethnic information. For the first time, Americans were able to identify themselves on government forms as members of more than one race. People with both black and white ancestry, for example, would be able to check both boxes. While hardly earth-shaking, these changes took four years of debate and testing to produce, which shows how politically sensitive the racial classification issue remains. Blacks in particular have consistently resisted multiple designations that would dilute their sole racial identity as African Americans. This change in reporting is an excellent example of the use of race as a political construct in resistance politics of which Gerda Lerner has written. But it is difficult to know what this new opportunity will mean. How will this new way of counting people affect enforcement of antidiscrimination laws and affirmative action policies? Traditional civil rights groups worry that allowing people to check more than one box will dilute minority numbers. If these "double-box individuals" are counted as whites, voting rights, equal employment, and fair housing cases might be harder to win.

Racial Politics and Affirmative Action in the United States and South Africa

Affirmative action is a main strategy of the ANC for addressing inequality. Strangely, it is often described by critics as "Africanist," when historically it has American roots. Affirmative action originated as a uniquely U.S.-focused initiative aimed at expanding opportunity for individuals from historically disadvantaged groups who suffered systematic discrimination. The concept spread quickly to other countries, particularly to South Africa, with its obvious similarities in racial oppression. The practice of racial privileging, however, has much older roots. For instance, the South African intellectual William Makgoba has described apartheid as "the worst, systematic and longest form of white affirmative action in the history of mankind."[18]

Affirmative action is a concept, a program, and a slogan as well as a crucial political issue in both societies. In current debates about affirmative action in both countries, stereotypes of blacks as incompetent and unworthy have surfaced. The context in which affirmative action is applied, however, is completely different: in South Africa it is part of a deep-seated transformation, but in the United States it is about racial inclusion in the mainstream. Affirmative action in the United States has become one of the most misunderstood and contested policies in the last fifty years of race relations and thus serves as the symbolic marker for the success or failure of American society to come to grips with persistent forms of racism. In the heat of debates over affirmative action, it is useful to remember that it is barely three decades old and was designed in a spirit of bipartisanship to remedy three centuries of particularly virulent racial discrimination.

Affirmative action began in 1965 with President Lyndon Johnson's Executive Order 11246, which directed federal agencies to draw up plans to increase the recruitment, hiring, and promotion of individuals from chronically underrepresented groups, including women from all backgrounds, African Americans, Latinos, and American Indians. Affirmative action requirements applicable to employment decisions of federal contractors, including universities, were substantially reinforced and extended under President Richard Nixon's administration. To this day, most regulations originate with the executive branch of the government, rather than Congress, and they require outreach plans, goals, and timetables. Since the seventies, state and municipal affirmative action regulations have been implemented, but some affirmative action—for instance in college admissions—is voluntary in the sense that it is not mandated by government. Although critics of affirmative action have portrayed it as providing preferential treatment for one group over another, that does not represent affirmative action's goals. Neither is it about quotas or giving something to blacks, other minorities, and women that they do not deserve. Instead, as the president of Stanford University, Gerhard Casper, has argued, "Affirmative action is based on the judgment that a policy of true equal opportunity needs to create opportunities for members of historically underrepresented groups to be drawn into various walks of life from which they might otherwise be shut out."[19] Thus, affirmative action is metaphorically about leveling the playing field, not lowering the quality of play.

In higher education in the United States, it has meant working harder to find, admit, and appoint a more diverse group of individuals into institutions and teaching faculties. Affirmative action encourages institutions to cast the net more widely than was the case historically, thus making these processes more, not less, competitive. Contrary to the way in which affirmative action has been characterized by its critics, it is not the opposite of meritocracy, but rather an enhancement of it. Having a greater number of candidates is likely to result in a more selective process and a better choice.

A more diverse student body or labor force can also lead to a more effective education or a better product. As the Harvard sociologist Orlando Patterson has persuasively written, "Affirmative action has made a major difference in the lives of women and minorities, in the process helping to realize, as no other policy has done, the nation's constitutional commitment to the ideals of equality, fairness, and economic integration. In utilitarian terms it is hard to find a program that has brought so much gain to so many at so little cost."[20] Despite this claim, affirmative action is under attack in the United States by those who reject it as contrary to the goal of creating a color-blind society. Critics argue that a policy cannot use race-conscious efforts to redress discrimination without inscribing a new form of discrimination against another group, namely white males. Proponents point out that a society cannot overcome a legacy of discrimination without taking that history into account in devising methods that compensate for the historic and systemic exclusion of individuals from these chronically disadvantaged groups. Importantly, the defenders of affirmative action are also saying that *fair* treatment in a society does not always mean the *same* treatment.

While few critics deny Patterson's point that affirmative action has worked to expand educational and economic opportunities, the backlash has grown. In a string of decisions in the nineties, the Supreme Court has made it easier for nonminorities to challenge remedies that take race into account and has applied strict constitutional standards to such policies. Applying those principles, lower federal courts have struck down affirmative action programs at the University of Texas and other educational institutions. At the same time, opponents of affirmative action at the federal, state, and local levels have advanced policy measures that ban or dismantle race- and gender-sensitive equal opportunity remedies. The most notable and successful is California's Proposition 209, which outlawed racial and gender preferences in state government, and a policy change by the Regents of the University of California, which eliminated the consideration of race in admissions.

Yet in a key referendum held in 1996 in Houston, Texas, voters upheld the use of affirmative action programs and policies. This suggests that large segments of the American public may not be as hostile to race- and gender-conscious remedies as critics claim. The leading proponent of affirmative action in Houston, the popular outgoing mayor Bob Lanier, a white male real estate developer, led the battle to preserve this policy, while the leader of the anti–affirmative action forces in California, Ward Connerly, an African American businessman, suggests that it is overly simplistic to conclude that Americans view affirmative action according solely to a race-based perspective.

Moreover, the controversy over affirmative action may have been "concocted," to use Patterson's somewhat loaded verb. Patterson blames the media, conservative intellectuals, and other pundits for exaggerating the degree to which affirmative action has resulted in "reverse discrimination" against whites. In a 1990 study, over 70 percent of whites asserted that other whites were being hurt by affirmative action, but only one-tenth of them, or 7 percent, claimed to have actually experienced any form of reverse discrimination. Furthermore, only 16 percent knew of someone close who had. Support for affirmative action among blacks (57 percent—slightly more than a majority) is not as high as we would expect and, indeed, is less than the previously reported percentages in the eighties. Patterson attributes this decline to the relentless attack on affirmative action by the media and politicians from the center to the Right.[21]

Interestingly, when one applies a feminist lens, the situation looks even more complex. Within the black community, women, who remain a disproportionately high percentage of the black poor, are more likely to support affirmative action than their middle-class black male or female counterparts. And within the white community, white women expressed the same level of fear as white men about affirmative action for blacks. This suggests that the "angry white male" is a myth. Whites appear to have equal levels of antipathy to race-based affirmative action.

What is especially troubling about this finding is that white women currently constitute the largest group of Americans to have benefited from affirmative action programs. Yet, they do not appear to connect affirmative action to their advancement. Polls revealing that large numbers of white women do not support affirmative action surely must trouble women's rights groups, which are trying to maintain their alliance with minority civil rights groups in the fight to preserve affirmative action. Clearly, proponents of affirmative action must reeducate white women if affirmative action is to survive this persistent conservative backlash.

Equally disturbing is that white women have been among the plaintiffs in recent challenges to affirmative action in Michigan, Maryland, and Texas. They clearly do not see this important effort to level the playing field in terms of gender or recognize that affirmative action policies have helped them advance. These examples and recent survey data indicate that many, if not most, white women do not feel a sense of solidarity with members of minority groups, whose historic exclusion from certain fields mirrors their own previously limited options. For the foreseeable future, it may be difficult for many whites to support a policy that could harm them or, at best, provide them with no obvious material benefit, such as admission to the most prestigious public university instead of one in the second or third tier. Affirmative action, however, is not fundamentally about preserving opportunities for historically advantaged individuals and groups, but rather the opposite. Its goal is to help societies become more just and fairer in allocating opportunities and redistributing resources, especially at the most selective public universities.

Thus, these universities around the United States are facing an *agonizing* dilemma: If they retain their affirmative action admissions policies, they face growing legal and political challenges, but if they move to a greater reliance on standardized tests, they will endorse racial segregation because test scores by black and Hispanic students remain stubbornly below that of whites regardless of the students' income level. The social and economic cost of wiping out an entire generation's educational opportunities because of a backlash against affirmative action would be very high—perhaps even catastrophic—for race relations.

In their exhaustive and controversial book on this subject, *America in Black and White,* the sociologists Stephan Thernstrom and Abigail Thernstrom argue that blacks have been making steady progress into the middle class since World War II and that affirmative action has been oversold as an effective remedy in reversing racially exclusive practices. Despite their claims, a more detailed review of the rate of black admissions into the most prestigious colleges and universities reveals that the real gains in racially and ethnically diversifying American higher education have occurred since the advent of affirmative action in 1965. In 1964, for example, approximately 4 percent of black adults had a college degree. By 1995, that figure had tripled to over 13.6 percent of black adults, even though the overall college completion rates for blacks tended to stagnate in the late eighties and early nineties. In predominantly white institutions, however, progress continued due to a commitment to affirmative action. For example, between 1984 and 1995, African American undergraduate enrollment grew by 33 percent in predominantly white institutions, and these institutions awarded 49 percent more bachelor's degrees to African Americans in 1995 than in 1984.[22]

Importantly, these figures do not focus on the effect of affirmative action policies themselves or on affirmative action as practiced by the most selective public universities, at which opponents have leveled their strongest and most effective attacks. It is one thing for less selective institutions to broaden access, but it is quite another for institutions like the University of California at Berkeley and the University of Michigan at Ann Arbor to employ affirmative action in cases where there are easily as many whites with strong qualifications as blacks. In these cases, admitting an individual from one group has the effect of denying a place to an equally qualified individual from another.

But this type of denial happens frequently in selective admissions situations, such as when children of alumni, students from certain geographical regions, gifted athletes, or talented musicians are admitted over other students with better test scores. Anti–affirmative action forces seldom discuss such choices, however, because they call into question the exclusive reliance on any single quantitative factor like the SAT test. To acknowledge this phenomenon would mean that the whole subject of meritocracy in college admissions has to be reexamined. Supporters of affirmative action, the political philosopher Michael Sandel contends, make their best case when they "challenge the sacred American myth that landing a job or a seat in the freshman class is a prize one deserves thanks solely to one's own efforts."[23] Proponents have a weak argument if they defend it as a compensation and remedy for past wrongs. After all, those who benefit are not necessarily those who have suffered, and those who pay the compensation are seldom those responsible for the wrongs being rectified. A more compelling argument for affirmative action, in Sandel's view, treats an admission less as a reward to the recipient than as a means of advancing a socially worthy aim. The aim is for a racially diverse student body because it enables students to learn more from one another than they would if they all came from similar backgrounds. Moreover, as Sandel indicates, "equipping disadvantaged minorities to assume positions of leadership in key public and professional roles advances the university's civic purpose and contributes to the common good."[24] This means that college admissions practices, as well as employment practices, have to be detached from a singular focus on individual merit and expanded to a multifocused approach that takes into account qualities that are required to advance societal goals. If supporters of affirmative action used this argument, they would appeal to a broader set of values that still may incorporate notions of meritocracy, but go well beyond it. For example, when the majority of the population has been historically underrepresented at a prestigious university, as is the case in South Africa, Sandel's greater social good argument is even more persuasive.

Affirmative action is just beginning to be implemented in South Africa, and already the community seems to recognize that the goal is not about advancing any single person's opportunity, but rather using this tool to build a stronger, more effective democracy in which the *majority* must assume positions of leadership. In contrast to South Africa, affirmative action in the United States has been tied too closely to an overly individualistic "merit-based" or "compensatory" analysis. If affirmative action in the United States is a tool of access to the mainstream—to the institutions that control power and resources—in South Africa it is understood as a means of transforming and recasting those institutions. In South Africa the myth of meritocracy has not obscured racial disadvantage. The installation of a democratic, nonracial government is only the beginning of a long process of reconstruction and development to foster social and economic equality. Despite this more positive context and the understanding that affirmative action means collective empowerment, not individual advancement, the policy is increasingly contested as a legitimate strategy in that reconstruction.

Clearly, racial politics in these two societies are divergent. While race-sensitive admissions policies in the United States are being dismantled, equity and redress policies are required by the provisions of the South African constitution and are supported by new legislation—but, it must be added, not without opposition by whites. Affirmative action is increasingly the subject of court actions in South Africa too. In March 1997 a group of white men, acting through the Public Servants Association, brought a case before the Pretoria High

Alison,

I was upset that more academics weren't at Babylon's graduation. I feel Babylon's career represents such a triumph over adversity. I'm also personally proud because I've put a lot into him. I've followed the admonition of Hugh Price in his keynote address to the Commonwealth Club that you sent me; Price talks about how if we are to make diversity work, then the mechanisms for apportioning opportunity must somehow take account of more than purely intellectual qualities. Moral courage isn't a conventional criteria for graduating with an M.A., but I *feel* that's the main quality that was rewarded tonight. Babylon as a Xhosa demonstrated enormous courage in going into the hostels (Inkatha strongholds at the time) and interviewing Zulu migrants about their experiences and understandings of political violence. He's shown perseverance too, and I think he will lead a really productive life. I had to fight for him because his analytical ability is not exceptional, but I'm pleased I did. I think Babylon's success says something important about affirmative action involving a new appreciation of diversity in that it takes account of a wider range of qualities, such as courage and energy and perseverance and commitment to one's notion of "truth." If marks and analytical ability had been my sole criteria I wouldn't have taken him on. We have this endless debate in the department over whether admission to our postgraduate program should be based strictly on grades or whether we should have race-based preferences in admissions. I think Babylon's case exposes the myth that diversifying the university means lowering standards; instead it means changing those standards and taking account of a wider range of criteria.

I've experienced two very different graduation ceremonies in the past week. I was invited to speak at a graduation ceremony on Robben Island arranged by an organization called Peace Vision for students who had completed its course. It seems like a weak organization. The board had sacked the executive director at a meeting the previous evening and there was no one at the airport to meet me. Then the organizers forgot the graduation certificates in someone's car and couldn't persuade the ferry boat captain to turn back for them. Having the graduation ceremony on Robben Island was appropriate, as it really is South Africa's "struggle university" in the sense that so many of our key political leaders were imprisoned and studied there. It's named Seal Island after the Dutch word for seal, *robbe,* and is a captivating and bleakly beautiful place. Eight miles from Cape Town, it was a place of exile for three hundred years for "lepers" (a category that included syphilitics and skin cancer victims), "lunatics," and political prisoners, including Nelson Mandela for eighteen years. On a visit there in February 1995, Mandela described it as "a towering monument of lessons for the future." The author Mtutuzeli Matshoba recently called it "the holy of holies," a place consecrated by the sacrifice of its victims. These include many generations of political prisoners, starting with the Khoi-Khoi leaders transported there by the Dutch colonizers in 1658. According to Jeff Peires, "the Dutch valued Robben Island as a prison not only because the prisoners found it difficult to escape, but because it concealed the terrible conditions under which the convicts lived, and the dreadful punishments they suffered. Convicted prisoners were often sentenced to whippings with the cat-o-nine tails, to branding and pinching with red-hot irons and to the chopping off of hands."

It was here that the Xhosa chiefs were imprisoned after their defeat by the British in the nineteenth-century frontier wars. On the journey back to Cape Town I watched the sea-wolves, as the fifteenth century Portuguese explorers called seals. I thought of the whales that used to swarm in Table Bay and of the Xhosa prophet Nxele, or Makana, who drowned with thirty comrades in a boat while trying to escape this gray, windy, and desolate place. As a child at boarding school in Grahamstown I often looked out at the hilltop called Makana's Kop. Makana surrendered to the British in 1819 in what was known as the Battle of Grahamstown after which the defeated Xhosas were driven across the Fish River. I also thought of how my ancestors had been part of this violent process of conquest and subjugation.

Court claiming that they had been discriminated against on account of their race and gender. They argued that the new codes in the Public Service Act, aimed at making the civil service more "representative," were invalid because they improperly discriminated against white men.

The presiding judge concluded that the official affirmative action policies did not satisfy the requirements of the Constitution. The judge said that under the Constitution the civil service was obliged to provide an efficient service as well as to become broadly representative of the South African community. Neither of these aims could be achieved at the expense of the other: "The efficiency of the public administration cannot be compromised by promoting a broadly representative public administration."[25] The case might set a precedent for further court challenges to affirmative action, as has been the practice in the United States for some time.

Despite these hurdles, affirmative action is being institutionalized in South Africa. In his public introduction of the Employment Equity Bill on September 5, 1997, the ANC minister of labor declared, "Apartheid has left behind a legacy of inequality reflected in disparities in the distribution of jobs, occupations and income. The government is of the view that it is necessary to redress imbalances and to inculcate within every work place a culture of non-discrimination and diversity. When it comes to jobs, training and promotion, we want a fair deal for all workers." The bill imposes regulations for black advancement in the workplace and places the onus on businesses to develop their own programs. The government will ensure that every business has a plan and will monitor the progress made after implementation. The bill also obliges employers to classify their employees by race and prioritize hiring black people, the disabled, and women.

Predictably, it has been criticized on a number of grounds, including that it is a step toward re-racialization. In practical terms, the implementation of affirmative action in South Africa challenges the premises of nonracialism because part of its focus is on racial groups—the very focus nonracialism had sought to overcome. But importantly, race is not the only category involved. The crucial point is that South African affirmative action targets three categories of excluded groups—blacks, women, and, unlike in the United States, the disabled. Under affirmative action, state investment in education, housing, health care, and job appointments aims to benefit the historically disadvantaged, which usually means just blacks. Even with South Africa's more inclusive view, however, its system ignores class considerations. If nonracialism is to continue to be an organizing concept in South African society, the marker of affirmative action must be *disadvantage* rather than just race or gender or disability.

Mamphela Ramphele, the former vice chancellor of the University of Cape Town and the first black African woman to head a major university in South Africa, argues for the concept of equity rather than affirmative action. "The key difference," she has written, "is that equity focuses on individuals, while affirmative action focuses on groups. Affirmative action runs the risk of becoming inequitable because it does not take individual differences or performance into account. . . . An equity approach assumes that individuals with talent and ability are spread throughout all sectors of society. It also recognizes that an individual's access to opportunities is determined by many factors, such as education, class, race, gender, social conventions and cultural norms. An equity approach seeks to overcome these barriers to opportunity in order to enable individuals to take responsibility for fulfilling their own potential."[26]

For Ramphele, this approach means removing obstacles to equal opportunity, and in her work she has focused on three main areas: broadening access, promoting personal development, and changing the institutional culture. For example, Ramphele stresses the importance of cultural change and diversity through allowing ululating at graduation ceremonies. She maintains that while good universities throughout the world share a common culture and values, other components of an institutions's culture, such as rituals, symbols, and shared events, play an important role in making people feel they belong. She explains: "At UCT we have a diverse campus community and so we strive to create a context in which people from different backgrounds feel comfortable. Our graduation ceremonies are good examples of our approach. We have relaxed our proceedings to enable families and friends of graduates to express their joy in ways appropriate to different cultures." Allowing ululating at graduation ceremonies "enriches our proceedings, assists in nation building and is a clear demonstration of our commitment to changing the cultural strictures of the past."[27] Some would consider this is trivial concession, however, since ululating amounts to a muffled sound in a ceremony modeled on Oxbridge and replete with British symbolism.

As Ramphele demonstrates, in the struggle to transform key South African institutions such as universities, programs aimed at diversity are shifting from an institutional to a personal level. Unfortunately, racism is making the same move. Struggles and controversies between blacks and whites cannot always be reduced to race issues, but they always have a race pertinency. It is in this sense that the charges of fraud and incompetence brought in 1995 by thirteen white South African academics against William Makgoba, the deputy vice chancellor of the University of the Witwatersrand, have been described as racially explosive. According to one source quoted in a newspaper account headed "Makgoba—South Africa's 'OJ Simpson Case,'" the charges had become a polarizing issue for the whole country blinded by the "rainbow nation" metaphor.[28] Once one probed below the country's surface tranquility, enormous racial tension emerged.

The response to the attack on Makgoba has also been interpreted as a threat to nonracialism in that the incident illustrates racial solidarity prevailing over principle. Despite this perception, many whites have also been offended by the charge that this distinguished medical scientist is incompetent. Judging from at least three similar cases it appears that faculty members at the University of the Witwatersrand have difficulty dealing with blacks in positions of authority. The attack on Makgoba has provoked solidarity among those committed to racial equality but alienated from the dominant institutional culture. The fruitful analogy is not between the individual persons of Makgoba and O. J. Simpson but between the racism operating in the informal culture of the university and in the Los Angeles Police Department. The challenge is for the legal and educational institutions to address the racial inequality that pervades both U.S. and South African society.

Alison,

For the first time I am finding teaching a strain—there is SO little cultural capital on which to draw in the classroom. E.g., when talking about how patriarchy predates capitalism I cited the examples of chastity belts and foot-binding. It then took me about fifteen minutes to explain each, something I didn't have to do in the past. Another example: talking about the origins of second-wave feminism I quoted from Stokely Carmichael, that "the only position for women in our movement is prone." The students all looked at me blankly—they didn't know what *prone* meant. I keep telling myself that this level of underpreparedness of black students is part of the legacy of apartheid—the other side of the privilege coin that whites like me enjoyed. But the reality is that teaching such underprepared students is a strain. Also, they don't watch television or read newspapers. E.g., there was a good program on a popular show (the local equivalent of Oprah Winfrey's) on Monday to mark National Women's Day. All the panelists (except Frene Ginwala) were incredibly affluent, successful businesswomen who were talking "sisterhood" and "women supporting" each other in a way I found sickening. One panelist was from a new women's empowerment company—the directors pay themselves R400,000 a year. No mention of poor, black rural women, some of whom earn R40 as seasonal farm workers. There was only one reference to domestic workers in passing. The whole program was a marvelous illustration of elitist or "right-wing" feminism. I have a reading about this concept in the package I give to the students but not one of them had watched the program. It feels like a struggle to deal with racial disadvantage in the classroom.

We left Cape Town early this morning feeling somewhat overwhelmed by yesterday's big event, Mamphela Ramphele's inauguration as vice chancellor of the University of Cape Town. Both of us found it emotional. I was proud to be there as Ford's rep because the foundation played a positive role in this extraordinary woman's life. Jackie felt almost tearful as she remembered her visit with Ramphele near Tzaneen twenty years ago, when she was banned and bereft, and contrasted it with the present affirmation from the audience of about two thousand people, including dignitaries like President Mandela and Archbishop Tutu. The shift from banned revolutionary to the head of one of the most distinguished universities testifies to the transformative possibilities of this place.

The ceremony was a wonderful statement of diversity with a praise singer (in the form of Ramphele's mother) as well as all the academic rituals and conventions. We sang both "Gaudeamus Igitur" and "Nkosi sikel'i Afrika." Jackie thought some moments were "kitsch," as when two racially separate choirs left their positions and merged, but I liked the symbolism.

Ramphele's speech was about the excellence-equity connection. She seems committed to excellence being enhanced by diversity and inclusiveness. She said that first among the challenges she faces is the "need to change the staff profile of the university which is largely white and male and also to transform the institutional culture into one which is more inclusive and affirming of all members of its community." Jackie especially liked her pointing to how many white South Africans still do not comprehend the depth of pain caused by apartheid. She said that the pain of being denied one's birthright is excruciating but the denial of the reality of that pain is even worse and contributed to the anger of black students. She also talked about the crucial role that universities could potentially play in the African renaissance. Mandela also emphasized the need to transform institutions so that they reflect our society, not only in terms of race, gender, and class, but also in terms of how their values and priorities seek to meet social needs. He spoke of the dangers of mediocrity and of the importance of excellence in teaching and research.

There was a long moment when Ramphele stood beaming in front of the packed hall when everyone clapped and cheered. Jackie said she felt proud of being South African with all its color and richness and I was exhilarated by the occasion.

Dear Jackie,

Finally, some hard data—the kind that economists like—supporting our side of the affirmative action debate! I have just finished reading a new book by Bill Bowen (president of the Mellon Foundation and former president of Princeton) and Derek Bok (former president of Harvard), *The Shape of the River*. It's an impressive study of how race-sensitive admissions—namely taking race into account when deciding who among many otherwise qualified applicants gets into places like Princeton and Harvard—has worked over time. To do this, the authors have tracked the college, career, and life experiences of more than 45,000 students of all races who attended twenty-eight academically selective colleges and universities in the United States starting in 1976 through the early 1990s.

The basic finding of the book is that minority students who were admitted using race-sensitive policies did as well as white students in many, if not most, academically rigorous institutions in the United States. There is abundant evidence that thousands of minority students had strong academic credentials when they entered college, that they graduated in large numbers, and that they have done very well after leaving college. In this retrospective look, Bowen and Bok do several neat things. For example, they construct a rough profile of the approximately 700 black matriculates in the 1976 entering cohort whom Bowen and Bok estimate would have been rejected by traditional so-called race-neutral policies. This analysis reveals that over 225 members of this group of "retrospectively rejected" black matriculates went on to attain professional degrees or doctorates. Seventy became doctors and 60 became lawyers. That more than 25 percent of a group that would not have been admitted but for affirmative action (i.e., race-sensitive admissions) went on to successful professional careers and made important contributions to civic life suggests that these so-called underprepared or unqualified students can, under the right circumstances, overcome previous educational disadvantage. And, this doesn't begin to deal with the hundreds of other black students in this cohort who completed B.A.'s and are leading productive lives.

The only quarrel I have with Bowen and Bok is that their study focuses on the success with race-sensitive admissions of a small number of truly elite universities and colleges, of which only three are public—Penn State, the University of Michigan at Ann Arbor, and the University of North Carolina at Chapel Hill. This seems a highly skewed view of American higher education since over 80 percent of all students are in public institutions. Moreover, surprisingly, there is no effort to disaggregate the statistics on race-sensitive admissions in the public research universities in the study. After all, these are the institutions that have been particularly targeted in the affirmative action controversies, and they are the most vulnerable to legal challenges because of their "public" status. In some ways, I feel the book is more a defense of the value of elite private education's approach to the issue than it is an examination of why affirmative action has made a positive difference more broadly.

To be fair, there is a suggestion in the book that diversifying the student bodies of these highly selective institutions is a good thing, not only for the black students, but also for the white students. Bowen and Bok's survey data throw new light on how positively the great majority of students regard opportunities to learn from those with different backgrounds and experiences. In their conclusion, the authors note cautiously, "Admission 'on the merits' would be shortsighted if admissions officers were precluded from crediting this potential contribution to the education of all students." Sadly, the education benefits of affirmative action for all students scarcely receives the attention it deserves in the controversies over the policy.

Lastly, I would have wanted more analysis that breaks down the findings not just by race, but also by gender. While all the data were collected by race and gender, there is no comprehensive effort to examine the gender differentials for black students who graduated from these institutions. For sure the data are there, but there is no effort to put a feminist lens on it. For example, for all socioeconomic levels from high to low, the data reveal that black male graduates of these highly selective schools make considerably more annual income than black female graduates. So, on the one hand, the opportunity structure for black students improves with graduation from these places, but on the other, gender inequities remain pretty fixed.

It makes me wonder—is any similar study being done in South Africa . . . ?

Alison,

I enjoyed William Makgoba's book launch yesterday. There were very few white people there, lots of intellectualizing with rather pretentious references to Kant and Sartre, knocks at Marx and Marxists, and a strong affirmation of an African intellectual identity. I felt very white and middle class and colorless in my suit, compared to people in their "traditional dress." There was also much talk about Mbeki's notion of an "African renaissance" taking root, which is exciting but glosses over issues such as military dictatorship, corruption, and armed conflict. I have finished reading Makgoba's book, *The Makgoba Affair: A Reflection on Transformation,* and found it moving. He's clearly an enormously proud man and with good reason—he's traveled such a long road from being one of nine children of a poor schoolteacher in a remote rural area to an eminent medical researcher in Britain. I like his pride in his achievements and his attempts to straddle the traditional and the modern. He talks about trying "to remain the village African boy but also to be a sophisticated modern scientist." There's also a lot of pain in the book and I feel bad that I didn't do more to support him. The trouble is that he leaves no space for progressive whites like us. He draws an analogy between the struggle at Witwatersrand in 1995 with the events of a century ago in 1895 when "Chief Makgoba, my great-grandfather, was involved in a similar battle of power and politics in the Northern Transvaal, defending his land against the 'Boer Kommandos.'" He clearly identifies with him as a figure who "lived and died for his principles: never to be taken prisoner and be defeated by Whites." But in the process Makgoba reduces the South African transformation to a power struggle between conservative white liberals and black Africanists. We've been written out of the script, and maybe this is the future. Maybe the anti-apartheid struggle was the glue that was necessary to hold the ideology of nonracialism together and Marxism provided some vision of an alternative society that is lacking now. He says that "the challenge to all African democracies today is the neo-liberal who from a racist society has internalized a sophisticated version of racism. It is typically that one who claims to have fought side by side with us, or that one whose sister or brother has African in-laws. These are the most dangerous threat to non-racism today." The trouble is that he lived out of South Africa for twenty years and was not part of the ANC's elaboration of what nonracialism means.

Makgoba wants a university that captures and encapsulates the essence of Africa. There's an unfortunate essentialism behind much of what he writes, which I find highly problematic. He writes of "the many fundamental features that are common to African identity and culture, for example the hospitality, friendliness, the consensus and common framework seeking principle, ubuntu, the emphasis on community rather than on the individual etc." Clearly, this homogenization is nonsense in the context of this vast, complicated, and diverse continent. Nowhere does he talk about class, and I think this is the most dangerous omission of all in the present context, where a growing black middle class is in danger of becoming as exploitative, materialist, and self-seeking as the previous white groupings.

Race in Post-Apartheid South Africa

There is general agreement that democratization has not abolished racism in South Africa. The post-1994 discourse on race has not focused exclusively on affirmative action but has included transformation, reconciliation, and the redistribution of wealth. As President Thabo Mbeki has often observed, the only solution for the country is real reconciliation between blacks and whites. But reconciliation requires redistribution. "National reconciliation," he emphasizes, "has to mean more than the simple fact that a black and white can drink a cup of tea together. A lasting reconciliation must obviously be based on a redistribution of wealth and equal sacrifices."[29]

The ANC has stressed its commitment both to deracializing South African society and to liberating black people in general and black Africans in particular. This is the main thrust of the "national democratic-revolution" now underway. A July 1997 ANC document defines the central task of the revolution as "the improvement of the quality of life of the especially poor" who are "by definition mostly black."[30] The ANC vision is of a single national identity built on cultural diversity and equality. The 1994 campaign document "A Better Life for All" referred to "a nation built by developing our different cultures, beliefs and languages as a source of our common strength." This is the vision embodied in Archbishop Desmond Tutu's phrase "the rainbow nation." Thabo Mbeki's powerful 1996 speech "I Am an African" on the adoption of the new Constitution was the embodiment of the "rainbow spirit." Increasing racial tensions, however, bring the "rainbow nation" notion into question. Although the rainbow does encapsulate the image of an inclusive nationhood, it is both class- and gender-blind.

Since 1994 some have argued that the rainbow image is unraveling under four pressures. First, whites' resistance to transformation and failure to understand reconciliation imply a refusal to come to terms with their past oppressive role. As Mbeki once put it, "The white population I don't think has quite understood the importance of this challenge. . . . If you were speaking of national reconciliation based on the maintenance of the status quo because you do not want to move at a pace that frightens the whites, it means that you wouldn't carry out the task of transformation."[31] Second, the assertion of ethnic identities has led to the growth of group self-consciousness. This has sometimes resulted, for example, in sporadic violence between Xhosa and Zulu workers. Ironically, this notion of the variety of African cultures, which was used to divide African peoples under apartheid, has reemerged despite the nonracial ideology of the ANC-led government. Third, the growing notion of "Africanism" typically entails a reassertion of pride in black identity, style, fashion, culture, even ideology. As the political scientist Irina Filatova describes this trend, "It is the rediscovery of 'Africaness,' if only in the form of renaming places and personalities, the re-invention and revision of a black legacy in search of a new, particularly African way forward."[32] Fourth, under President Mbeki, fewer whites are in positions of authority. Many critics, both within the ANC and outside it, interpret this phenomenon as a repudiation of nonracialism. Some go even further, suggesting that nonracialism is fading under the impact of black racism. Proponents of this position point to the declining political influence of the white Left as evidence, but a leftist position in general is seriously in decline. This change in politics, we would argue, is part of a global trend that began in 1989 rather than evidence of the failure of nonracialism in South Africa, though it no doubt contributes to a narrowing of white participation in government positions.

The concept of "Africanism" has taken on a fresh meaning during the Mbeki presidency because of its focus on "the African renaissance." This notion is mobilized in a range of arenas, from AIDS to foreign policy to defense policy, to underpin a new dominant role for Africa and to make South Africa the moral leader and voice for Africa in the world. The "African renaissance," as Mbeki appears to use the term, refers to the establishment of stable democracies, economic development, respect for human rights, an end to violent conflicts, and an assertion of Africa's influence in international forums, such as the United Nations and the World Trade Organization. The emphasis is on breaking the image of Africa as a "basketcase" and on the reconstruction—by its own energy and resources—of Africa's social, political, and economic relations. This concept was endorsed by President Clinton during his 1998 visit, when he claimed that the core values driving Africa's renaissance—democracy, diversity, free enterprise—are shared by the United States. Despite such glowing support, the South African Communist party theorist Jeremy Cronin has warned about the concept's potential elitism: "There are obviously very positive elements associated with the notion of a renaissance. This marginalized continent needs to be reconstructed and developed and the end of the cold war has offered some space for democratization in Africa. However, the African renaissance can become associated with a project led by the elite for the elite. The Italian renaissance was a process led by a humanist elite on behalf of the Italian city-state masses. In a similar vein we could have an African renaissance led by a new South African male and falsely nonracial elite."[33] Many share his fear that "the African renaissance" is—like "the rainbow nation"—a class-blind concept, a movement of the African black middle class interested in advancing its own agenda. In the final analysis, changes in class relations are as much at the center of the reconstruction of South African society as is establishing a nonracial democracy.

Conclusion

The central challenge facing post-apartheid South Africa is that transformation is not limited to the creation of a nonracial middle class or an elite that includes some black people. As the social analyst Ran Greenstein has explained, "The evasions of race, and the use of the language of 'standards,' 'quality' and 'excellence,' can serve to retain academic privilege and resources in white hands; equally, though, the focus on race and the use of the language of 'empowerment,' 'redress' and 'relevance' can serve to accumulate privilege and resources in elite black hands."[34] Similarly, the existence of a growing black elite in the United States does not meet the demands for social justice that a race-blind society entails. In both countries redress is in the interests of social justice and social stability. Historically, both the United States and South Africa formally constitutionalized white supremacy. Despite its efforts throughout the second half of the twentieth century, the United States has yet to transform adequately the institutions and dominant culture that still perpetuate white power and privilege.

One-third of all African Americans continue to live below the poverty line; more than half of all black South Africans live in poverty.[35] It follows that inequality, which historically has been racialized in both societies, is the most serious problem plaguing both countries. Both societies have wide income and wealth gaps. In South Africa inequality assumes a racialized and gendered form because power and resources are mainly controlled by white men. Under the apartheid regime South Africa had the worst distribution of income across households among countries for which similar studies had been conducted. In 1991 the poorest 40 percent of households earned a mere 4 percent of the income, while the richest 10 percent earned in excess of half. This inequality followed racial lines. People in the poorest households were most likely to be black, live in rural areas, and have a female head.[36] As South Africa moves away from a race-based society to a class-based one, inequality within race groups is increasing. Four years after the advent of democracy, President Mbeki warned that South Africa was "still divided into two nations: one of relatively rich whites and another larger nation of the black poor."[37] In 1998, 61 percent of black Africans were poor while the figure among whites was only 1 percent.[38]

The phrase *two nations* thus has deep resonances in both societies. As Andrew Hacker pointed out in his book of that title, the United States is still a substantially segregated society. Overall, black poverty has actually increased slightly since the end of the sixties. The current one-third of blacks living in poverty are mostly confined to the inner cities, which are riddled with high unemployment, crime, gang violence, drugs, and welfare dependency.[39] Conversely, the U.S. Department of Labor's Glass Ceiling Commission in 1998 found that 97 percent of senior managers at Fortune 1,000 industrial corporations were white males and only 5 percent of top managers at the Fortune 2,000 top industrial and service companies were women, virtually all of them white. According to Orlando Patterson, white men in the United States still control more than 99.9 percent of the top positions in private and public institutions.[40] This racially inscribed inequality requires a fresh examination of class relations that also takes account of racial and gender discrimination. Racial injustice has a material base; it is not simply a matter of altering perceptions and attitudes, though they matter too, as racial profiling of police suspects attests. We have consistently tried to emphasize both this material base and the interlocking character of race, class, and gender relations in understanding why one cannot speak of diversity without understanding disadvantage and domination.

Jackie,

I didn't want this weekend to go by without writing to you about the Amadou Diallo verdict. Diallo, a Guinean immigrant, was standing in his vestibule in a crime-ridden part of the Bronx on February 4, 1999. Four plainclothes white policemen saw him and claimed he reminded them of a mug shot of a serial rapist in the neighborhood. They surrounded him and before words were spoken pumped forty-one bullets in his direction, nineteen of which struck the unarmed black man. In the trial, the defense and prosecution witnesses argued over which bullets killed him! Can you imagine? This trial's outcome testifies to so much that is wrong with the United States, despite the rhetoric of healing that Clinton and other liberals use. First, it's a case of racial profiling—that is, blacks commit a disproportionate amount of crime in the area so an innocent black who mistakenly puts his hand in to get an ID from a wallet is perceived to be a potential murderer. Then there's the deadly force—guns that rapid-fire sixteen bullets in less than thirty seconds. Last, the trial was moved to upstate Albany, where it was said that the policemen would get a "fairer" trial. The result was acquittals on all counts. I believe that even if the cops did not intend to kill, they behaved in a racist fashion and used undue force. Surprisingly, there has been no riot like after the Rodney King beatings that Anna Deavere Smith memorialized in *Twilight: Los Angeles.* There are calls for a federal court to take up the case on civil rights grounds. I hope that happens but I am not optimistic. Diallo never had a chance, considering the way black males are perceived. Ironically, I am pretty certain that a black female would have fared better. Fewer black women meet this fate at the hands of cops. But of course sexual violence and abuse is rampant in all communities, including among African Americans. Black men show no greater empathy toward wives and girlfriends than their white counterparts. But the police, of course, weren't looking for a black female serial rapist, so racial profiling also has a gender dimension. This kind of incident makes me realize that beneath a thin exterior of presumed racial tolerance, there is little deep understanding and social justice in the United States. For the first time ever, I felt a momentary positive feeling that O. J. Simpson beat the odds! That's pretty pathetic.

Alison,

During the Cease Fire National Conference this last weekend, there was a very interesting debate on the notion of a "shame tax" to be imposed on all white people. The crucial question is whether it is a form of reverse racism. I argued for it on the grounds that all whites benefited in some way from apartheid and needed to make reparation. This seems an appropriate moment for the debate since the Truth and Reconciliation Commission has estimated that it needs R3 billion to pay compensation to the twenty-two thousand eligible victims. These are all individuals who have given eloquent testimony to the commission about the human rights abuses they suffered under apartheid, many involving torture by the security police—wet bags over the head, electric shocks to the genitals, sticks forced up anuses, and such like. What is extraordinary is the modest nature of the "compensation" many victims have asked for: a tombstone, reburial, a wheelchair, or even simply "the truth." For example, the widow of an activist who was tortured to death and had his body thrown into the Fish River stated, "I want-ed the truth. I've heard the truth. Now I'm so happy."

However, others are upset about the amnesty provisions, which violate their conception of justice. Apparently the amnesty provisions are unique. One condition is a political motive and a crucial question is whether racism constitutes such a motive. Several white applicants found guilty of murdering black people have argued for amnesty on the ground that in wanting to rid South Africa of "mud races" they had a "political" motive. It's been said that the amnesty provisions are the most generous in the world for political offenses—for example, perpetrators are not required to show remorse, only to tell the full truth.

It was pointed out to me at the conference that a racially discriminatory tax would be "unconstitutional," and of course a small minority of blacks, such as "homeland" leaders, benefited from apartheid as well. The minister of justice has said that the provision of resources for reparation and rehabilitation is "the responsibility of all South Africans" and "will have to come from the taxpayer." But I think there should be a strong appeal (if coercive measures are not possible) to all those who acknowledge that they benefited unfairly from apartheid.

2

Biodiversity:
Species Differences and
Human Domination

In the middle of the day in the Amazonian rain forest we could only lie in the shade, panting for breath, mopping perspiration, and swatting insects. We were doing so when an excited shout from the Indian guide brought us out of our reed hut onto the jetty of Heron Lake. A little distance away a twenty-foot anaconda lay sunning itself and moving in slow, sinuous coils along the twisted roots and branches of the lakeside vegetation. The awe and fascination we had felt since leaving Quito peaked at that moment. We felt like intruders in a frightening and alien world.

The Amazon is a world of extraordinary richness. The visitors' book at our lodge told us, "Just around you at the lodge, in a typical four square mile patch of rainforest, one should be able to find 1,500 species of flowering plants, 750 species of trees, 125 species of mammals, 400 species of birds, 100 species of reptiles and 150 species of butterflies." "Ten thousand years in the making, a survivor of the last ice age, the Amazon basin and its diversity is a symbol of all that is good and right on our planet."

But so much threatens that symbol. While traveling down the Napo River in a motorized canoe, we had been struck by the destruction caused by loggers and oil drillers. Oil pipeline ruptures have spilled more oil in Ecuador's Amazon than was released from the

Exxon Valdez. In global terms, the scale of this destruction has been described as "a biological holocaust." Scientists estimate that at least thirty thousand different species are lost each year and warn that if we allow this mass extinction of species to continue unchecked through habitat destruction, global warming, acid rain, and other human-caused changes to the environment, it will surpass the "great dying" of the dinosaurs and associated species 65 million years ago. One such scientist, E. O. Wilson, has argued that we verge on a mass extinction of life caused by human action. He argues that "every scrap of biological diversity is priceless, to be learned and cherished and never to be surrendered without a struggle."[1]

The Meaning of Value and Biodiversity

Biodiversity means the collective diversity of all living things and includes the life-support systems and natural resources upon which we all depend. More formally, it is defined by the 1992 Convention on Biological Diversity as "the variability among living organisms from all sources, including, inter alia, terrestrial, marine and other aquatic ecosystems and the ecological complexes of which they are part; this includes diversity within species, between species and of ecosystems." The extent of this diversity is amazing—at least 10 million species coexist on our planet.

Biodiversity is also a contested concept. For some, the notion is grounded in a conception of rights—the "Noah Principle"—which maintains that every species has an inalienable right to exist. For some, other species have no rights or fewer rights than humans and no or little value apart from their ability to fulfill human needs. While debate centers on the status of human beings in this biological collectivity, there are strong ethical, economic, and ecological arguments for protecting biodiversity. All imply redefining our relationship to the other forms of life with whom we share this small, blue planet.

In *Silent Spring* Rachel Carson presented the most powerful ecological argument for preserving biodiversity in her notion of a web of life that binds together all organisms. The implication of this interconnectedness is that even small change in one area or species will reverberate throughout the ecosystem. It is a web of life or death. Or as Aldo Leopold put it, "The first rule of intelligent tinkering is to save all of the bits and pieces."[2] Complexity is vital because the earth functions as a whole, with each of its ecosystems and landscapes playing their part in the maintenance of the processes that sustain life.

But even looking from a superficial or surface level, from what Bill Devall terms a shallow ecology or a reform environmentalism that views nature only as a collection of natural resources, a case can be made for preserving biodiversity.[3] According to such an argument, the world's diversity of plant and animal species should be protected so that it may be tapped for human benefit because the extinction of species will deprive future generations of new medicines and new strains of food crops. Currently, 80 percent of people in the developing world rely on traditional medicine based on wild plants and animals for their primary health care. At present over 40 percent of pharmaceuticals are derived from natural sources. Yet only 5,000 of the 250,000 flowering plants in the world have been analyzed for their potential pharmacological properties.[4] A microscopic bacterium first discovered in a pool in Yellowstone National Park in 1965 eventually led to DNA fingerprinting technology. Vast numbers of life forms remain unknown to us; this means there are thousands of plants whose human benefits are not known.

Biodiversity also has clear economic value. The collection of a wild species of tomato in South America in the sixties resulted in crossbreeding with domestic species to create a new tomato with marked commercial improvement over other varieties. The discovery of a virus-resistant species of wild maize in Mexico in 1979 has revolutionized maize cultivation. Conserving biodiversity can also be translated into direct economic value through ecotourism. For example, it has been estimated that each elephant in Addo Elephant National Park in South Africa is generating R1.5 million in economic activity per year. Ecotourism, however, will perpetuate the dependence of countries in the Southern Hemisphere on the rich tourists of the Northern Hemisphere. This raises important questions about linking conservation to human benefits.

The 1992 United Nations Convention on Biological Diversity, which was signed by over 150 countries (including South Africa but excluding the United States) at the United Nations Conference on Environment and Development in Rio, requires that signatories

We visited the Rachel Carson Salt Pond Preserve on the shores of Muscongus Bay this morning. Apparently this one-quarter-acre tidal pool was one of her favorite spots. It was dedicated to her in 1970 and is marked by a bronze plaque.

I feel I've learned a lot from Rachel Carson but couldn't finish the collection of letters between her and Dorothy Freeman. At one level it's a really affecting account of a deep, apparently asexual love, and clearly this love was a source of enormous strength and support to Rachel in the last twelve years of her life. I was moved by her last farewell letter: "Never forget, dear one, how deeply I have loved you all these years." I hadn't realized how lonely Rachel was and how much she struggled to write, so this support was clearly crucial. At another level I was incredibly sad that they had so little time together, and I feel angrily determined that Alison and I will be different. The book has given me a new appreciation of Rachel as a person— her generosity and kindness, her total lack of vanity, her devotion to her family. But what has depressed me most is how small the range of communication in Rachel and Dorothy's letters is. There's good stuff

about birds and bird calls, animals, tides, and the tidepools of the Maine coast—things that were important to both of them—but the letters are quite dull. They are full of domestic minutiae to do with visits to the hairdresser and their cats and domestic arrangements and plans for visits. I liked reading that Jeffie (Rachel's kitten) "had a grand play, ate a lamb chop, and is now sound asleep in his basket on the bed," and of her nephew Roger's baby antics, but surely there was more in their lives that they could have shared. There's nothing (at least in the one hundred pages I read before giving up) about some of the major events in the world, and there was so much happening in the United States at this time (1952–64)—like McCarthyism and the rise of the military-industrial complex. Certainly Carson spoke out strongly about radioactive waste and the hazards of "the atomic age" on numerous public occasions, and paging through the rest of the book I came across a few references to the world—for example, Rachel was deeply upset by Kennedy's assassination. But their relationship does feel somewhat narrow. Perhaps they had rich telephone conversations instead.

One of the most impressive qualities is that there was no false separation in Carson between people and nature. Patricia Hynes wrote about how Carson brought together a love of nature and a concern for human beings in a complex unity, rarely if ever achieved in conservationist and humanist circles. Hynes also speaks of "the rich, discerning capacity for friendship with women which marked her life." So much is only now beginning to emerge about how women sustained each other—Eleanor Roosevelt and Lorna Hickok, Sarah Orne Jewett and Annie Fields, to mention only two examples.

I was distressed by Dorothy's anxiety about their love being labeled lesbian. I'm not sure whether this was a sexual love but they certainly felt the need to camouflage the intensity of their mutual affection.

PERINET, MADAGASCAR
OCTOBER 23, 1998

The call of the indri has been described as "one of the most exciting and neck-tingling sounds in nature," an "eerie, wailing sound somewhere between the song of a whale and a police-siren." We spent hours watching them; the largest of the lemurs, they stand about three feet high, look a little like pandas, are among the 3 percent of mammal species that are monogamous, and are capable of amazing leaps through the treetops. The Malagasy call them *babakota,* meaning "the father of man," which suggests an indigenous understanding of evolution. They live up to ninety years of age in small family groups. Tragically, only an estimated 280 indri remain in the world, and they are all found in this reserve. And this is also one of the few densely forested areas left in Madagascar.

This great red island, famous for its unique plants and animals, is also one of the poorest countries in the world and illustrates all the tensions between saving habitat to preserve biodiversity and the needs of indigenous peoples for land to cultivate foodstuffs like rice. Tourism does have the potential to link the two but is embryonic. For example, Perinet Reserve

provides employment for only twenty-seven local people trained as guides, and half the small entrance fee goes to the local community. We spent two days at the hotel Feon 'Ny Ala (the name means "window of the forest") and walked to the nearby hotel Buffet de la Gare, where Gerald Durrell and David Attenborough both stayed. The lack of tourist development means that these establishments are rudimentary.

Later in our visit we felt somewhat schizophrenic when we flew to Nosy Be—"the perfumed island"— so called because it is scented with vanilla flowers. Its an area that does seem to attract more tourists, mainly rich Germans and Italians. We went snorkeling on a coral reef and ate grilled fish served on banana leaves and crab cooked in coconut milk on the beach. Our hotel room had a view of the sea and we spent one entire day lying under the coconut palms sipping rum and Coke and feeling like rich, spoiled tourists ourselves.

Tourism may help to protect both lemurs and human beings but we were told that at present only about 20 percent of tourists visit a national park or reserve. Overall there are only six national parks and the latest, Ranomafana, seems to have been established largely through the efforts of an American woman, Patricia Wright, who, in 1985, first described the golden bamboo lemur. Pictures show a little creature with big, watchful eyes and gray fur that lives on the cyanide-laced shoots of young bamboo and can consume amounts of the poison that would kill a grown man. According to a profile in the *New York Times* of August 11, 1988, Wright's "extraordinary contribution has been her ability to see the intimate link between the beauty and fascination of the animals and the lives of the people. . . . It's so easy to say that what matters is the animals or what matters is the people. Pat has been able to say that what matters is both."

Established in 1991, Ranomafana National Park protects 108,000 acres, is home to twelve types of lemurs, and is linked to the establishment of new schools and health care centers. It provides employment for 133 villagers, though this is a tiny amount given that some 77,000 people live in the vicinity.

Madagascar was the site of one of the first Debt for Nature swaps whereby part of the country's debt was written off against the establishment of protected areas. In the meantime the number of lemurs, unique to Madagascar, and ranging from the indri to the two-ounce mouse lemur, continue to dwindle, and Madagascar is one of the ten poorest countries in the world.

adopt methods to conserve the variety of living species and ensure equitable sharing of the benefits from sustainable use of biological diversity. To achieve the latter goal the Biodiversity Convention stresses the need for involvement of adjacent communities in the development and management of protected areas. Many of these adjacent communities lack access to power and resources. A feminist analysis is grounded in trying to understand power and how it operates in gendering the world and thus is useful in understanding the contest over biodiversity.

A Feminist Lens on Biodiversity and Environmentalism

Looking at biodiversity through a feminist lens means recognizing how our interaction with nature is shaped by gender relations that operate to privilege men and subordinate women. Women's responses to environmental issues are strongly mediated by gender ideologies, the gendered division of labor, and women's access to resources and power. Women and men do have different relationships to nature, but a feminist lens on environmental issues is different from an ecofeminist perspective. Whereas a feminist lens is grounded in the material conditions and lived experience of women, as these are structured by gender relations, ecofeminism asserts women's closeness to nature. In their writings, ecofeminists such as Susan Griffin and Mary Daly have argued that the bond of women with nature represents a significant and empowering bridge for women—a route to "natural" cycles. This perspective thus implies an essentialism that devalues differences in women's material conditions and other social divisions—such as those of race, class, ethnicity, and age. Furthermore, the gendering of nature as a nurturing mother or goddess by some ecofeminists has fostered a romanticism that diverts attention from confronting material conditions. In its favor, ecofeminism has succeeded in mobilizing women on behalf of biodiversity and sustainable development. For example, India's Chipko movement, which aims to save forests from becoming fuelwood, has its historical roots in ancient Indian cultures that worshipped tree goddesses and sacred trees as images of the cosmos. A feminist lens, rather than an ecofeminist one, demonstrates that while women bear the brunt of environmental problems and are largely excluded from attempts to formulate policy solutions, they also provide some of the models and much of the energy for grass-roots environmental movements.

The main victims of environmental degradation are the poorest people, and the majority of these everywhere are women. In South Africa black peasant women deal directly with the resource base. They gather wood, carry water, and struggle to provide food for themselves and their dependents. They do so in a position of powerlessness and vulnerability. In South Africa black women's lack of access to land is due to the land shortage, the overcrowding of the apartheid homeland system, and traditional patriarchal practices. These practices exclude women from community decision making, from power and control over their lives. Customary law, to which rural, black women were subject, excluded them from citizenship because it designated them minors subject to the authority of their fathers and husbands. Traditional systems of land tenure enabled families to claim land from the greater community and granted the male head of the household certain powers in community decision making. The breakdown of traditional household and community organization, however, has left women in an invidious position. Instead of gaining formal status in decision making by assuming responsibility for land management, they are merely perceived to be operating on behalf of their husbands or fathers.

Women everywhere manage the daily interaction their families have with the environment. In South Africa black working-class and peasant women organize most household consumption of resources in both rural and urban areas. Because of the disruption of black family life caused by apartheid and the migrant labor system, they often do so alone. Across South Africa, 26 percent of households are headed by women, and in the cities the figure is 35 percent.[5] The majority of black South African women need to support themselves economically; even those with male partners are usually unable to support themselves and their families on only the low wages these men earn. This emphasis on women's poverty and vulnerability does not mean that these women are helpless victims. In fact, women were in the forefront of the struggle against apartheid and are a major source of energy in the emerging environmental movement.

Increasingly, women are providing the commitment in environmental struggles around the globe, such as that of Chipko in India and the anti–toxic waste movement in the United States. Women's voices on environmental issues emerged strongly and clearly at the World Women's Congress for a Healthy Planet in Miami in 1991, one of the preparatory meetings to the United Nations conference. Miami seemed an appropriate location because it is the scene of one of the worst environmental crimes of the century—the destruction of the Everglades. Once a vast ecosystem that covered 4 million acres, the Everglades now occupies a mere 10 percent of its original expanse. What remains is largely due to the conservation efforts of the Florida Federation of Women, who in 1916 acquired the 4,000 acres that became the nucleus of Everglades National Park, and to one woman in particular, Marjory Stoneman Douglas. Her 1947 book, *The Everglades: River of Grass,* transformed public perceptions of the wetlands, which were then primarily considered useless swamps that should be drained and developed for farming and housing. Many now believe that without Douglas the Everglades would probably be little more than a memory.

The damage done to the Everglades is a warning about the destructive power of irresponsible and greedy "development." But instead of dwelling on the past, the Miami conference looked to the future. It was intended to assert their creative power and strengthen the power of women to address global environmental degradation. Perhaps the most moving moment in the Congress came at the opening ceremony when Marjory Stoneman Douglas, then one hundred years old, was wheeled into the auditorium and received a standing ovation from the almost nine hundred women present.

Marjory Stoneman Douglas, along with Rachel Carson, highlighted the two main threats to the preservation of biological diversity— habitat loss and pollution. Rachel Carson has been criticized of late for her "political softness," for perpetuating conventional beliefs about nature, and for failing to question the capitalist interests shaping pesticide production at the time. However, despite (or perhaps because of) *Silent Spring*'s missing politics, it acted as a catalyst to the modern environmental movement. Even so, world pesticide production has increased dramatically.

In *Silent Spring* Rachel Carson revealed how the war on people and the war on nature were connected and often employed the same weapons. Nerve gases developed for World War II were used as pesticides in agriculture in peacetime. Similarly, herbicides developed for agriculture before the Vietnam War were used as defoliants in Vietnam. Carson's biographer, Patricia Hynes, has pointed out that the destruction of people and nature with chemical poisons constitutes the same failure to solve problems other than by violence.[6]

Carson's central message was that the methods employed for insect control were so violent that they would destroy people too. In a new wave of concern some biologists in the United States are cautioning that trace amounts of pesticides and other human-made substances may be interfering with the action of reproductive hormones and are therefore damaging the fertility of various animal populations, including humans. At least forty-five synthetic chemicals, most of them pesticides, have been found to affect hormones. Many scientists agree that these endocrine disrupters pose a potentially serious threat to conserving biodiversity. The current discussion among scientists is, in some ways, a replay of the one in *Silent Spring,* since Carson argued that fat soluble pesticides in the bodies of birds were interfering with reproduction.[7]

Increasing numbers of women are involved in these environmental initiatives, and increasingly women's voices are warning that since wars against nature and people are connected, militarization is a major threat to the preservation of biodiversity. But true voices are in danger of being silenced under the impact of a growing backlash directed against the green movement. In the United States, "for conservatives, a green scare is replacing the red menace."[8] One American critic, George Reisman, a professor of economics at Pepperdine University, "condemns environmentalism as every bit as menacing to capitalism as Bolshevism or Nazism. The movement's contention that nonhuman nature possesses intrinsic value is a thin cover for its true goal, which is, according to Reisman, 'nothing less than the undoing of the Industrial Revolution, and the return to the poverty, filth and misery of earlier centuries.'"[9]

This backlash has taken some extreme forms, and many environmental activists—including women—have paid heavy penalties. Scorn is a commonplace weapon of the powerful. Rachel Carson was pilloried and called a spinster who should have no concern with genetics. The persecution of environmental activists is worse in the poor countries of Brazil, India, and Kenya, where environmentalism has become linked to the struggle for human rights. A case in point is that of Kenya's Wangari Maathai, founder of the Green Belt movement that has planted millions of trees worldwide. Also a pro-democracy activist, Maathai has been tear-gassed, clubbed by police, and imprisoned for her activities.

A feminist lens also implies a sensitivity to how women (along with powerless men) are excluded from policy formulation and conventional decision making on environmental issues. For example, the largest environmental impact assessment ever done in southern Africa—the proposal to mine the shores of Lake St. Lucia—largely excluded local people apart from the local tribal authority that is limited to men. The environmental movement may also be in danger of reproducing the structures of elite male dominance. In the United States Patricia Hynes has pointed to "the tradition of women in the conservation and environmental movement functioning as the supporters and helpmates of the heroic male leaders. This role has rendered the majority of women invisible, understated, or mute to history."[10]

Feminist environmentalists, however, have not paid sufficient attention to women's varied complicity in the structures and practices that abuse the environment, specifically their role in promoting excessive consumerism and animal abuse. For example, the feminist geographer Joni Seager acknowledges that even though women wear most of the consumer furs produced in the United States and the United Kingdom, fur-wearing by women is largely the vehicle of men's fantasies and men's sense of self-importance. "The fur trade is a big business, run by men, for men, with enormous profits reaped by men."[11] It is not enough, then, for an individual woman to stop wearing fur; women must change the thinking that leads to such exploitation of animals and women. Feminism must provide a political platform to challenge women's complicity and support for practices such as the fur trade and battery farming that involve confining animals to small spaces. This challenge depends on a new understanding of our relationship to other living creatures.

The Politics of Biodiversity

Debates on biodiversity and environmentalism need to be related to the main fault line dividing our planet today—the divide between the Northern and Southern Hemispheres. Biodiversity is richest in the South, but arouses most concern in the North. In this increasingly polarized world, biodiversity and environmentalism are understood very differently in these two areas. For instance, the American social anthropologist Anna Tsing has delineated two environmentalisms: an environmentalism of the rich countries, which attempts to manage global resources for the benefit of nature lovers and consumers, and an environmentalism of the poor countries, which builds from grass-roots awareness of the dangers of misusing natural resources and aims for social equity in resource management. Possibly this is too stark a contrast since both forms exist in South Africa at present—the one oriented to preservationist conservation, the other to social justice.

But in all forms of environmentalism "nature" and "wilderness" are constructs with contrasting meanings in different cultures. Mainstream environmental groups from the North too often argue for a notion of wilderness as a region empty of human habitation and activities. This notion is foreign to many grass-roots environmental activists in the South, where wilderness accommodates humans. For example, the Green Belt movement in Kenya planted trees to fight desertification and soil erosion to protect local communities; there is little notion of the wild as a place apart or even clear demarcations between nature and culture. In their daily activities many rural peasants in the South avoid both the claim that nature should be preserved free from human intervention and the opposite claim that nature exists only for human consumption.

Some of these diverging perspectives surfaced at the Earth Summit in Rio in 1992—the largest gathering of world leaders in history. But participants did agree on the need for sustainable development in which economic growth no longer results in the net destruction of natural resources. The Rio Declaration on Environment and Development stresses the necessary interconnection between economic progress and environmental protection, a connection that informs

Agenda 21, the action plan for the declaration's implementation. Agenda 21 recognizes the need to eradicate poverty by increasing poor people's access to the resources they need to live sustainably and the need for wide public participation in environmental issues.

The disparate conceptions of biodiversity emerged sharply again in 1997 during the debate on the elephant downlisting proposal at the Convention on International Trade in Endangered Species of Wild Flora and Fauna (CITES) in Harare, Zimbabwe. At this meeting representatives from 139 countries debated the future of eighty-nine species. The most contentious issue was whether the controlled sale of ivory would lead to the salvation or the extermination of the African elephant, of which there are now some 500,000 throughout the continent, down from roughly 1.3 million in 1979. Representatives from Namibia, Botswana, and Zimbabwe submitted proposals to CITES for downlisting their elephant populations from Appendix 1 (a category of animals whose products may not be traded) to Appendix 2 (a list of animals whose products may be the subject of limited international trade). Since elephants and ivory are a natural resource of African countries, they argued that these resources should be used in a sustainable way to benefit local communities. They argued that because of an abundance of the mammals, herds can be safely culled and their ivory used to generate desperately needed funds for conservation and rural development. For example, Zimbabwe's president, Robert Mugabe, whose country has about R18 million worth of stockpiled ivory, maintained that the animals must pay for themselves. Such arguments about the sustainable utilization of wildlife are often framed by a notion of "African conservation." The main opposing argument from groups such as the Species Survival Network, a consortium of over thirty nongovernmental organizations mainly based in Europe and North America, was that any relaxation of the ivory trade ban would send a message to poachers and illegal traders that an open market is imminent and will spur the slaughter of elephants in anticipation of a wider relaxation of the trade ban. The landmark decision was to relax the ban on the international ivory trade. In a secret ballot CITES voted that Zimbabwe, Namibia, and Botswana could sell ivory to Japan. An animal rights group called the decision a death sentence for thousands of elephants.[12]

The debate had ethical dimensions, a stark expression of which is whether elephants are a natural resource to be used to benefit humans—illustrating sustainable utilization—or sentient mammals capable of feeling pain and fear that are members of a biotic community—illustrating animal rights. To many in the North, elephants are objects of awe and admiration; to many in the South, they are pests who damage crops and homes. The struggle is to transform elephants from economic liabilities into community assets. The debate also had practical dimensions regarding whether lifting the ban would lead to increased poaching (a connection difficult if not impossible to measure) and whether the countries of the South in which elephants live and the consumer countries of elephant products in the North, such as Japan, have the capacity to control the trade.

In the last few years CITES has become a battleground for the contrasting notions of conservation put forward by the North and the South, with the South accusing the North of trying to turn its countries into natural history museums. Characteristically, the South African and the U.S. representatives at the 1997 meeting took opposing positions, with South Africa coordinating broad agreement among the African states. Overall, South Africa and the United States illustrate the two poles of environmental approaches.

South Africa is a microcosm of current global challenges. With its mix of Third World environmental problems, such as soil erosion, and First World environmental problems, such as air pollution, it dramatizes the conservation challenges facing the planet. With one of the most unequal distributions of income in the world, South Africa is also a microcosm of the injustice that divides the planet into the rich countries of the North and the impoverished ones of the South. South Africa's natural resources are exceptionally diverse, with over 240 species of mammals (including the world's largest land mammal, the elephant), 887 different species of birds (including the world's largest bird, the ostrich), 1,200 kinds of trees (Europe has about 300), and over 20,000 species of flowering plants. But these diverse forms of life are not adequately protected. Protected areas cover only 6 percent of the land area. Almost 200 mammals, birds, reptiles, amphibians, and fish are threatened with extinction, as are over 2,000 plant species. The threat to these range from the destruction of their habitat through the spread of urban and industrial infrastructure to pollution, illegal trade, and the irresponsible use of poisons by farmers. All these threats are anchored in social practices and understandings that fail to value different life forms.[13]

At the same time the United States highlights the problems of consumerism and pollution that threaten the preservation of biodiversity. This country consumes almost half of the earth's resources and emits half of its pollution. According to the President's Council on Environmental Quality, in 1992 nearly 600 plant and animal species were listed as threatened or endangered in the United States, about 4,000 were under consideration, and as many as 9,000 were at risk.[14]

While biodiversity is highly valued in the North, it is arguable that the majority of people in the South—and Africa specifically—do not yet have a living standard sufficient to make them willing to give up anything to ensure the survival of an endangered species. There is no known way of measuring the value of any species to the world. The concept of "protecting biodiversity" is especially problematic in a country of people struggling to survive. The man who snared the last leopard in a remote mountainous area of South Africa has described pride at his deed. For years these animals had been killing his sheep and now they were gone. Herbert Monnye was then asked how he would feel if that had been the very last leopard left on earth? Monnye's grin only widened. His replied that the one who finally eliminated this vermin would be a true king among men.[15]

At a debate entitled "Do Animals Have to Pay to Stay" held in Johannesburg in 1997, some argued that "the extreme 'use it or lose it' school, which assumes that sustainable use can easily be achieved, will lead to a homogeneous, biologically depleted and socially and economically impoverished world."[16] On the same occasion the paleoanthropologist Richard Leakey argued that preserving biodiversity was a state responsibility that could not be left to the whims of the marketplace.

Protected Areas of Biodiversity

Protected areas are the front line in the battle to conserve biodiversity. Strictly protected areas—in the form of national parks and game and nature reserves—form a small proportion of the total landscape, only

A disappointing evening at the dam, as not a single crowned crane appeared. The flocks of tall, golden, crowned cranes who used to fly in to roost here in the evenings, celebrating the end of the day with their weird croaking calls, used to carry the hopes of this little town in the foothills of the Drakensberg Mountains. It is the only place in the world where three different varieties of cranes—blue, wattled, and crowned—coexist. In a talk here some years ago the head of the International Crane Foundation from the United States referred to this as symbolizing the peaceful and harmonious coexistence of English, Afrikaner, and Zulu communities in the area. But any "peace" or "harmony" is illusory. Recent reports of cruelty to black farmworkers by white farmers and the continuing terrible poverty of the majority of the black population dispel the happy facade. It is hoped that the promotion of Wakkerstroom as a birdwatching destination (reportedly there are 350 species in the area) will generate employment in various ecotourism projects. But the place also provides us with two examples of how such efforts can backfire. One reason the crowned cranes no longer roost at the dam is that a hide for birdwatchers was built too close. And last week a local youth offered a captured crowned crane and a chick for sale for R20.

about 3 percent of the earth's surface. South Africa currently has only 5.5 percent of its land area conserved.[17] This is well short of the internationally accepted figure of 10 percent to which South Africa is committed as a signatory to the Convention on Biological Diversity.

The inclusion of local people in both material benefits and decision making in protected area management is essential to the conservation of biodiversity. It is in this sense that, as the South African minister of land affairs said in 1994, "conservation is far more a social challenge than a biological one. . . . National Parks should not be seen as isolated islands of biodiversity, but part of an overall land use policy."[18] In a similar vein, Robbie Robinson, the former executive director of the National Parks Board in South Africa, maintained that poverty in South Africa was the greatest threat to biodiversity and environmental integrity and emphasized promoting the relationship between conservation and rural development.

This concern with the development of rural communities is recent and involves an element of redress. In both the United States, largely in the nineteenth century, and in South Africa, establishing protected areas often meant dislocating, dispossessing, and removing local people. For example, the Makuleke were forced from the area that became part of Kruger National Park. In the 1850s U.S. troops flushed the final Ahwahneechee out of the Yosemite Valley. Thus, in both the North and the South, dispossession was often the other side of conservation.

The United States pioneered modern Western-style conservation in two senses: in passing the first law to protect wilderness, which established Yellowstone as the first national park in 1872, and in passing the Wilderness Act of 1964. While this act was the product of a long campaign and was hailed at the time by protectionists as a "benchmark" it was extremely limited. Though the legislation set aside wilderness areas, it also allowed significant exemptions for water development, livestock grazing, recreational uses, and mining.

Yellowstone and Kruger are the two oldest national parks in the world, but their images have been used to do more than preserve biodiversity. Each park has been employed to promote an ideology that historically involved the oppression and exclusion of indigenous populations. In the United States the establishment of national parks has been described as "an attempt to forge a national identity out of natural grandeur."[19] In South Africa Jane Carruthers has documented how the notion of conservation was used to mobilize an exclusive Afrikaner nationalism in which the mythologized figure of Paul Kruger, after whom the Kruger National Park is named, was central. Although both Yellowstone, championed by John Muir, and Kruger are associated with charismatic individuals, these men seem diametrical opposites— Kruger is a crude politician compared with the gentle pantheist Muir. The effect of these men's efforts is the same, however: "As in their formation a century or more ago, today's parks remain a powerful cultural statement fusing notions of nature and nation."[20]

Fortunately, managers of national parks in both societies are rethinking their relationships to local communities. In South Africa acceptance is growing for local communities to have rights to park resources. They are shifting away from a colonial model of conservation focused on preservation to an indigenous community–based model of conservation focused on human benefits through traditional practices of sustainable utilization. Although national parks in both countries face ongoing threats from industrial and commercial developments, particularly mining, the United States, pioneer of Western-style conservation, is leading the way in wilderness destruction through commercial interests. The relationship between conservation and commercial interests is a complex and contested one, but a more holistic understanding that links biodiversity to sustainable development in a new form of environmentalism is emerging.

Environmental Initiatives in the United States and South Africa

In South Africa, as in the United States, race intersects with class to create special environmental and health vulnerabilities. The phrase *environmental racism* has been used to describe the disparate impact of environmental hazards on communities of color, as well as racial discrimination in the enforcement of environmental regulations and laws. In the United States race has been found to be an independent factor (not reducible to class) in predicting the distribution of air pollution, contaminated fish consumption, municipal landfills and incinerators, abandoned toxic waste dumps, and lead poisoning in children.[21] White communities see faster action, better results, and stiffer penalties than communities where blacks, Hispanics, and other minorities predominantly live. Armed with this evidence of "environmental racism" a loose alliance of church, labor, civil rights, and community groups led by people of color is emerging to demand environmental justice.

In South Africa a similar development has taken the form of the Environmental Justice Networking Forum, a coalition of over five hundred organizations united in their commitment to environmental justice. This is defined as "social transformation directed towards meeting basic human needs and enhancing our quality of life—economic quality, health care, housing, human rights, environmental protection, and democracy. In linking environmental and social justice issues the environmental justice approach seeks to challenge the abuse of power which results in poor people having to suffer the effects of environmental damage caused by the greed of others."[22]

Environmental racism in South Africa still has to be systematically documented. Poor black people confined to townships such as Soweto suffer most from air pollution—not only from power plant emissions but also from coal stoves—though the government has not taken adequate note of such disparities. Disregard for black people led to the siting of polluting industries nearby, but left them legally unprotected from the health consequences. For example, the Indian township of Merebank, near Durban, is surrounded by two oil refineries, a paper mill, a chromium processing plant, and several smaller chemical factories. Merebank's children are ten times more likely to suffer from respiratory disorders than children who live nearby.[23] But the worst example of environmental racism in South Africa is that of the nuclear waste facility situated in Vaalputs in Namaqualand. Although the area is sparsely populated, the communities in the vicinity have existed for generations. The place was deliberately chosen to ensure that no white towns were in a fifty-kilometer range of the waste site.

In South Africa the notion of environmental racism is powerful, especially in the reconfiguration of the discourse on environmentalism, and contributes to addressing another serious legacy of the apartheid regime—the absence of a mass-based environmental movement. Most environmental organizations in South Africa have three characteristics: their social composition is largely white and middle class, their understandings of environmental issues are largely class-biased, and their approaches are superficial in the sense that they deal with effects rather than causes. Until very recently the dominant approach toward environmental issues in South Africa was an authoritarian conservation one. This focused on the preservation of wilderness areas and particular species of plants and animals and presented itself as operating "outside of politics." Within this perspective overpopulation was often identified as the main environmental problem. People were perceived as responsible for destroying trees and creating waste and conservation efforts were divorced from the issue of development. Only very recently has an alternative progressive perspective begun to emerge. This perspective views environmental issues as deeply political in that they are embedded in access to power and resources in society. It is critical of the victim-blaming approach inherent in earlier movements and insists on the need for development to overcome poverty.

However, the legacy of the authoritarian conservation perspective is that many black South Africans view environmental issues with suspicion as "white middle-class concerns." Farieda Kahn has pointed to "the negative environmental perceptions and attitudes of many black people, ranging from apathy to hostility."[24] This hostility is often grounded in the many conservation projects of the past that disregarded human rights and dignity and in which "conservation" meant dispossession. Put simply, if conservation means losing water rights, losing grazing and arable land, and being dumped in resettlement areas without even the most rudimentary infrastructure, vigorous anticonservation ideology results. Further, resistance to creating game and nature reserves must be understood in the context of the Land Acts of 1913 and 1936, which restricted black land ownership to 13 percent of the country and forced relinquishment of community and family lands and thereby livelihoods. Kahn maintains that "feelings of alienation and disconnection from the land" are at the root of "the problem of negative environmental perception and attitude."[25]

Clearly, what is needed in both the United States and South Africa is a convergence of two movements that, in both societies, were historically splintered. The first is the movement for the protection and conservation of wilderness, which developed quite separately from the second, whose focus is on issues generated by urbanization, such as water quality, sewage and sanitation, solid and hazardous waste generation and disposal. To make environmental concerns relevant to everyone means taking an all-encompassing view that links issues of wilderness and biodiversity to issues of human health and pollution. Fortunately in both societies there are signs of an embryonic but developing "new environmentalism." This rejuvenated movement in South Africa is beginning to address urban issues, particularly those of occupational health and pollution. It was estimated that by the year 2000 two-thirds of the South African population would live in cities. The focus on the traditional "big five" of tourism—lion, elephant, leopard, rhino, and buffalo—is being expanded to include the new "big five" of the urban environment—housing, electricity, water, sewerage, and refuse removal. This represents an important new synthesis.

To make this synthesis effective, our starting point must be an understanding of power relations in our society. Many conservationists fail or are reluctant to view environmental issues as fundamentally political and deeply embedded in relations of power. Their naivete causes them to overemphasize the potential of the environment to serve as a unifying issue. To overcome this weakness they must attend to varying material conditions and competing class interests. Much of our present environmental crisis is comprehensible only in terms of the pursuit of power and profit. For instance, Joni Seager has shown how large-scale environmental degradation is the product of militaries and multinationals, both male-dominated institutions. The understanding of power that is at the center of current feminist thinking could strengthen this emerging new environmentalism in both the United States and South Africa.

Conclusion

It is not men exclusively but *Homo sapiens,* a primate risen in Africa from a lineage that split away from the chimpanzee line 5 to 8 million years ago, that most threatens biodiversity. This understanding of our origins is not commonly accepted. Jonathan Weiner refers to a 1995 poll demonstrating "that nearly half of the citizens of the United States do not believe in evolution. Instead they believe that life was created by God in something like its present form, within the past ten thousand years."[26] Many people not only reject evolution but also hold to a stereotyped view of other animals as completely different from ourselves, totally deficient in intelligence and emotion. The reality is that nature is fluid, and the new science of ethology is revealing a surprising repertoire of competencies and activities among other animals. Species are not fixed, as many scientists once believed, and the differences between them are becoming increasing blurred as we make discoveries. As Darwin argued, one animal species can shade into another; there are no rigid and immutable species barriers; hybridization is far more common than we had supposed: "The borders between species are as fluid and adaptable, as sensitive to changes in pressure, as the heaving waves in a high sea."[27]

Much of our earlier, rigid categorizations were anchored in ignorance. Benjamin Franklin called our kind "Homo faber," Man the Toolmaker; even in the 1960s tool-making was considered a distinctively human capacity. We now know that chimpanzees, as well as certain species of Darwin's finches, use tools. Nor are humans exceptional in learning new tricks from one another; all animal behavior cannot be explained simply by instinct. Mammals such as lions, apes, and elephants learn from their elders. The notion that human behavior is shaped by culture, in contrast to animal behavior that is driven by rigid patterns of instincts, is now open to question. Evolutionary biologists have shown us that natural selection can shape sexual preferences, so mating patterns can shift, change, and evolve. As Weiner notes, "arrangements between males and females—arrangements and behaviors we think of as primary, as given, fixed, almost immutable—these are not permanent at all. Behavior is the product of forces, contending forces that are still contending today, struggling within each generation. The borders between species are continually tested and redefined."[28]

Like many others, Richard Leakey views the division between species as not black and white, but rather an infinite gradation. He admits that he does not know exactly what it is to be human.[29] Similarly, Holmes Rolston remarks, "We cannot draw as comfortable a line between humans and animals as we once thought."[30] Over a century before Leakey and Rolston, Charles Darwin addressed species differentiation: "Man in his arrogance thinks himself a great work, worthy the interposition of a deity." Why should we assume that consciousness is a uniquely human quality? "It is our arrogance. . . . It is our admiration of ourselves."[31] Similarly, Sigmund Freud declared, "Humanity has in the course of time had to endure from the hands of science two great outrages upon its naive self-love. The first was when it realized that our earth was not the center of the universe, but only a speck in a world-system of a magnitude hardly conceivable. The second was when biological research robbed man of his particular privilege of having been specially created, and relegated him to a descent from the animal world."[32]

This human concern with distinguishing ourselves from other animals on the grounds that we speak, reason, imagine, love, fear, anticipate, worship is what Pierre van den Berghe calls "the vanity factor": "Since Copernicus, science gradually displaced man and his planet from the comfortable center of the universe. The myopia of anthropocentrism is generic to our species, but doubly acute among social scientists who base their livelihood on claims of human uniqueness. It was difficult enough to accept that man was animal and thus evolved by natural selection, but a last line of exceptionalism was erected to save the human ego. Sure man was an animal, but a very special and unique kind of animal, an animal with a soul, a psyche, a mind and culture."[33]

This "human exceptionalism" paradigm is increasingly being brought into question by mounting evidence from ethological studies. We are beginning to understand that other animals have equally complex patterns of social organization. Anna Rasa's evidence of role allocation and conformity among a dwarf mongoose community is a powerful illustration. These animals have complex social interactions, clearly demarcated divisions of labor, and tightly defined roles. They demonstrate unmistakable qualities of altruism and affection; their warning calls can convey what type of predator has been sighted, how high, the degree of danger, and the distance; they exhibit "the nearest to human language that we know among mammals."[34] The work of women such as Anna Rasa on mongeese,

I took Jackie to hear Jane Goodall lecture at the Museum of Natural History. Goodall came across as very warm, modest, and likable. She told marvelous stories of how as a child she took earthworms to bed with her so that she could see how they moved without legs and how, at the age of four, she sat for hours in the henhouse to see how a chicken laid an egg. We were both touched by how she paid tribute to her mother's support and encouragement, which dated back to these childhood experiences. It's interesting that all three of "Leakey's angels," the "trimates" Jane Goodall, Dian Fossey, and Biruté Galdikas, were women who lacked the scientific training that Leakey feared would blinker their observations. Leakey thought that women's patience, intuition, and persistence would make them better students of primate behavior than men were. Jackie says that apart from promoting an essentialist view of women, this is not quite fair since some of the longest studies (for example of the bonobos) have been conducted by men. But it makes you wonder why women dominated the field of primatology even before Leakey chose his three women.

We loved Goodall's slides and accounts of chimpanzees—our closest living relations. Goodall grew up believing that humans were toolmakers, that this was what distinguished human beings, but of course her observations over the thirty-five years she spent in Tanzania have challenged that notion. She listed a total of ten ways in which chimps use objects as tools. Her account of what social creatures chimpanzees are reminded Jackie of Anna Rasa, another woman who spent years in the African wilderness, in this case observing mongoose behavior and social organization. Both women, in a totally convincing, unsentimental fashion, demonstrate that mongeese and chimpanzees have emotional capacities and experience grief as well as joy and affection. That knowledge makes the cruelty inflicted on caged animals in zoos and laboratories even more difficult to accept. Goodall argues that chimps are capable of rational thought, simple problem solving, planning for the future, altruism, and developing a sense of self. In her words, chimps are like a bridge linking us to the rest of the animal kingdom. She stressed that all the great apes share a common ancestor with humans that is evident in their similar body structure, behaviors, and DNA. Chimps share almost 99 percent of our genetic material. She also emphasized that, sadly, there are only 250,000 chimpanzees left in twenty-one different African countries and that they are disappearing across most of Africa.

Cynthia Moss on elephants, and Dian Fossey, Biruté Galdikas, and Jane Goodall on primates suggest that human beings are less distinctive and unique than has been commonly supposed.

Even "face-to-face intercourse" was once thought "uniquely human, a cultural innovation reflecting the dignity and sensibility separating the human race from 'lower' life forms." We now know that bonobos—the least understood of the apes—follow the human pattern. Bonobos also "seem capable of taking the perspective of someone else," which Francis De Waal and Frans Lanting point out is "an advanced capacity, which some believe unique to our species."[35]

Research has revealed the complex emotional lives of animals, including their feelings of altruism and love. Jeffrey Moussaieff Masson and Susan McCarthy have demonstrated how denying such "anthropomorphism" and maintaining the species barrier is related to maintaining domination. They ask why the distinction between humans and other animals should be so important to humans and argue that examining the distinctions humans draw among ourselves—among whites and blacks and men and women—may point to the answer: "Dominant human groups have long defined themselves as superior by distinguishing themselves from groups they are subordinating. . . . Thus the distinction between man and beast has served to keep man on top. People define themselves as distinct from animals . . . in order to keep themselves dominant over them. Human beings presumably benefit from treating animals the way they do—hurting them, jailing them, exploiting their labor, eating their bodies, gaping at them, and even owning them as signs of social status."[36] Such abuse is highlighted in the case of vivisection, which involves millions of animals a year in South Africa in cruel and often unnecessary experiments, most of which are performed without anesthesia. In many contexts throughout history, oppressed classes and races have been presumed to be equally insensitive to similar treatment.

A biocentric vision of people as part of the natural world, but not its center, is in sharp contrast with the worldview of technocratic societies, which have become obsessed with control and dominance: humans over nonhuman nature, masculine over feminine, the wealthy and powerful over the poor. In the process of opposing this mindset and moving toward a biocentric vision, one risks incurring the same kind of scorn that was meted out to the antislavery radicals for insisting that slaves were human beings with rights.

A number of contemporary thinkers have drawn a connection between human and animal rights. For example, Alice Walker's response to those who dismiss the concern with animal exploitation as "sentimental" is that they are people who have "destroyed great tracts of feeling in themselves."[37] Gary Snyder suspects that "many of the problems within the human community—racism and sexism, to name two—reflect back from confusion about our relation to nature. Ignorance and hostility toward wild nature set us up for objectifying and exploiting fellow humans."[38]

One danger the planet faces is that this "nature" is interpreted very differently above and below the equator. "Radical environmentalism in South Africa is firmly part of a broader socio-economic and political critique, an anthropocentric approach with the interests of the less privileged at its heart. Radical environmentalism in the United States, by contrast, has tended to be more biocentric, championing the vulnerable and violated members of the natural community."[39] Recognition of this web of interconnectedness implies a decentering of people, which is viewed by some as threatening. Still, things are changing. The World Charter for Nature approved by the United Nations General Assembly in 1982 recognizes that humans are "a part of nature" and that every form of life should be respected.

The biocentric notion of a "natural community" of which people are a part takes us beyond dualistic conceptions of "culture" and "nature." Care and respect for animals as well as other life forms need not necessarily mean a disregard for human needs. For example, common ground exists between the proponents of "sustainable utilization" and those of "animal rights" in the sense that both are committed to the survival of the African elephant. While a tightly controlled trade in elephant products may generate significant material benefits for impoverished rural communities, its impact must be carefully monitored (difficult as this may be) so that most benefits accrue to the rural poor and not to Japanese ivory traders or hunting operators in the United States or international ivory smugglers, whom the International Fund for Animal Welfare have rightly termed "vicious, greedy, selfish and devious people who care for nothing except profit."[40] Empowerment is not incompatible with the expansion of protected areas when local communities participate in their management and benefit in material terms. When approached carefully, conservation can be linked to poverty alleviation. But hunting and culling should be done as humanely as possible and with respect for the animal's social organization and place in the ecosystem. Indigenous cultures of the South—such as that of the San—provide models for such respectful relationships.

This biocentric understanding of humans as neither separate nor dominant but part of the natural world is central to many indigenous cultures that have been subjected to violent conquest. For example, the Amerindians of Guyana have a saying: "The sky is held up by trees. If the forest disappears the sky, which is the roof of the world, will collapse. Nature and man then perish together." Promoting this biocentric understanding involves restoring people's sense of embeddedness in nature so that nature is no longer commodified as an object, outside of and separate from human existence. It also requires changing our understanding of biological difference and extending our appreciation and caring beyond an anthropocentric perspective that is person-centered and concerned exclusively with our own species. The strongest case for preserving biodiversity is an ecological argument that recognizes the interconnectedness of all life forms. All species are related, descended from a common ancestor that lived billions of years ago. Therefore, we are all part of the same biotic community.

Alison,

I just finished reading Biruté Galdikas's book about her work among wild orangutans. Nothing was known about orangutans before her. As recently as the 1960s few scientists had even seen an orangutan in the wild. They once numbered in the hundreds of thousands and roamed throughout Asia. Now fewer than thirty thousand remain in the rapidly disappearing tropical rain forests of Borneo and northern Sumatra. Galdikas has also struggled with the boundaries between animal and human. She notes that the word *orangutan* comes from the Malay term for "person of the forest." To her the distinction between humans and orangutans has begun to blur; she argues that "more than other species, great apes remind us of our unity with nature."

"Leakey's angels"—Biruté Galdikas, Dian Fossey, and Jane Goodall—are all amazing women and have taught us almost everything we know about apes. Quite alone over eighteen years, Fossey changed the public image of the gorilla from monstrous King Kong to peaceful vegetarian. The giant four-hundred-pound silverbacks turned out to be family-oriented patriarchs, patient fathers, and protective mates. Fossey and Galdikas had angry confrontations with loggers and poachers that embittered them both and apparently led to Fossey's murder. I'm not sure that they were always as sensitive to indigenous peoples and their needs as they should have been. For example, Galdikas tried to persuade the authorities to move a whole village outside the orangutan reserve across the Sekonyer River, even though this would have meant enormous social and economic disruption. It's hard to find writers who seem equally sympathetic to people and animals. This is what I'm looking for.

3 Cultural Diversity: Difference without Domination

Hiking in the Kwazulu/Natal Province in the Drakensberg Mountains on a rainy, wintry July day in 1994, we came upon some faded pictures painted on rocks above our heads. The pictures were of hoofed animals—antelope or eland. They had an almost modern, Picasso look, though they possibly dated back to the Stone Age. These rock paintings were contemporary with the better-known cave art of Europe and were one of the few known material reminders of the so-called Bushmen or San peoples in this vast, mountainous region of what is now South Africa. What happened to the San in southern Africa is not that different from what happened to other indigenous peoples around the world. While no one can say with exact certainty what cultures are becoming extinct, estimates suggest that at least one-third of the world's inventory of human cultures have disappeared completely since 1500—their languages, their traditions, their ways of life, their worldviews, and their very identities. These peoples faced extinction for many reasons. Principally, they got in the way of technologically superior cultures and, at the same time, were considered (as were certain racial groups) sub-human.

Cultural differences have always divided people. At the end of the twentieth century, these differences—often of race, ethnicity, religion, class, and language—have been mobilized politically in the form of ethnonationalisms that have ultimately led to armed conflict in such places as Northern Ireland, the former Yugoslavia, the Middle East, and central Africa. And yet, cultural diversity is increasingly valued by artists, scholars, scientists, and even politicians. Seen as a repository of human creativity, such variances can enrich all societies and deepen appreciation of the meaning of being human.

At the beginning of the twenty-first century, cultural diversity is, nevertheless, still under threat worldwide. From the seizing of lands of Yanomani Indians in Brazil to the displacement of the Wanniya-laeto, perhaps better known as the Veddahs of Sri Lanka, cultural diversity is slowly disappearing. In this chapter, we argue that cultural preservation is a complicated issue not only in terms of what constitutes authenticity and who is being represented but also because the goal of preserving diverse cultures has often become synonymous with the struggle for human survival and self-determination.

The San of Southern Africa

The art on the rocks of the Drakensberg constitutes one of South Africa's most important historical records. They are the clearest form of what remains of the original culture of the San peoples. It is estimated that between thirty and ninety thousand San lived in southern Africa before colonialization, and now less than three thousand are left in South Africa, though higher numbers still dwell in neighboring Botswana and Namibia. Who were these "first South Africans" and what happened to them?

The most pervasive reminders of their once lively communities in South Africa are these remarkable rock paintings. According to R. Townley Johnson, who had spent a quarter century tracking down rock painting sites throughout southern Africa, some one thousand such sites currently exist.[1] Some paintings have been dated by various technological methods to at least 25,500 B.C., while others depict scenes from the mid-nineteenth century.

Despite the absence of a written language system, the San graphics provide many clues to the lives of these people. For example, food remains from the archaeological sites indicate that the artists were not depicting animals commonly eaten. The prominence of the

Dressed in brightly colored robes of red and blue and wearing tall yellow headdresses, the dancers whirled and twisted to the beat of a gong. We felt privileged to be witnessing a demonstration of an ancient shaman ritual. It was a dramatic scene, dominated by the powerful peak of Snow Dragon Mountain and witnessed by some hundred villagers, mostly old and bent, wearing faded Mao trousers and jackets. While this ritual excluded women, it reflected the efforts of a small minority to preserve their cultural practices against Han dominance. We talked about this province of China, where the greatest concentration of ethnic minorities—twenty-two distinct peoples—live. But even here, these ethnic groups constitute less than 25 percent of the total population of Yunnan. Nevertheless, this ethnic diversity gives Yunnan its character and has helped to make the old city of Lijiang a UNESCO-sponsored World Heritage Site. One reason China has remained so united and successful, despite its vastness, is the predominance of the Han culture. Nearly 90 percent of the more than 1 billion Chinese are Han, and, if you add all the other ethnic minorities together, of which there are approximately thirty-six, you still would not begin to have the kind of culture clashes that characterize most of Africa or the Americas during the height of colonization, when so many indigenous communities were either wiped out or dispossessed of their lands. Now China sees the value of "exotic" ethnics like the shaman dancers and has decided to develop a tourist industry to "show off" these peoples to Westerners like us. Even the Han from the northern provinces vacation down here to take in the "local color" at Las Vegas–like restaurants with Naxshai showgirls.

Our deepest experience of a different culture, admittedly through the shallow nature of "the tourist gaze," probably came in Bali. Jackie met me in the Singapore airport and we had a marvelous few days on holiday there. Bali is an incredibly colorful and diverse place of golden beaches, volcanoes, and emerald rice fields. We walked through magical rain forests, explored some amazing temples—especially one that is situated on a cliff top high above the ocean—and marveled at the beauty and color of the people, especially the processions of women carrying towering offerings of fruits, flowers, and rice cakes on their heads to present to the Hindu deities at the ubiquitous temples.

The spirit of Hinduism is everywhere—baskets of flowers offered to placate evil spirits and stone figures draped with black-and-white checked cloths, which symbolize the balance between good and evil. Linked to this pervasive spirituality is a simple beauty and attentiveness to detail in everything: clothes, buildings, the way food was served on banana leaves, and the flowers decorating all the stone figures. For instance there

are the *penjor,* which are tall decorated bamboo poles placed in front of each Balinese household and temple for the Galungan holiday. Hanging from the end of every *penjor* are beautifully plaited palm leaf decorations called *sampian.* It made me think of Gerda Lerner's assertion that all human beings are practicing historians; in this case, every Balinese woman is a practicing artist. Much of what we saw was incomprehensible—especially the complex meanings of the *wayang wong* and *legong* dances—and we promised to prepare better for our next trip.

We specifically vowed to try to learn more about Raden Kartini, an early Indonesian feminist pioneer who believed that "the freedom of women is inevitable" and who challenged Dutch colonial rule and many of the patriarchal practices in nineteenth-century Javanese society, such as arranged marriages. A woman's destiny at that time was, in Kartini's words, "to marry, belong to a man without being asked when, who or how." After reading a translation of Kartini's letters, Eleanor Roosevelt commented, "If we are to become cognizant of the oneness of humanity, regardless of race or creed or color, this will be one of the ways that we will learn." In 1964 the government of Indonesia posthumously awarded Kartini the title Heroine of National Independence.

There's a peaceful, tolerant feeling about Bali. There are also lots of thin dogs, but these walked with their tails in the air, unlike in India, and the monkeys are regarded as sacred and are bold and confident as a result. Some parts of the island seem spoiled by large, rich tourist hotels, and Kuta was a nightmare of noise and foreign shoppers. I'm not sure whether this kind of mass tourism is a good or bad thing for indigenous peoples. We are really the first generation of middle-class people who are able to explore the world in this way. It's left us with a lot of questions about the impact of mass tourism and whether it provides a shallow, cheap experience of the exotic, which distances the "other," or a new appreciation of the extent of cultural diversity in the human community.

eland, a large imposing buck, in the Drakensberg art points to a more spiritual dimension to the San's daily existence. It has been argued that this splendid animal was not thought of simply as a source of food, but that it had mythological symbolic meaning. What does this archeological evidence tell us about the lives of these people, a group who were considered by colonizers to be "subhuman" and incapable of abstract thinking?

At the beginning of the twentieth century, German settlers poured into southern Africa. This settlement was made possible by the expansion of the railroad into lands that were previously the exclusive domain of the San. Ignoring the indigenous peoples' land claims, the settlers demanded the removal or, in many cases, the extermination of the San. Their solutions included setting aside distant lands as reserves and, more typically, declaring San to be "vermin" that had to be wiped out. Newspapers of the time described them as "parasitic," "like wild animals," a "deteriorate race."[2]

The situation of the San scarcely changed when the South African government replaced the German colonial administration following World War I. The San were still in the way of progress and few whites or blacks took up their cause, though their numbers were declining precipitously. In 1941, for example, the South African minister for native affairs referred to the San as follows: "It would be a biological crime if we allowed such as peculiar race to die out, because it is a race which looks more like a baboon than a baboon itself does. . . . We look upon them as part of the fauna of the country."[3]

As recently as 1957, it was still possible for a South African anthropologist to characterize the San as a different type of human: "From an anthropological point of view, both racially and culturally, the Bushmen occupy a place quite apart in the human family."[4] This position eerily echoes the dehumanization of blacks under institutional racism. Given this persistent perception, it was not surprising to find a 1996 *New York Times* headline noting that "Endangered Bushmen Find Refuge in a Game Park." In Kagga Kamma Game Park, approximately 160 miles north of Cape Town, tourists pay seven dollars to "view" a group of about forty San. "In a country that has treated them savagely for centuries, being in what feels very much like a zoo may seem like a step up," wrote the reporter.[5] Perhaps San chiefs learned a paradoxical lesson in the late twentieth century. Refuge for humans in a game park may ward off their extinction because endangered animals are often more highly valued than endangered peoples. How does this seemingly disastrous history of the San relate to the fact that these peoples have, nevertheless, given South Africa the richest treasuries of Stone Age art in the world?

Is it not unusual to appreciate the "primitive" culture of a people while, at the same time, ignore their dire economic and social circumstances. It is happening across the world in our times. In 1995, for example, as the world witnessed ethnic genocide in various parts of Africa, the Royal Academy of Arts in London mounted an extraordinary exhibit, "Africa: The Art of a Continent," in collaboration with the Guggenheim Museum in New York. Over eight hundred pieces of African cultural expression were displayed from eight regions of the continent in what has been called the greatest single collection of African art ever assembled. But even the phrase "African art" has to be examined with a critical eye. In his thoughtful essay in the catalogue accompanying the exhibit, the noted Ghanaian philosopher Anthony Appiah instructs the reader that "we might as well face up to the obvious problem: neither Africa nor Art—the animating principles of this exhibition—played a role as ideas in the creation of the objects in this spectacular show."[6] Indeed, the very concepts of "Africa" and "art" have their origins outside Africa, are recent, and, equally important, are not relevant to what these craftspeople were thinking of creating in the first place. The creators belonged to various cultural communities so diverse across the land mass we now call Africa that it is a dangerous shorthand to claim to capture a topic so vast as "African art" in a single, so-called comprehensive show. And, as Appiah usefully reminds us, "what goes for art, goes, even more, for life."[7] The preservation of African art, however, seems to be an easier concept to embrace than the preservation of African peoples.

The diversity of African peoples is every bit as stunning and complex as the diversity of Africa's biology and range of its species, yet this cultural complexity hardly commands the attention of the world as a precious resource. When "Africa: The Art of a Continent" displayed the art of southern Africa, the catalogue did not hesitate to claim, "The best known arts of southern Africa are the rock paintings and engravings that were produced by the San peoples."[8] This statement seems all the more ironic because the least known peoples of the same region were the San, who were suffering near physical extermination while their "art" was being chipped away by vandals from the rocks that housed their world. The most famous artifact of rock art, the Linton Panel, was removed in 1918 from a rock shelter in the southern Drakensberg range and now is housed at the South Africa Museum in Cape Town. It was loaned for use in the exhibit. This enabled thousands of museumgoers throughout the West—the show began in London and traveled to Berlin before coming to the United States in the summer of 1996—the chance to see this remarkable panel. The panel is composed of various linked human and animal images that float in space and are accompanied by religious symbols. This complex imagery suggests that it was not created to depict a realistic scene. But now the Linton Panel had lost something essential about its meaning because it was taken from its original natural context. Like the artists themselves, much of the rock art of the San people has been destroyed in the process of removal, and those paintings that were left in the rock shelters across southern Africa have been badly damaged by the ravages of weather as well as grasping tourists seeking souvenirs.

The fate of San rock art in South Africa has not been all that different from the fate of similar forms of cultural expression by American Indians in the U.S. Southwest. Over the same time period, newcomers to the lands of these indigenous peoples tried to eliminate them by whatever means possible, including establishing reservations, but not excluding physical annihilation. One route toward understanding the parallel histories of these "first" people—original South Africans and American Indians—focuses on comparing their cultural legacies.

Threats to Cultural Diversity: Contrasting the San and American Indian Tribal Survival

The rock art in the American Southwest may be even older than the oldest San artifacts. The timeframe for these extraordinary examples of human expression may extend back to when Paleo-Indians hunted now extinct animals at the close of the Ice Age throughout a vast part of the North American continent. Figures of mammoths carved on cliffs have been found in the same canyons where the bones of these Indians were excavated. Like the tribal communities in Africa, no southwestern native culture has a word that matches the Western concept of art. So even the phrase *Indian rock art* is misleading and irrelevant to understanding what this activity meant to the creators of it.

In the American Southwest, like in South Africa, a contemporary scholar or simple tourist desiring to see these works is more likely to find them in one of the many national parks or in a museum than among Indians. While not as victimized as the San, most of the Indian peoples of the Southwest no longer inhabit the same cliffs and mesas as their forebears. In fact, a less intrepid person wishing to look at Indian rock art need not climb up a mountain or wander into the desert to find extraordinary examples of southwestern native rock art. Over fifteen thousand petroglyphs (forms pecked, incised, or ground into a rock surface) can be found right in the greater metropolitan Phoenix area at Deer Valley Rock Art Center, which is operated by Arizona State University.[9] As the population of the Southwest grew, rock art vandalism increased in much the same way as in South Africa. Clumsy efforts at removal, defacing, and careless damage had been done to sites, sometimes even in the name of learning more about the rock art and the peoples who created them.

Knowing that we were walking in the shadow of a now near-extinct population in South Africa recalled for us the contrasting histories and struggles of two distinct minority peoples, one who had populated vast areas of what is now the world's oldest democracy and the other, one of its youngest. But understanding what happened to the San of southern Africa and to American Indians in the United States requires more than just remembering where these peoples had once lived. It also demands that we understand the contemporary challenges to ensure not only biological diversity—protecting and sustaining animal and plant species—but also cultural diversity—protecting and sustaining diverse forms of human life.

Culture is one of the most complicated words in the English language. By *culture* we mean everything acquired by and uniting a group of people or a population. Culture encompasses language, symbols, and images as well as systems of values and social norms. At the beginning of the twenty-first century, the peoples most at risk are like the San—those who are indigenous, the original inhabitants of the land. David Maybury-Lewis, an anthropologist at Harvard University, has warned that "the roughly 5 percent of the world population who are indigenous people are seriously being threatened worldwide. Cultural diversity is an important world resource, as essential to the resilience of the human race in the long run as is biological diversity."[10] The long decline and then reemergence of American Indian populations in the United States presents an important case study that may have parallels in other world contexts.

A hundred years ago, the Indian population in the United States had reached an all-time low—less than 240,000 individuals or less than 5 percent of the total population said to have lived in this area before Columbus set foot in the West Indies in 1492. Since 1900, the American Indian population has made an extraordinary comeback and now stands at over 1 million, according to the U.S. Census. This renewal has been termed by at least one prominent American Indian demographer, Russell Thornton, as a "holocaust and survival." Thornton uses the term *holocaust* because he regards the arrival of the Europeans as the beginning of a long holocaust, the Indian equivalent of the Nazis coming to power for the Jews. He has written that "the holocaust that consumed North American Indians were fevers brought on by newly encountered diseases, the flashes of settlers' guns, the ravages of 'firewater,' the flames of villages and fields burned by vengeful EuroAmericans. The effects of this holocaust, like that of the Jews, was millions of deaths."[11] In fact, as Thornton notes, the holocaust of the North American tribes, was, in a way, even more destructive than that of the Jews since many of these groups became extinct.

The most likely explanation for the rejuvenation of American Indian tribal life and culture has been recognition by governmental agencies and institutions such as the U.S. Supreme Court of a legal concept called "tribal sovereignty." Tribal sovereignty grants Indians dual citizenship: they belong to the larger American nation, but they also belong to their own nations—their respective tribes—and can independently govern themselves and their lands. And, because

An amazing place . . . armed with three different, annotated guide books and works by Thomas Mann, Jan Morris, and Mary McCarthy, we were probably too serious and conscientious. I had trouble following Alison physically and aesthetically in her appreciation of Tintoretto and—by the end of the week—felt I would scream if I heard Vivaldi again. But we did have some fun just wandering around, climbing the Campanile, going down the Grand Canal in a waterbus. And best of all, drinking Bellinis (peach juice and champagne) while traveling in a gondola. What affected us most deeply was visiting the ghetto. Established in 1516, it is the origin of the term. We talked about how the Jews in medieval Venice had some rights but that these were totally divorced from any notion of equality; they had a position "half-way between protection and persecution," as Jan Morris expresses it. They had to wear a special costume (first a yellow hat, later a red one) and were cruelly taxed and locked into the walled and windowless ghetto at sunset.

We also visited the old Jewish cemetery on the Lido. This dates back to 1386, when the Jews obtained permission to bury their dead on this plot of ground. According to one of our guidebooks, Goethe, Byron, Shelley, and George Sand all wrote of the melancholy beauty of this cemetery abandoned in the eighteenth century. Its deep green silence was a strong contrast to the color and bustle of the rest of the Lido. Back near San Marco, we were struck by two pieces of graffiti—one calling for "Death to the Jews" and the other proclaiming that "Nazis were homosexuals." A tantalizing place and quite like Virginia Woolf's description of seventy years ago—"the playground of all that was gay, mysterious and irresponsible."

these tribes were able to maintain some of their land, the physical basis for a rebirth of Indian life and culture existed.

There has been no such revival of the San in South Africa. Unable to mount even a modest form of resistance to their enemies, the San were outnumbered and outarmed even compared with the African tribes with whom they first came into contact. By the end of the nineteenth century, the San were no match for both the English and Afrikaner settlers who hunted them down as if they were human "game."

How do we explain the Indians' survival? Neither the southwestern Indians nor the San had the technology to resist the encroachments of white civilization. Both peoples' cultures stood in the way of "progress" as defined by the dominant colonial cultures. Even black Africans viewed the San as simply lower versions of the Hottentots (Khoi-Khoi) and inferior to great tribal powers like the Zulu, who dominated the cultural conflicts of the nineteenth century. While the African tribes left no written record of their views of the San, a 1852 report by an English adventurer claimed that the Namaquas—the name used in aggregate to describe partly "civilized" Hottentots—"looked down on the Bushmen with the greatest contempt . . . and caught them for slaves."[12] Recent scholarship, however, suggests that the San descended from the first fully modern humans, who evolved in southern Africa hundreds of thousands of years ago. They probably were the ancestors of the pastoral Hottentots.

Although the San had been struggling against seemingly insurmountable odds to retain their culture throughout the nineteenth century, the real era of extermination did not occur until the early decades of the twentieth century. In addition to new railway lines bringing settlers to southern Africa, the lands and livelihoods of San hunters were appropriated by legislation that eventually led to the establishment of the first game reserves in 1907. Bans on the hunting of giraffe, buffalo, eland, and kudu were quickly implemented. San who tried to live inside the reserves were rounded up and forced to find work as laborers on white settler farms. As the anthropologist Robert Gordon observes about this move to create game parks, "the political implications . . . were transparent. All the proclaimed royal game, by coincidence, happened to be those that were already easily hunted by the local indigenous without firearms."[13] By 1911, relations between settlers and the San had deteriorated badly. Unable to hunt for their usual game, San males were typically accused of stealing stock. Headlines in the newspapers of the day referred to the "Bushmen Plague" and the "Yellow Peril."[14]

To calm white settlers, the government promulgated policing measures to subdue the San accused of criminal acts. These included using firearms in the slightest case of insubordination against officials, and when patrol officers were searching San areas, they were permitted to have their weapons ready to fire at all times. Interestingly, these rules pertained to the pursuit of men only, not women. Since it was common knowledge in those days that San males would run at the sight of colonial police, the ordinance constituted, in effect, a warrant for genocide. The wanton killing of San ensued as patrols shot men on sight, according to journals of the police troopers.[15]

When in 1919 South Africa took over the former German territory of southwest Africa, the San "problem" was well on its way to a dire solution. The population had declined by over a half, from a little over eight thousand people in 1913 to thirty-six hundred in 1926.[16] The attitude of most South African settlers was summed up in 1926: "The Bushman, with his wrinkled skin, bloated stomach and sly, cunning eyes, looks like a beast of prey himself. . . . They seem to be dying out and no one will be any worse for their loss."[17] By the late thirties, no concerted government effort provided economically for the San or set aside land. Despite pleas from a small group of anthropologists and other academics, South Africa's policy toward the San remained unchanged up through World War II. The overwhelming majority of the San had "disappeared"—many died and others went unnoticed into southwest Africa's rural workforce.

The post–World War II period saw a virtual explosion of white ranches on the lands formerly occupied by the San and the beginning of a long and acrimonious debate over whether the San were "authentic" hunter-gatherers, as Laurens van der Post concluded in his influential 1958 book, *The Lost World of the Kalahari.* Van der Post's critics, however, maintained that the San were more or less acculturated into the regional economy as a marginal underclass. This revisionist argument was most forcefully presented thirty years later in

It's an exciting time to be here because a land claim from the San has been resolved. It's been agreed to buy some additional land and to cede some land from the national park to the San to create a "contract" park that will be jointly managed. The San inhabited this area before the turn of the century. When the Kalahari Gemsbok National Park was proclaimed in 1931 they were allowed to remain and continue their nomadic lifestyle, but these rights were later removed when the park authorities decided that they had acquired "Western lifestyles and habits." Under the new arrangement the San should benefit from ecotourism projects. At present ecotourism is limited to San trails organized by a lodge in the vicinity and a young man in an animal skin loincloth standing next to a sad San grass shelter at the side of the road, where he tries to sell a pathetic display of three ostrich egg shell necklaces and a dead pangolin. We visited the place where most of the remaining San community of about two hundred households live and found it depressing—just tin shacks and extremely thin people, some of

whom looked and sounded as though they had TB. Most of the San men, including their traditional leader, were away being filmed. The whole project raises fascinating questions about heritage and cultural authenticity. It seems that none of the San want to return completely to their former lifestyle, yet they want to preserve their cultural traditions and generate some income from displaying them. I suppose a Williamsburg-style San settlement would not be inauthentic if they lived elsewhere without pretenses.

It's shameful that the park authorities have done nothing for the local San community. The officials are mostly enormously carnivorous Afrikaners with legs like mahogany tree trunks—I watched one young man consume six big lamp chops one evening. They are clearly struggling to come to terms with political changes. Because the ecosystem includes an adjoining park in Botswana, the area has been declared a transfrontier park that will be jointly managed by both countries. It's the first transfrontier park in Africa and signals peaceful and cooperative relations with neighbors instead of the armed conflict that has predominated throughout the continent. At present the park runs at a R2 million loss but administrators are planning to build more tented accommodations and establish various trails to attract tourists, including a honey badger trail, which could be great. It's a moving desert landscape of red sand teeming with enormous herds of springbok, gemsbok, eland, and wildebeest. Last night a glimpse of a bat-eared fox while driving back to camp under a large and starry sky was a thrill.

Edwin N. Wilmsen's controversial 1989 monograph, *Land Filled with Flies*. This debate was focused only on men's roles since San women's roles had remained largely unchanged.

In the fifties, the South African government took beginning steps to establish a San reserve. The rationale was to keep these laborers from moving to Bechuanaland, now Botswana, where they had better opportunities under the British protectorate. But in finally creating a "Bushmanland" reserve for the San in 1970, the South African government severely restricted the means by which the San could live. They were not allowed to grow crops or raise cattle for food and instead were forced to rely on hunting and gathering, which, following van der Post's assessment, government officials believed represented the "authentic" way of life for San males. Unfortunately, this romanticized view had the effect of further reducing the San's economic options.[18]

Complicating this history is that in the seventies, the war for liberation in southwest Africa—now Namibia—began to heat up. In 1974, South Africa recruited San men to serve in the South African Defense Force (SADF) in its campaign against the South West African Peoples Organization (SWAPO). Founded by black Namibians in 1960 as an anticolonial movement, SWAPO successfully increased the level of armed struggle against South African rule. In response to the SWAPO insurgency, the South African government moved fifty thousand troops into northern Namibia and established a major military base and airfield in the area near the San reserve. By 1981 almost one thousand San soldiers were serving in the SADF. At the time, this was among the highest rates of military service of any designated ethnic group in the world, according to the SADF's own figures. That the San would find soldiering a positive alternative to the dire economic circumstances on their reserve is not surprising. Other forms of paid employment were scarce and military pay was excellent by comparison. Life surrounding the comforts of an army base had much to recommend it, including schooling for children and better health care for families.

Ironically, whereas whites had formerly tracked down the San as "vermin," the dominant white culture now prized the "natural" soldiering traits of the San and their reputation for being the best trackers in the world. White soldiers claimed that the San were "natural trackers. . . . If you have never seen a two-legged bloodhound at work, come to South Africa and watch the Bushmen. Actually the Bushmen put the bloodhound to shame."[19] The SADF hoped that the San would both inspire fear among the SWAPO guerrilla forces and boost the morale of its soldiers. "With Bushmen along," one trooper told *Time* magazine, "our chances of dying are very slight."[20]

This romanticization of the San as soldiers is eerily reminiscent of the ways in which the U.S. military eagerly recruited American Indian soldiers for service during World War II. Over twenty-five thousand American Indians served from 1941 to 1945, creating the largest single exodus from reservations in history.[21] Like the San, these American Indians were also assumed to be natural trackers and bush fighters, capable of stalking prey with animal-like instincts. That both groups had been first hunted down and then, paradoxically, later valued for their supposed "natural" hunting and warlike traits suggests that stereotypes are fluid and can be reworked in both negative and positive forms depending upon the dominant culture's needs.

Once the indigenous population is subdued, a mythologizing of the positive qualities of the victim emerges, replacing the older, more negative qualities. It is as if the conquest should not be seen as easy or simple because that would nullify the significance of the victory. This time-worn historical narrative was captured, in part, by Margaret Mead in 1966: "Today the principal plot enacted on the worldwide political stage derives from a clash between the guilt of those who have combined technical superiority with a sense of racial arrogance and the assertion of the rights of those who in different ways experienced that arrogance. . . . This association of racial superiority arises from man's capacity to symbolize and, in so doing, transform members of his own species into non-men, predators or prey."[22]

By the late twentieth century, the San were so dispossessed and marginalized in South Africa that a comprehensive anthology, published in 1996 and entitled *Miscast: Negotiating the Present of the Bushmen,* contained no direct contribution from the San. In contrast, it would have been almost unthinkable to publish a similar volume about American Indians in the United States without at least significant input if not editorial influence by scholars who were also American Indian.

In southern Africa and in the United States, the indigenous "first peoples" suffered as a result of the overwhelming technological superiority of the settler cultures that sought their lands. The similarities in their situations have been noted by other scholars, especially the historians Howard Lamar and Leonard Thompson in their pioneering 1981 anthology, *The Frontier in History: North America and South Africa Compared.* Lamar and Thompson were interested in examining the "opening and closing of the frontier." This concept describes the time when distinctly different peoples initially make contact—the "opening"—and then, when one of the peoples gains ascendancy over the other—the "closing." Typically, this comparativist view examines white/black relations in South Africa and white/Indian relations in North America. But the San's experience is often ignored in such narratives. Seen as neither white nor black, the San were more perplexingly seen as the "other," somehow a different and less than human form of life. Moreover, unlike expansive indigenous societies such as the Sioux in the United States and the Zulu in South Africa, each of whom was engaged in its own form of colonization, subjugating groups such as the Pawnees, Crows, Ndwandwe, and Ngwane, respectively, the San showed little interest in dominating other indigenous peoples.[23]

The Sioux and the Zulu represent two expansive, aggressive preindustrial societies that gained hegemony in their respective regions. Each also developed highly effective military systems that scored significant victories over their colonizing opponents. As a result, they became widely feared, hated, and respected among other indigenous peoples. In contrast to the Zulu, the San's seeming lack of territorial ambition was interpreted by whites as yet another sign of their unadaptive, "hunter-gatherer" culture and their distance from and dissimilarity to other human groupings. Among North American Indians, few groups were thought to be like the San. The hunting societies of the Plains, such as the Sioux, were judged serious threats to white expansionism. More vulnerable and isolated groups like the Hopi and the Pueblos in the Southwest were considered passive agriculturists and were largely ignored by expansionist policies. In contrast, the San had neither the credible expansionist aims of the Sioux, which elicited respect, nor the unthreatening passivity of the Hopi, which encouraged benign neglect. This resulted in a situation in which the San's survival as a people hardly mattered until late in the twentieth century, when calls to "preserve" the San led to somewhat more enlightened governmental policies. But as the South African sociologist Robert J. Gordon recently wrote, "small in numbers, divided as to whether to accentuate their 'Bushmen-ness' or integrate with the wider population, the few remaining San speakers seem unlikely to obtain the redress which similar indigenous populations elsewhere have begun to achieve."[24]

Cultural Preservation as a Politics of Identity

On the eastern tip of Long Island, approximately 130 miles from New York City, a group of seven hundred people who call themselves the Montauk Indians are fighting to maintain (some might say reestablish) their cultural identity as a distinct people even though they have lost their ability to speak a distinct language and govern their tribal lands. Given these losses, the Montauks, originally called Montauketts by the colonial settlers, are not an "officially recognized" tribe in the eyes of the U.S. government. That is, they are not entitled to a set of programs and earmarked funds that have been allocated to "federally recognized Indian peoples." Yet, they persist in their efforts to force the federal government to declare them a legal entity, an "authentic" tribe. A law firm in Chicago, Illinois, which has helped other unrecognized Indian tribes gain this crucial legal standing, is helping the Montauks' chief, Robert Pharaoh, with his petition, but the outlook is grim. Even though Pharaoh can trace his lineage to generations of chiefs of the Montauks, including an ancestor who was sketched by the eminent nineteenth-century artist Winslow Homer in 1874, the Bureau of Indian Affairs, which has the sole authority to accept or reject such petitions, remains unsympathetic. The small tribe has no communally held land, and court records document that key tribal leaders gave up titles in land deals at the end of the nineteenth century. Furthermore, most Montauks left the area decades ago for employment in other parts of the country, most notably, Brotherhood, Wisconsin, over one thousand miles away.

While Robert Pharaoh waits for federal recognition, he is working on another front to establish Montauks' legal claim. He has recently negotiated for half of a small county-owned building to house a museum documenting the Montauks' history and culture. Thus, if his legal argument is not accepted, he can still make progress on restoring a tribal identity. This museum project, along with a cultural center, establishes the Montauks' claim to having a distinct cultural identity. When it is opened, the museum will display artifacts discovered in an early burial site that held decorative beadwork, fabric, tools, and household objects, along with maps depicting the location of the nineteenth-century Montauk population. "What concerns me is the preservation of our culture," Pharaoh was quoted as saying. "I'll do whatever I can to accomplish this."[25]

Across the United States and in South Africa, marginalized and often minority peoples are using institutions, especially museums, to establish their claim to having a recognized cultural identity. As a result, the concept of cultural preservation has taken on a fresh political meaning. It is no longer a term describing efforts by "outsiders," usually anthropologists, archaeologists, and museum curators, who hold the image of a people in a "timeless, static past," as the American Indian intellectual Vine Deloria commented in 1969.[26] Instead, "cultural preservation" has become shorthand for cultural revitalization and political survival. More individuals representing those communities whose past culture and present identities are being "preserved" are taking over the leadership of cultural institutions and are thus making decisions about how to "represent" the changing culture of their own communities.

Perhaps the most significant mainstream example of using a museum to reclaim or control who represents the culture and identity of indigenous peoples in the United States has been the establishment in 1994 of the National Museum of the American Indian (NMAI). This museum is a constituent part of the larger, government-chartered Smithsonian Institution, which also operates the most popular museum in the United States, the Air and Space Museum. The NMAI has a branch in lower Manhattan in New York City and the main exhibit space will be built on the Mall in Washington, D.C., just adjacent to the Capitol Building. American Indians have rallied behind the creation of this national cultural institution because they believe it is a powerful way to reclaim control over how they wish others to see them and their cultures.

The New York branch opened in October 1994, and the centerpiece of the collection is 300 items selected by tribal leaders and artists from among 1 million objects collected decades earlier by an oil heir, George Gustave Heye. For the first time, several parts of the Heye Collection, one of the largest and most diverse collections of American Indian culture in the world, were presented and interpreted by Indians. Even though Heye paid for boxcars full of skeletons and religious artifacts, the fact that these items were either private remains or sacred to Indian peoples means that they belonged in some moral sense to the tribes and the heirs. Curators estimate that eventually about 10 percent of the Heye Collection will be returned to the tribes from which they came. In some cases, the loss to the museum has been significant—about half of the artifacts from the small Jemez Pueblo in New Mexico have already been returned.

Throughout Indian country in the United States, the subject of repatriation—the return of bones, skeletons, and sacred artifacts to the tribes and families—is becoming a important test of cultural and religious preservation and revitalization. Under the 1990 Native American Graves Protection and Repatriation Act, tribes can claim remains discovered on their lands. And, as the Pulitzer Prize–winning Indian novelist N. Scott Momaday has observed, "they are doing so with a vengeance."[27] This federal act and similar legislation in many states represent the clearest extension of the concept of "tribal sovereignty" into U.S. culture. As W. Richard West, the NMAI director, puts it, "Repatriation is the most potent political metaphor for cultural revival. . . . Political sovereignty and cultural sovereignty are linked inextricably, because the ultimate goal of political sovereignty is protecting a way of life."[28]

In the years since the passage of the repatriation act, some tribes have also stopped archeological research on hundreds of prehistoric remains. In part, their effective rationale is grounded in a religious view, which for lack of a better term, is akin to "creationism." This view holds that Indians did not come across a land bridge over the Bering Strait some twenty thousand years ago, as many archeologists and evolutionary biologists now believe. Instead, Indian traditionalists argue

Dear Jackie,

What a relief. The board meeting is over. The best news is that Wilma Mankiller is back. Next to Olesegun Obasanjo's return—he has just rejoined the board after over three years in prison in Nigeria—Wilma's return following a two-year struggle with cancer and kidney disease is nothing short of miraculous. Indeed, her story serves as a kind of metaphor of American Indian survival. Mankiller is a little younger than I am. In 1985, before she was forty, she took over the leadership of the second largest tribe in the United States. At the time there was a lot of hype about how marvelous it was that this woman ascended to leadership in such a patriarchal environment. Much was made of her name and she handles it rather well. In a recent speech at the opening ceremonies of the new $130 million Mashantucket Pequot Museum in Connecticut she joked that Mankiller was a nickname and that she "had earned it." (The truth is always more complicated. Mankiller is a somewhat common name among the Cherokee and probably has its roots in some fight between two males!)

Mankiller, like many other less prominent Indians, has had her share of struggles. As a child and young adult, she and her family moved back and forth between the reservation and the city looking for jobs and a better life. They were continuously disappointed in the white world. In time, her family, furnished with the infamous one-way bus ticket to leave the reservation, went to San Francisco. It was gladly provided by the Bureau of Indian Affairs in the early 1950s because official government policy advocated relocation to get Indians off the reservations. This seems like the opposite of the apartheid government's pass system. In South Africa blacks weren't allowed to relocate, but here Indians were forced to. Mankiller eventually received a B.A. in social work, got involved with urban Indian politics, and joined the protests that led to the takeover at Alcatraz in 1969. Following years of protest and advocacy, Mankiller decided in 1977 to relocate permanently back to Oklahoma and her tribal community. Since then her life has been focused on gaining tribal council control of the remaining resources of the Cherokee and promoting self-determination among American Indian peoples and indigenous communities around the world. She was elected to a third term as principal chief in 1991. She's a powerful force with a sure sense of grass-roots politics and provides an uncompromising yet gentle feminist analysis of development issues wherever we work. Lastly, one cannot comprehend Wilma without realizing how much a spiritual dimension dominates her worldview. Its not *Dances with Wolves* romanticism or sentimentality. She wouldn't come across in that p.c. kind of way. It's just that you know when meeting her and talking with her for the briefest time, as I did yesterday, that she sees the present as deeply connected to the past through ancestors and their dreams of revitalizing their way of life. As she wrote in her speech about the Pequots—a tribe that was virtually decimated by the Massachusetts Bay Colony over three hundred years ago—"As we approach the twenty-first century, the Mashantucket Pequot Nation is not only surviving—it is marching confidently into the next century with one hand firmly on the future and the other hand softly touching the ancestors. Our ancestors can no longer speak for themselves. It is up to us to speak for them. . . . But today if they could talk to us across time, I am sure they would talk among themselves and say, Look at this museum. We survived, after all. They have not forgotten us."

The Pequots' museum was made possible by gambling—the tribe owns one of the world's biggest casinos. Quite an irony and yet who among us can cast stones? . . . the state of Nevada? Atlantic City? the Catholic church with its bingo profits?

Alison,

We had a really interesting National Park Board meeting last week. The shift from a colonial mode of conservation that excluded people (fences and fines) to a community-based model that recognizes human needs is really dramatic.

The highlight of the whole year came Tuesday when I flew along with other board members to Parfuri (in a military plane, which wasn't such fun) to the north of the Kruger Park for the opening of the Thulamela archeological site and to see the remains of Chief Ingwe. It's a wild and beautiful place; the stone buildings are situated high on a hilltop with a view of the lush Limpopo River valley and surrounded by enormous baobab trees. The site was a village dating back to 1460 A.D. and there is clear evidence of gold mining and trading by people who lived there for almost two hundred years. The occasion really did feel like a celebration of the "rainbow nation" with conservationists, corporate types, and about eight hundred people from the local Venda and Tsonga communities eating and drinking and dancing together. The music came from traditional instruments, which included skin drums and a buffalo horn; the local women wore traditional grass skirts and the men shuffled in a circle doing "the reed dance." The Thulamela site is important because its development involved extensive consultations with the local people, believed to be descendants of the cultural group who had inhabited the site five to six hundred years previously. They agreed that the graves should be excavated, and the skeleton remains should then be studied and send for radiocarbon dating to obtain scientific information about their ancestors. The remains would then be returned to the site for reburial so that the necessary respects could be paid to the ancestors. Apparently, this is a unique arrangement in the history of archaeology here—marrying local cultural wishes for respect for the ancestors with scientific inquiry.

that their peoples emerged from a spirit world that surrounded them on the North American continent. "We did not come from elsewhere. We were always here," declared a Hopi leader to Momaday.[29]

The importance of this issue rests not so much on a rejection of Western-oriented science but on a deep suspicion of non-Indian researchers and scholars. Historically, many of these scientists had wantonly excavated Indian burial remains and treated the human remains they found carelessly, stacking them in boxes in the basements of some of the most respected museums in the world. As Momaday suggests, "Indians have endured massacres, alcoholism, poverty. The desecration of spiritual life has been no less an assault" that American Indians feel they must fight.[30]

The battle to resist efforts to use their ancestors' remains to understand prehistory is simply another manifestation of the drive to preserve culture, and thus Indian identity. It has emerged from the long-standing effort to preserve the diversity of Indian cultures, but it is more threatening to dominant U.S. culture because it conflicts with one of the most deeply held tenets of Western liberalism, namely the value of unfettered scientific inquiry. Thus, the issue of repatriation reveals a stark gap between traditional religious belief and scientific modernism. Indians and non-Indians can be found in both camps. Many non-Indians who oppose the theory of evolution support denying archeologists' access to Indian remains.

Thus, trumpeting cultural diversity is not always an unalloyed good. It can be interpreted by any culture to deny the right of others to explore, examine, or intervene in issues deemed private. For example, with female genital mutilation, which is still practiced in parts of Africa, defenders of cultural diversity can easily undermine and thus counteract feminists' calls to abolish this tribal right that most Westerners and many Africans have deemed sexist, brutalizing, and backward. Despite good intentions, protecting the multiplicity of cultures does not always result in a harmonized world order in which all peoples are treated fairly or equally. Under sovereignty statutes that the U.S. Supreme Court has persistently upheld, American Indian tribes have the authority to deny women members the same rights as men. Similarly, in South Africa, customary tribal law discriminates against women in denying wives' right to inheritance. In contrast, however, the passage of the South African Constitution allows the state to intervene on behalf of women in these customary law cases and directly challenges the primacy of cultural diversity over women's equal rights.

Conclusion

Throughout this essay, we have argued that the world's cultural diversity is persistently threatened by efforts to control the lands, livelihoods, and cultural resources of indigenous peoples. We have suggested that societies are stronger and more democratic when they encourage variety in human experience and tolerate difference through policies that protect vulnerable ethnic, racial, religious, and other groups whose values and belief systems diverge from those of the dominant majority. Typically, the case for cultural diversity does not interfere with majority rights. Even so, it has often led to violent clashes, whether between Nazis and Jews, Hutu and Tutsi, Serbs and Muslims, or Catholics and Protestants. When these confrontations occur, it is not enough to defend "everyone's right to be different." Difference is always contextualized and operates historically and politically. Diversity must exist without domination. The acknowledgment of "difference" also cannot be a justification for separate development, as it was in apartheid South Africa.

Perhaps difference and diversity are inherently weak concepts because they cannot signify connection or engagement or mutual respect between peoples. The concept of "cultural pluralism" may capture more accurately the elusive goal to which we must all strive. Pluralism means more than difference because it implies an engagement with the diversity of cultural forms. It also means that difference has to be historicized and linked to disadvantage. Otherwise, cultural diversity will be a politically correct way to maintain the status quo rather than transform unequal and discriminatory social, cultural, and economic relationships.

4

Differences in Sexual Orientation: "Flying the Rainbow Flag"

In the summer of 1963, the Reverend Martin Luther King led a nonviolent protest called the March on Washington for Jobs and Freedom. This march brought almost a quarter million Americans, white and black, male and female, to the capital. It was hailed then as the largest political gathering in U.S. history. Defying conservatives' predictions of a drunken riot, the march was peaceful and dignified. On the carefully chosen steps of the Lincoln Memorial, King delivered a speech that combined Christian ethics and a secular philosophy of equal rights. "I have a dream," he preached, "that one day this nation will rise up and live out the true meaning of its creed . . . when the sons of former slaves and the sons of former slave owners will be able to sit together at the table of brotherhood." Today, despite his choice of exclusively masculine imagery, King's words still have the power to summon reservoirs of energy and commitment to the unfinished agenda of the civil rights movement, which has given rise to other contemporary equal rights struggles in the United States—those of women, Latinos/Latinas, Asian Americans, American Indians, the physically challenged, and, perhaps most controversial of all, gay men and lesbians.

Thirty-one summers after King's March on Washington, another unprecedented crowd—this time of 250,000—participated in a different kind of march. Instead of descending upon the national capital, this June 1994 march of gay pride took to the streets of New York City, the site of the Stonewall Inn riots. The Gay Pride March commemorated a protest that had occurred twenty-five years earlier in June 1969, when police raided a well-known gay male bar named the Stonewall Inn. Instead of allowing themselves to be treated as victims, the largely gay male patrons resisted by throwing beer cans and bottles. While not dignified or carefully planned, this protest reflected deep-seated resentment of police surveillance of one of the few spaces in which gay men could be themselves. Most U.S. historians consider the Stonewall riots the event that led to the establishment of the first open political movement to secure civil rights for gay men and lesbians in America.[1] Indeed, it gave rise to a new organization, the Gay Liberation Front, and the theme of "gay power" that catalyzed the movement for gay rights throughout the world.

King's march was specifically focused on the U.S. government's failure to secure jobs and a full measure of political participation in American life for blacks. Thirty-one summers later, the theme of this gay rights march was pride, not protest. This simple distinction says a lot about this "rights" movement and similar modern efforts to secure civil rights for disadvantaged groups. Even though there is much to protest about the ways federal and state legislation stigmatizes and criminalizes certain homosexual practices, and especially fails to address adequately the scourge of AIDS, this march was more a commemoration and a celebration than a protest and a call to action. Gay men and lesbians came out to proclaim and reclaim their sexual identities, but whether any government took notice or action as a result was not the point.

The 1994 march celebrated the diversity of human sexuality. Homosexuality and bisexuality were being shown as other forms of sexual expression within the human species. No form was considered more "natural" than another. Interestingly, the march organizers took no positions on even more controversial sexual practices such as pedophilia or sado-masochism. Perhaps this is because these practices are not exclusively used by lesbians, gays, and bisexuals and

Alison,

I watched a fascinating television program—"The Man Who Drove Mandela." It suggests one answer to the question of how we came to be the first country in the world to give constitutional equality to lesbians and gay men. The program included an interview with Albie Sachs in which he maintains that the progressive stand of the ANC toward gay rights was largely due to one person—Cecil Williams: "He raised our consciousness on these matters." Williams was a white teacher and theater director who was openly gay as well as active in resistance politics in South Africa after World War II and throughout the 1950s. He experienced both banning and house arrest before going into exile in London, where he died in 1979. He was driving Mandela from Durban to Johannesburg when Mandela was arrested. I am not sure about Albie's explanation for the ANC's progressivism on this issue, however. There was a telling interview with Walter Sisulu, who described Williams in positive terms as "kind," "friendly," and a "perfect gentleman" but goes on to admit: "I am a bit conservative about that

[Williams's homosexuality] . . . but he was accepted by the movement." In other words, I think people maybe bracketed (rather than accepted) his sexuality. The commitment of white people like Cecil Williams and Joe Slovo and Ruth First and Hilda Bernstein and Rusty Bernstein strengthened the ANC's commitment to nonracialism. That notion seems increasingly fragile now, as does much in our Constitution. For example, it abolishes the death penalty, which is an important gain given that at one time we hanged more people than any other country in the world. A recent opinion poll sampling three thousand South Africans found that 91 percent of the respondents thought the death penalty should be reintroduced. I am afraid that a large percentage would vote for the abolition of the gay rights clause if they got the chance.

because celebrating them would diffuse the more acceptable message of the rally. Hundreds of thousands of gay men and lesbians marched under the flags of their native countries past the United Nations headquarters on New York City's East River. But importantly, they also marched under one unifying banner—a carefully stitched two-mile-long "Rainbow Flag" representing the diversity of all who attended and, thus, "came out" together. Regardless of nationality, gay marchers used this extraordinary symbol to assert a common transnational humanity and new solidarity committed to fighting against repressive measures wherever they exist.

One of the most moving sights came when dozens of South Africans strode past the United Nations building. Only four years earlier, when the first gay rights march was held in Johannesburg, organizers offered paper bags for shielding identities to marchers who feared reprisals. But in just four years South Africa could boast a large, multiracial contingent. Its presence reminded bystanders and marchers alike that this nation, so recently among the most racist and undemocratic in the world, is the first and only country to specify the protection of gays and lesbians in its Bill of Rights.

King's 1963 march protested the continuing exclusion of blacks from mainstream American life, while the 1994 Gay Pride March celebrated the politics of inclusion. Its theme was that being sexually attracted to and loving a member of one's own sex was no barrier to full citizenship. In this assertion, gay rights was claiming a place alongside women's rights, black rights, Latino/Latina rights, disability rights, and rights for the aged in the political mainstream. The mood of the day was playful and welcoming as thousands watched and cheered on the sidelines.

But what does joining the gay rights movement really mean? Is it simply another civil rights struggle, as Michael Nava and Robert Dawidoff forcefully argue?[2] Or is there a difference to this struggle that distinguishes it from other U.S. civil rights movements? How similar were the gay rights agendas during the past decade in the United States and South Africa?

Historical Roots

The word *homophobia*, the hatred of lesbians and gays, was only recently introduced (1988) into *Webster's New World Dictionary* and its first recorded use is 1969, but the concept is nevertheless as old as patriarchy and surely as widespread as racism. Since the ancient Greeks, some level of discomfort, prejudice, and outright discrimination in Judeo-Christian societies has been directed against people who have sexual relations with members of their own sex. But any society's tolerance of homosexuality ebbs and flows depending on a variety of factors, most of which have nothing to do with the nature of any homosexual act but may have something to do with levels of tolerance for a variety of sexual practices, including homosexuality.

That most gays and lesbians cannot be identified by some external physical characteristic means societies use strategies of repression rather than exclusion to persecute them. For example, following World War I, the Weimar Republic ushered in a decade of sexual freedom and tolerance in Germany. The relaxing of Victorian sexual mores came not just in this vanquished nation but throughout the western world. Germany's revolt against sexual freedom took a horrific turn when National Socialism in the early thirties claimed that homosexuality was a symptom of racial degeneracy and destructive to the white race. In Hitler's Germany, thousands of lesbians and gays were sent to concentration camps because they engaged in practices once tolerated by the state.[3] At first, since so many outspoken voices for tolerance of homosexuality were Jewish, Nazi attacks were interpreted by many gay men and lesbians as prompted by anti-Semitism. Gentiles quickly learned, however, that they were not immune from Nazi charges that homosexuals were eugenic inferiors. Like Jews, lesbians and gay men had previously enjoyed a climate of tolerance, but unlike Jews, who could be traced by heredity, gays and lesbians were hunted down in bars or were betrayed by former friends and lovers. To distinguish them from Jews, gay men and lesbians had to wear pink stars instead of yellow ones. The well-documented, but little discussed fact that Erich Roehm, one of Hitler's early trusted subordinates, was gay, suggests at least some willingness to ignore sexual difference in National Socialism. Although few historians have endeavored to explain this anomaly, at the very least it means that one must dig deep to find the roots of prejudice against homosexuality. One cannot simply assume that this form of bigotry is similar to racism, anti-Semitism, sexism, or any other xenophobic fear of the "other."

In 1992 the feminist literary scholar and public intellectual Catherine Stimpson predicted that the struggle over acceptance of gays and lesbians in U.S. society would be one of the great issues of the decade. With the exception of Wisconsin and Massachusetts, which passed laws barring discrimination based on sexual orientation in 1982 and 1989, respectively, other states did not do so until the nineties. These are Hawaii and Connecticut (1991), New Jersey, Vermont, and California (1992), Minnesota (1993), Rhode Island (1995), and New Hampshire and Maine (1997). Not surprisingly, as more gay men and lesbians found the courage to come out, the number of bias incidents directed against them rose concomitantly. As the gay rights movement has gained strength and legitimacy over the past thirty years, so has the organized opposition to it. One stark example of the volatility around gay rights are growing movements to repeal legislation passed to protect gay men and lesbians from discrimination. In February 1998, Maine became the first in the nation to repeal its law.

Before Stonewall, lesbians and gay men used a variety of defense mechanisms to cope with prejudice and social ostracism, chief among them silence, social isolation, and self-denial. In the post-Stonewall era, gay men and lesbians have come out of the closet and claimed their sexual identities openly. Moreover, the broad political agenda of the gay rights movement has focused on equal treatment, even though most gay men and lesbians assert that their sexuality is significantly different from that of heterosexuals and that this difference is one they will fight to defend. Thus, one conundrum of the contemporary gay rights movement is whether one can proclaim difference and not expect that to lead to discriminatory treatment.

Before the seventies, gay men and lesbians lived largely invisible lives except in large cities like New York, where they had ways of co-existing with and being tolerated by the mainstream heterosexual community. As histories such as George Chauncey's *Gay New York,* Charles Kaiser's *The Gay Metropolis,* and Lilian Faderman's *Odd Girls and Twilight Lovers* have so brilliantly described, lesbians and gays developed subcultures in the pre-Stonewall period, but had practically no effective organized civil rights movement. The post-Stonewall era marks a historical break for gay men and lesbians whose covert social worlds and sexual identities were largely unknown to their family, heterosexual friends, and co-workers. They were never victims of legally enforced segregation, and yet theirs was often a form of social segregation from loved ones, sometimes by choice, but more often by unspoken subordination to dominant sexual mores.

The gay rights movement emerged in the seventies in the United States as the next logical step in the broader equal rights struggles for blacks and for women, but its issues and claims for tolerance of difference are not the same. Similarly, in South Africa, gay liberation emerged in the late eighties and early nineties after the national liberation movement finally began to overtake the legally enshrined system of apartheid. Exploring the paradoxes and contradictions inherent in these contemporary movements in these two contexts can broaden our understanding of difference, diversity, and disadvantage at the end of the twentieth century.

Up through the seventies in the United States, as long as gay men and lesbians remained silent about their sexual identity and did not openly engage in affectionate gestures or homosexual practices, they were typically not noticed, harassed, or discriminated against. In the closet, they often held leading positions in government, industry, the military, sports, and the entertainment industry. Gay men typically married for convenience. Lesbians more commonly denied their sexuality and assumed the public identities of childless spinsters lucky to have their "Boston marriages."

During the twentieth century, prominent gay men and lesbians from Willa Cather to J. Edgar Hoover to Cole Porter were part of the American scene—prominent for their accomplishments and virtually unknown as private citizens. Before Stonewall, the most famous American lesbians were Gertrude Stein and Alice B. Toklas. Though born in the United States, their unconventional lives were on display in faraway Europe, so they were thought to be eccentric expatriates who played out the roles of a heterosexual married couple, with the "male" Gertrude dominating the "female" Alice. Alice was perceived to be so subordinate to Gertrude that no one thought it odd that Stein would write Toklas's autobiography for her.

During the fifties and sixties Hollywood whispered that "macho" movie stars like Rock Hudson and Tab Hunter were gay, but studio executives usually found ways to throw the press off course. And in pre-Stonewall literary society, although gay men such as Tennessee Williams, James Baldwin, Gore Vidal, and Truman Capote could flaunt their sexual liaisons with men, there was little space or freedom to be a gay person outside bohemian, artistic circles. Not until the eighties could sports figures like Billie Jean King and Martina Navratilova openly acknowledge that they were bisexual or lesbian and not be ostracized. When she came out, Martina Navratilova was already "different"—as a Czech who defected, she was disliked by tennis fans who favored the more "winning" and "normal" image of a Chris Evert. As Navratilova began to be viewed as a world-class athlete, she won grudging respect despite her outsider status.

Although many public figures have announced their sexual orientations since the seventies, two stories of sexual identity disclosure during this time violated public personas in highly charged ways. In 1984, when Rock Hudson died of AIDS, the Hollywood press corps no longer hid what many had known for decades. Hudson, the female heartthrob of the fifties, was the last person mainstream America would expect to be gay. Having a crush on a gay man impersonating a straight man signifies nothing about one's own sexual identity, but it does call into question easy assumptions and demonstrates the skill many gay men and lesbians develop to "fake" heterosexuality. Perhaps the most tragic part of the Hudson story was his inability to acknowledge either the cause of his illness or his sexual orientation.

The other story concerns Lt. Col. Margarethe Cammermeyer, who brought the most celebrated legal case involving homosexuality since Oscar Wilde was sent to prison in England more than a century ago. Cammermeyer's "crime" was that she admitted to being a lesbian during a security clearance interview. Importantly, she did not admit to engaging in homosexual practices, but the military code does not allow an admitted lesbian or gay man to serve. Most of Cammermeyer's fellow officers and colleagues in the Army Nurse

Wonderfully, we are visiting Llangollen the same month as Eleanor Butler and Sarah Ponsonby first did 220 years ago. It is a sunny May day filled with the smells of wild garlic and the sounds of the river Dee. It is an enchanting place. We were prepared to be irritated by the class eccentricities of "the ladies" when we visited their home and instead found ourselves delighted. Clearly they were awful snobs (especially Eleanor) but their servant, Mary Carlyle, is buried with them in the local churchyard. Clearly they were arrogant—for example, they removed a font from the nearby Cistercian ruin (Valle Crucis Abbey) but it is reverentially placed along a riverside walk on their property.

Their defiance in escaping from their respective conventional Irish families, their journey to Wales, and their creation of a home together at Plas Newydd, where they lived for almost fifty years in their "new way" as their "own guides," is touching. When they moved there in 1780 it was an unpretentious cottage. Much has been changed over the years and the present property seems imposing with its fine stained glass windows and elaborate carved oak panels. It

hardly fits Doris Grumbach's description of "a cave of oak and stone." But it does have some quality of a refuge for hunted quarry; Eleanor wrote, "Plas Newydd is a thicket, affording cover for us, two Lady birds."

We were faintly annoyed by the coy descriptions of their relationship. For instance, the guidebook describes how "the two friends slept together in a capital four-post bedstead" but they were "the most famous virgins of Europe," who lived "a life of sweet and delicious retirement" in "a model of perfect friendship," much of their time devoted to gardening and entertaining visitors such as the Duke of Wellington, William Wordsworth, and Sir Walter Scott. Obviously, they were popularly perceived as the embodiment of "romantic friendship," a literary ideal of the eighteenth century.

Romantic friends from the privileged classes could retire from the world together to devote their lives to cultivating themselves and their gardens but without any hint of a deviant sexuality. According to one source they were "shocked and appalled" at the suggestion by contemporaries that they were lesbians. But they certainly loved one another and affirmed that love in their shared life.

After visiting their house we climbed the hill to see the view from the ruins of Dinas Bron Castle, which they described in their 1778 journal as "the beautifullest country in the world," and traveled a short distance along the Llangollen Canal in a long boat— which was marvelous. Bought some postcards including one of St. Winefride, the seventh-century Welsh virgin martyr who was apparently beheaded by a rejected suitor.

A marvelous though exhausting day mostly spent walking the streets of Paris. We went first to the rue de Fleurus and looked up at the building where Gertrude and Alice lived for all those years. We tried to imagine the incredible people—Picasso, Matisse, Braque, Apollinaire, Gris, Hemingway—who'd been where we stood. Tomorrow we plan to drive to the Rhone Valley to see Belley, Gertrude and Alice's summer holiday place, and maybe we'll get a stronger sense of their presence there. We talked a lot about them and why we find them so attractive. I think the main quality is their courage to be themselves. Apparently soon after arriving in Paris, Gertrude removed her corset, symbolizing her stepping out of the conventional restraints on women.

We also like their shared capacity for joyous living. In *Wars I Have Seen,* Gertrude wrote, "I liked to eat I liked to eat . . . and see a great deal of eating as an excitement and as an orgy." We also like the food Gertrude lists in *Everybody's Autobiography:* honeydew melons and oysters, corn muffins and apple pie. Indeed, we share

two of their favorite things: "but most of all there were books and food, food and books, both excellent things."

The conventional view of the relationship as exploitative and conventional, with Alice nothing but the servant-shadow, seems mistaken. There was much sharing and mutual admiration. As a critic points out, "Gertrude Stein's most successful book is a monument to the equal spirit of her companion."

One comment in *The Autobiography of Alice B. Toklas* reminded Alison of me: "She [Gertrude] was not efficient, she was good humored, she was democratic, one person was as good as another, and she knew what she wanted done." A comment from one of their guests about Gertrude reminded me of Alison: "She had the easiest, most engaging and infectious laugh I have ever heard . . . straight from the heart." I like the image of Gertrude as an overweight, middle-aged woman dancing with her dog, as I do.

The downside is that theirs was a defiant courage cushioned by the privilege of a private income; Gertrude came from an affluent German-Jewish family and always received a family allowance. We talked about what this meant for feminism. So many of the women we admire—Elizabeth Bishop, for example—enjoyed class privileges and independent incomes. It comes back to Virginia Woolf's two conditions for women's creativity—a private income and a room of one's own.

We wished we had the time to explore the personal connections among the other foremothers; apparently in 1934 Gertrude attended a reception given by Eleanor Roosevelt at the White House. What did they say and think of each other?

We had a somewhat scratchy exchange over dinner as Alison wanted to splurge on a grand marnier soufflé that I thought was extravagant. Eventually, we ordered one without noticing the word *glace*, so what finally came (at an enormous price) was a round helping of faintly orange-flavored ice cream.

Corps knew about her private life but it had never been an issue for her or for them. That she had once been married and was the mother of four sons no doubt made it easier to identify with her, so her relationship later in life with a woman was accepted or at least tolerated. Had she remained silent in that job interview, she would have been granted a promotion and finished her career unnoticed by the public. Instead, she took her case to the highest military authorities, who upheld the army's regulations. Her appeal to the U.S. Supreme Court was denied.[4]

Cammermeyer's case and the service of gay men and lesbians during the 1991 Gulf War led newly elected President Clinton to support the abolition of the military's ban. He eventually backed down following a firestorm of opposition, including the outspoken rejection of lesbians and gays in the military by Colin Powell, then chairman of the Joint Chiefs of Staff. The tortured compromise, a military policy that goes by the shorthand "don't ask, don't tell," remains the subject of numerous court cases brought by gay servicemen and women.

These high-profile examples illustrate the many facets of discrimination and the fight against it. Unlike Rock Hudson, Cammermeyer was not famous. Even though she was highly respected in her profession, she was stigmatized by her sexual orientation anyway and lost a promotion over her unwillingness to lie. Her legal battle, however, brought her fame and public recognition for her strength. Although Hudson was a loved and respected actor, he died unable to acknowledge that he was gay to all but a few personal friends. In contrast, Cammermeyer has decided to spend the remainder of her life as a gay rights advocate.

There are no analogous controversies in South Africa, even though some white gay men have achieved prominence in public life. For example, Edwin Cameron, an openly gay man, was named in 1994 to the South African Supreme Court. Pieter Dirk Uys, a highly popular gay female impersonator, had his own television show years before Ellen DeGeneres came out on her prime time U.S. sitcom in April 1997. It is hard to know how to explain these divergent societal responses to homosexuality.

The Current Legal Context

The mere fact of being gay is not illegal in the United States—or anywhere else in the world, for that matter. But governments do intervene in private sexual practices between men. For example, sodomy, which is defined as any sexual intercourse held to be abnormal but specifically refers to anal intercourse between two men, is outlawed in twenty-three states. To engage in this private sexual practice is to engage in criminal activity, according to the 1986 U.S. Supreme Court decision *Bowers v. Hardwick,* which upheld Georgia's sodomy laws. Sexual acts between women, however, have never been criminalized. The truth is that being a gay man or a lesbian is not a crime, but proclaiming or practicing your sexuality can get you thrown out of the military or fired from your job or worse. Moreover, the United States does not have a federal law protecting the civil rights of lesbians and gay men as does South Africa. Individual states have passed laws banning discrimination based on sexual orientation, but these laws can be easily overturned by statewide referendums, as was the case in Maine. The lack of broad-based federal protection means several things. First, discrimination is legal. For example, a man caught performing a private sexual act in his own bedroom with a consenting member of his own sex can go to prison in those states with sodomy laws still on the books. Second, attempts by municipal governments and states to provide legal protections in housing and employment have been challenged in federal courts.

In 1995, the U.S. Supreme Court heard arguments over whether Colorado violated the U.S. Constitution in 1992 by adding an amendment to its state constitution that nullified all state and local laws protecting gays and lesbians and barred such laws from being enacted in the future. In May 1996, the U.S. Supreme Court voted six to three to throw out the Colorado state constitutional initiative. The majority opinion argued that the Equal Protection Clause of the U.S. Constitution "requires us to hold invalid a provision of Colorado's Constitution . . . because a state cannot so deem a class of persons a stranger to its laws." In a dissenting opinion, Justice Scalia paradoxically offered the best description of the historic significance of this case, which came to be known as *Romer v. Evans*. Scalia wrote that the majority view "placed the prestige of this institution behind the proposition that opposition to homosexuality is as reprehensive as racial or religious bias."[5]

Despite this important victory, gay men and lesbians still frequently choose to remain closeted. By blending in, they can go and come as they please, sit anywhere on the bus, and take any job. In fact, prior to the 1996 Supreme Court decision, a lower court had used the Equal Protection Clause to eliminate rights aimed at gay men and lesbians. And while the U.S. government has not made being gay illegal, it has, as recently as 1967, affirmed the constitutionality of a 1952 act that excluded homosexual immigrants from becoming citizens on the grounds of mental illness.[6]

When they openly reveal their sexual identities or chose a partner of the same sex and live as a couple, lesbians and gay men experience everything from ostracism to outright legal discrimination. Therefore, it might be argued that discrimination against lesbians and gays exists most obviously in the social sphere, since they are being denied the right to express their behavior in public as well as in their own homes. Because what makes a person gay are sexual feelings for someone of the same gender, not an arguably physical characteristic like race or gender, behavior is at issue. So long as they hide their sexual behavior, they are welcome in any social setting. If this is true, does the social nature of discrimination faced by gays and lesbians make it a different kind of civil rights struggle?

It would seem so, if we are to believe the U.S. Supreme Court in its most recent decision regarding gay rights. In June 2000, the court ruled in a highly publicized ten-year battle that the Boy Scouts of America has a constitutional right to exclude gay members because opposition to homosexuality is part of the organization's values and because the Constitution protects its right of free association. The decision overturned a New Jersey lower court ruling that had applied the state's law against discrimination to require a Scout troop to re-admit a longtime member and assistant scoutmaster dismissed for being gay. What made this case so troubling is that the Supreme Court seemed to be drawing a distinction between the gay rights argument and other previous civil rights rulings from the eighties that denied that all-male organizations, such as the Rotary Club, had a First Amendment right to exclude women. As the legal expert Linda Greenhouse pointed out, "While none of the court's free association cases have dealt with exclusion by private organizations on the basis of race, the court's analysis would presumably permit a white supremacy group to exclude blacks if racial exclusion was an inherent part of the group's identity and message."[7]

No state laws mandate that all citizens must be heterosexual, though one suspects that religious fundamentalists would surely desire them. But heterosexual unions are currently the only marriages that receive legal recognition in all fifty states. In 1993, the Hawaii Supreme Court surprisingly held in *Beahr v. Levin* that its state constitution might require recognition of same-sex marriages and thus denying marriage licenses to same-sex couples was unconstitutional. This matter is still being litigated. If same-sex couples are permitted to marry legally in one state, however, such unions might become legal elsewhere since a person's legal marriage in one state is usually recognized in other jurisdictions. This possibility no doubt prompted Congress in 1996 to pass the Defense of Marriage Act, which was supported and signed into law by President Clinton. This legislation defined marriage as a legal union between a woman and a man, thereby short-circuiting attempts to legalize same-sex relationships, even as some municipalities, universities, and private employers have recognized domestic partnerships to ensure equal access to benefits policies.

In 2000, Vermont became the first state to pass legislation approving marriage-like civil unions for gay couples. What makes the Vermont law so significant is that it came despite widespread opposition from citizens expressed in town meetings and public polls. The battles for gay marriage reveal an interesting tension in the gay rights movement, namely, the desire to assert a different identity while at the same time claiming a legal status based on sameness. It is the ironic place where gay rights liberalism meets "family values" conservatism. Gay men and lesbians are also receiving support from churches and synagogues performing same-sex commitment ceremonies and gay marriage rites.

Opposition to gay rights in South Africa is led primarily by church leaders, including many in black African churches, and they remain

An exhausting but exhilarating weekend in The Hague. Cora Weiss managed to bring together some eight thousand people from one hundred different countries for her Hague Appeal for Peace conference. Jackie felt there wasn't enough tough analysis of the material basis to war, but overall there were inspiring moments. It's great to be resting here with Rosi and Annicka in their sixteenth-century house. They took us for a walk along the canals shaded with enormous horse chestnut trees and past the medieval cathedral before feeding us a wonderful dinner with different kinds of herring. They're a great couple and we were sad to have missed their wedding. It sounded like an extremely affirming event with many of Rosi's and Annicka's family, including Annicka's eighty-plus-year-old parents, who from photographs look like a nineteenth-century farm couple out of Ingmar Bergman's film *Wild Strawberries.* Rosi's colleagues from the University of Utrecht, led by the vice rector, also came to celebrate this state-blessed gay union, one of the first in the Netherlands. Looking over the photographs, we thought both women looked blissfully happy, but Jackie and I had almost opposite reactions. We differed strongly over whether Rosi and Annicka's wedding was a conformist or a revolutionary act. For Jackie, reproducing bourgeois heterosexual rituals like marriage is a perversion of the revolutionary potential of the gay rights movement. The right to marry is nothing we should aspire to since it has been a time-honored way to treat women as second-class citizens. But for me, having the opportunity to enter into this sanctioned legal union undermines a key Judeo-Christian homophobic taboo, namely, that love between members of the same sex is unnatural, and thus illegal.

formally opposed to efforts to treat gay men and lesbians as the equals of heterosexuals. One such church-related group, the African Christian Democratic party (ACDP), unsuccessfully tried to abolish the clause in the Constitution securing civil rights for gays and lesbians. Its stand proclaiming that "homosexuality, lesbianism, sodomy and bestiality are unnatural, abnormal and immoral and do not deserve constitutional protection," however, never received much formal political support. The ACDP's submission to the Constitutional Assembly's Theme Committee on Fundamental Rights in 1995 stated, "The Bible literally and clearly forbids homosexuality. . . . The practice of homosexuality is a lifestyle, a subculture, like gangsterism. If we call for the protection of this one subculture, on what basis are other subcultures excluded?"[8] A similar view was expressed nearly a decade earlier in 1987 by one prominent member of the ANC's National Executive Committee, Ruth Mompati. She justified the ANC's silence on gay rights by stating, "We don't have a policy on flower sellers either." Mompati expressed skepticism and even contempt for gay rights, claiming it was a Western-imposed concept. "The gays have no problems," Mompati argued. "They have nice homes and plenty to eat. I don't see them suffering. No one is persecuting them. . . . We haven't heard about this problem in South Africa until recently. It seems fashionable in the West."[9] Mompati accused gay activists, whom she saw as "single-issue" leaders, of detracting attention from the struggle against apartheid. Although her views were highly publicized, they did not prevail at the highest levels of the ANC.

How can we explain the ANC's championing of the Constitution's gay rights clause? The answer lies in the discourse on discrimination in the late eighties and early nineties. Because discrimination was widely understood as a multidimensional phenomenon, denying gay rights was perceived as just another limit on individual freedoms. This linkage between discrimination in general and gay rights in particular can be traced to the successful advocacy activities of such groups as the Organization of Lesbian and Gay Activists (OLGA), the predominant activist alliance in the Western Cape, which lobbied the ANC in exile in the eighties, and the United Democratic Front (UDF). This version of coalition politics succeeded in defining the gay rights movement as part of the broader anti-apartheid struggle.

In this process, the role of particular gay rights activists, such as Peter Tatchell in England and Simon Nkoli and Ivan Toms in South Africa, was crucial. A member of the London-based gay rights group Outrage, Tatchell was an effective publicist on gay rights issues as well as a long time anti-apartheid activist. He published excerpts of Mompati's statements in Outrage's London newsletter, *Capital Gay,* and called upon the ANC leadership to disavow them. Writing in 1987 to Thabo Mbeki, then the ANC's director of information in Lusaka, Tatchell reminded the ANC that "both in SA and here in Britain, many lesbian and gay people have been involved in the anti-apartheid struggle." Mbeki replied with a letter stating, "sexual preferences are a private matter" and the ANC "has never been opposed to gay rights."[10] Tatchell then sent the letter to leaders of OLGA and the UDF, thus helping to strengthen the coalition between the gay rights leadership and the ANC's key human rights policymakers. He also helped arrange a meeting in England in 1990 at which Albie Sachs, one of the ANC's framers of the proposed constitution, conferred with gay activists. Tatchell even claims to have written a draft of the gay rights clause. This kind of personal contact proved persuasive. Tatchell later wrote, "Sachs' backing was significant in winning over most of the ANC's leadership."[11]

Around this same time Simon Nkoli became instrumental in linking the gay rights agenda to the broader goals of the anti-apartheid struggle. In 1984, Nkoli was arrested and charged with high treason following mass antigovernment protests in the black townships. Along with others, he became part of the "Delmas" treason trial and was the only openly gay person among the twenty-two defendants. After being acquitted and spending nearly three years in jail, nine months of which were in solitary confinement, Nkoli noted in 1987 that he had not received support from the largely white middle-class Gay Association of South Africa (GASA). GASA, in its newspaper, *Exit,* urged gay men and lesbians to vote for the ruling National party candidate. In opposition to this stance, the Rand Gay Organization was founded in 1986 and quickly became the largest association of lesbians and gay men in South Africa and had a primarily black membership. To demonstrate solidarity with the anti-apartheid cause, the International Lesbian and Gay Organization suspended GASA from membership. Nkoli praised other gay anti-apartheid leaders such as Tatchell and Ivan Toms, an openly gay white physician who, along with Archbishop Desmond Tutu and Winnie Mandela, provided consistent support during Nkoli's trial and imprisonment. Nkoli also succeeded in shifting the attitudes of UDF organizers. After Nkoli was released from jail, he became chairperson of the Gay and Lesbian Organization of the Witwatersrand (GLOW), which joined forces with the UDF and became part of the broad movement against apartheid.

Like Nkoli, Ivan Toms served as a bridge between gay rights struggles and the broader anti-apartheid movement. Toms was a gay conscientious objector who, along with Sheila Lapinsky, a lesbian organizer, was a founding member of OLGA. He was jailed in 1986 and then imprisoned for twenty-one months after refusing to serve in the South African Defense Force. Toms's case revealed the close, if not always easy, collaboration between the End Conscription Campaign (ECC) of the UDF and lesbian and gay activists. In a June 1987 letter to the ECC leadership, these activists protested efforts to "downplay" Toms's homosexuality and commitment to gay rights. They called for Toms's membership in the Lesbian and Gay Organization (LAGO) to be mentioned in press publicity and for including his experiences as a gay man in his official statements at the trial and thereafter. Finally, the letter to the ECC stated, "as progressive lesbians and gays, we are acutely aware of the interconnections between various strands of the struggle for a democratic South Africa."[12]

During the late eighties and early nineties, gays and lesbians who played an active role in the anti-apartheid movement allied with leading ANC figures like Sachs and Mbeki. As Edwin Cameron wrote to Ivan Toms in 1989, "My feelings of hope arose from the fact that the ANC members seemed to be real democrats and many of them humanitarians as well. . . . Albie Sachs is a real hero and I warmed to Mbeki because of the liberal minded things he has been saying about gays and lesbians. He really put sourpuss Ms. Ruth Mompati in her place about poefter-bashing."[13] Nelson Mandela also became a hero to South African gay rights activists when he mentioned freedom from discrimination based on sexual orientation in his presidential address in May 1994.

The first national Gay and Lesbian Legal and Human Rights

Alison,

I watched a fascinating debate on television between a gay rights activist and the Reverend Kenneth Meshoe, who is the leader of the African Christian Democratic party. Meshoe argued that homosexuality is against both biblical principles and African culture. It's alarming how references to African culture are used to legitimize oppressive practices. I have heard the same reference used to argue that African men should not have to do their share of housework. The sexual orientation clause is in the Bill of Rights, which is part of the final Constitution, and this homophobia is a puzzle to me. Admittedly, his party got only eighty-eight thousand votes in the 1994 election, but I think this stigmatization is widespread. Apparently Khosian X of the Pan-African Congress also regards homosexuality as "un-African." The Reverend Mr. Meshoe argues that the clause is there because the Constitution involved an "undemocratic" process. I suspect that it all depends on how one views a democratic constitution—as an aspirational document of the kind of society we want to create or as a reflection of the views of the majority or as a protection of minority rights. I don't know if the lobbying of the gay coalition could have prevailed against a grass-roots mobilization around "traditional African culture" or "family values."

Conference met in Johannesburg in December 1994 and launched a coalition dedicated to retaining the equality clause, as it was called, in the new permanent Constitution. The coalition involved forty-two separate gay organizations, and Simon Nkoli and Sheila Lapinsky served on the Executive Committee. In its major submissions to the Constitutional assembly's Theme Committee on Fundamental Rights in February 1995 and June 1996, the coalition argued that, apart from the ACDP, all major political parties had supported the inclusion of lesbians and gays in the Bill of Rights. Equally important, the submissions looked to the international human rights community, and U.S. case law, in which the right to nondiscrimination on numerous grounds, including sexual orientation, was increasingly gaining wide international recognition.

The South African Constitution, passed in 1996, contains a section that states, "No person shall be unfairly discriminated against . . . on the grounds of sexual orientation." This victory probably stands more as a testament to the power and influence of the international human rights community's acceptance of gay rights, which was inscribed into the Constitution by its framers, than an expression of the black majority's support for equal protection for gay men and lesbians. In fact, despite noteworthy submissions by anti-apartheid leaders such as Mamphela Ramphele and Desmond Tutu, many submissions were orchestrated by the religious Right, with most echoing the ACDP. Four years later, South Africa's Law Commission took on same-sex marriage because the existing Marriage Act did not recognize gay unions. The battle to legalize gay marriages will likely end up in the Constitutional Court, which has already ruled in favor of a gay man's ability to get a permanent residence permit on the basis of his committed relationship with his partner.

Gay rights activists in South Africa face unusual challenges because both white and black fundamentalist religious leaders have argued that homosexuality was brought to Africa by white colonialists. It is small wonder that black gay men and lesbians are among the most invisible members of South African society. And yet, as Nkoli correctly observes, "Ever since laws against sodomy were promulgated in this country, it's been African men in the main and coloured men who have been at the brunt of prosecutions. Over the years, a silence has been maintained around these statistics. We want to ensure that people understand that there are more African and coloured gay men and lesbians than white gays."[14] Regardless of the logic of this position, many Africans refuse to acknowledge homosexuality as part of their traditional or even contemporary cultures.

In both the United States and South Africa, discrimination based on sexual orientation becomes clear and pervasive in social settings. For example, openly gay men and women are subjected to assault and derision, denied custody of their biological children, not recognized as their partners' legal dependents in health insurance plans, evicted from homes previously shared with now-deceased partners, and not recognized as heirs to their lovers' possessions regardless of wills' provisions. By living separate lives, alone and apart from loved ones, lesbians and gay men can avoid these forms of discrimination. Once they enter the public sphere, however, they quickly discover that their societies permit few deviations from heterosexuality. The truth is that gay men and lesbians can and do "pass" in whatever culture or society they inhabit as long as they do not reveal their sexual identities. Because they cannot be identified by a physical characteristic like race or gender, they are the invisible minority, "apparitional," as the literary critic Terry Castle has described lesbians in the literary canon of Western culture.[15] Blacks, women, and other disadvantaged peoples of color have no such choice.

Because being a gay man or a lesbian is not visually self-evident but must be acknowledged, the struggle for gay rights diverges in several fundamental ways from other civil rights movements. Much as gay rights leaders would argue an easy correspondence between equal rights for gays and lesbians and equal rights for all other disadvantaged groups, too facile a correspondence can be drawn between them. For example, no empirical evidence demonstrates that gay men and lesbians are disproportionately economically disadvantaged because of homophobia—though with the rise of AIDS-related discrimination that statistic may change, particularly among gay men. Being in a committed gay relationship that is not treated legally as a "marriage" or "civil union" can create material disadvantages, such as higher taxation, fewer benefits, and less legal protection in matters like inheritance. Although in 1996 women in the United

States on average made 75 cents for every dollar men made, no research indicates that lesbians make proportionately lower salaries than heterosexual women.[16]

Gay men and lesbians may achieve higher levels of education than the population in general does, and their disposable income is assumed to be among the highest in the world because many do not have children. No law has ever denied housing or accommodation to individuals based on their homosexuality. Golf, social, and professional clubs could easily deny membership to blacks or women or Jews based on looks alone, but how could they possibly exclude closeted lesbians and gays, especially members of families whose ancestors can be traced back to the *Mayflower?*

Thus, the kind of disadvantage gay men and lesbians experience cannot apply to other disadvantaged minorities. And this, in part, has led to fissures within the mainstream gay rights movement about the degree to which gay men and lesbians should identify with and make common cause with other equal rights activists. Led by Bruce Bawer, author of *A Place at the Table,* and Andrew Sullivan, a British citizen living in the United States who formerly edited the *New Republic* and is the author of *Virtually Normal: An Argument about Homosexuality,* a school of thought among largely white middle-class gay men is gaining wider credence. The cornerstone of this critique is that "gays have indiscriminately linked the movement for gay equal rights with any left-wing cause to which any gay leader might happen to have a personal allegiance. Such linking has been a disaster for the gay rights movement. They falsely imply that most gay people sympathize with those so-called progressive movements, but they also serve to reinforce the idea of homosexuality itself as a 'progressive' phenomenon, as something that is political in nature."[17]

It is difficult to argue that being a gay man or a lesbian is inherently a political choice (rather than a personal one) or that gay men (especially white middle-class ones) are more economically impoverished than heterosexuals. Nor can one make a comfortable or convincing argument for including sexual orientation in affirmative action schemes in colleges and universities since anecdotal evidence suggests that openly gay men and lesbians may be better represented on faculties than as a percentage of the general population. While

countless gay men and lesbians have lost their jobs (or, more commonly, cannot obtain a more visible leadership position once their
sexuality is acknowledged or widely known), this form of job discrimination is probably not a sufficiently compelling reason to offer them
special or preferential treatment. The only issue, so goes this argument, is one of fairness, since being gay should have no bearing on
the outcome of any job-related decision. In reality, contrary to the
positions of fundamentalist opponents, gay males and lesbians have
never demanded "special or preferential treatment," but rather, constitutional protection to ensure fair treatment.

Opposing this neo-conservative viewpoint that gay rights should
be about fighting for individual liberty, not social justice, is Tony
Kushner, the Pulitzer Prize–winning gay playwright. Kushner sees in
various equal rights struggles the possibility for a natural coalition of
all discriminated persons fighting for everyone's right to be treated
fairly and share a piece of the economic pie. Kushner contends that
"openly queer GIs and same sex confectionery couples on wedding
cakes won't be enough" since gay men and lesbians are more than
"heterosexuals with a difference."[18] Kushner notes that although gay
men and lesbians do not require nor have they ever demanded special or preferential treatment, their marginal status means that their
struggle is more akin to that of other groups whose physical characteristics have been the basis of discrimination.

One piece of evidence for Kushner's position is that gay men and
lesbians, whether they remain closeted or are open, have so internalized homophobia that gay teenagers are now six times more likely to
commit suicide than straight teens.[19] Gays and lesbians are daily
bombarded with media messages and advertising that either deni-
grates them or denies their identities and experiences. If they adopt
unconventional forms of dress or behavior, they can be the object of
even greater derision or physical attack. This kind of treatment often
leads to a self-loathing that the eminent black psychologists Kenneth
B. Clark and Mamie Clark first exposed in their pioneering studies of
black children's preference for white dolls over black ones.[20]

Discrimination based on race or gender focuses on a characteristic that is largely unalterable, immutable, and undeniable. Anti-

Semitism, similarly, regards a person's Jewish identity as immutable. But what about being a a gay man or a lesbian? How immutable is this identity?

Homosexuality: A Condition or a Construction?

The current theory in the mainstream gay rights activist community is that being homosexual is neither a sickness nor a sin, but the preferred sexual identity of a minority of human beings. Some gay rights advocates, relying on the Kinsey Report's findings among men, have claimed that about 10 percent of the human population is homosexual. Recent studies, however, put the figure at considerably less than this.[21] While scientists will continue to debate these numbers and their meaning, a more fundamental question has yet to be definitively answered, namely, whether homosexuality is an unalterable biological condition, socially constructed, freely chosen, or some combination of these. Opposition to gay rights shifts depending upon how much weight is given to any one of these explanations.

Opponents generally use two contradictory arguments, both based on a supposedly fundamentalist reading of the Bible. The first is that gayness is a "lifestyle," a term that implies it is chosen. According to certain interpretations of Scripture, lesbians and gay men make a choice to join a group whose members engage in sinful acts. They are deliberately disobeying God's will. And, if gayness is simply a matter of choice, then gay men and lesbians can be condemned for knowing the "right" way but rejecting it. The theologian Bernadette Brooten has found ample evidence for this argument in early Christian texts.[22] A second argument, which is a variant on the first, assumes that homosexuality is not a choice, but rather a pitiable but unnatural condition according to God's law and therefore cannot be condoned. In this scenario, gays and lesbians are "lesser" beings, barely tolerated and surely not entitled to the same treatment as other members of a community. At the very least, they should not engage in homosexual acts and they should never be granted social legitimacy.

The Christian Life Commission of the Southern Baptist Convention in the United States declared in a 1993 newsletter that it opposed homosexuality "because it is clear in the Bible, God condemns it as a sinful lifestyle harmful to the individual and society. . . . The CLC opposes the granting of civil rights normally reserved for immutable characteristics, such as race, to a group based on its members' sexual behavior." Moreover, just in case homosexuality is not a choice, the group goes on to observe, "The Scriptures declare the Lord Jesus can change homosexuals. To accept homosexuality as an appropriate, alternative lifestyle would betray the life-changing sacrifice of Christ and leave homosexuals without hope for a new and eternal life."

It is not an exaggeration to claim that some of the most virulent anti-gay sentiment is found in literalist interpretations of Leviticus (see 18:22, 20:13). But historians and theologians such as Brooten, the late John Boswell, and Peter Gomes of Harvard Divinity School have found ample evidence for a more sympathetic interpretation of the Gospels when it comes to tolerance of male homosexuality, but not female homoeroticism.[23] The existence of divergent biblical exegesis may seem esoteric, but religious attitudes toward homosexuality influence public attitudes, even in a country with a formal distinction between church and state. Biblical revisionism may help to move us closer to an acceptance of gay behavior as not unnatural or sinful. And, it can help to undergird a legal framework in which consistent and fair treatment of all citizens helps to guarantee their individual rights.

In the minds of many progressives, combating the discrimination and disadvantage that gay men and lesbians face does not engender the same respect and support as fighting for other forms of equal rights. One need only think of contemporary controversies such as lesbians and gays in the military or hiring openly gay teachers to re-alize that there is no easy correspondence among liberals between gay rights and the rest of the civil rights movement. Many leaders who would never question the integration of blacks in the military still argue that openly gay people should not serve in combat because they would make heterosexual service members uncomfortable. Others fear that gay teachers might introduce or encourage tolerance for their way of life in their classrooms. If one were to substitute *Asian* or *Hispanic* for *gay* in these previous examples, the argument would be universally viewed as indefensible. Similarly, there is no easy cor-respondence between a "progressive" notion such as demilitarization and gay rights. As Cynthia Enloe has demonstrated in her brilliant book *Maneuvers,* the nineties gays-in-the-military debate advanced gay rights but deepened the militarization of American culture by valorizing the image of the patriotic soldier as the ideal citizen.

Interestingly, during the constitutional deliberations in South Africa, many argued that a general equality clause would be sufficient, but one of the key framers, Albie Sachs, now a member of the Constitutional Court, did not agree.[24] He insisted on specifying the fundamental right to sexual orientation because he wanted all citizens to be protected by the Constitution.

Thus, the question that must be squarely asked is why have gay rights proven to be the hardest civil rights to secure in the United States? South Africa's Constitution provides one kind of answer. But is there a difference of kind, not simply of degree, in advocating gay rights in the long, mantra-like credo that celebrates difference and diversity? Few would disagree that being gay puts a person at a disadvantage in what Adrienne Rich has bravely called the "compulsory heterosexuality of late 20th century America."[25] At best, lesbians and gays are tolerated in cities like New York and San Francisco; at worst, they are attacked and murdered. As recent Justice Department statistics confirm, the only hate and bias crimes on the rise in the United States are ones involving violence against gays and lesbians. Even in South Africa, Winnie Mandela's effective defense against a murder charge was that she was protecting a young black teenager from a white homosexual's advances. This defense echoed the homophobia of many South African black church leaders and fed into the argument that homosexuality is imposed upon blacks by white oppressors.

The gay rights effort focuses on overcoming repression, a problem Puritan-based American culture has trouble facing. Gay men and lesbians can function readily in heterosexual society as long as they repress a central aspect of their identity. If the state does not ask and the individual does not tell or if the individual does not relate to another in a sexualized way, there is no problem. The same cannot be said for skin color or gender. In race or gender discrimination one's identity cannot generally be hidden or altered. Conventional wisdom wrongly sees race and gender as largely inherited biological categories, even though we now know that they are not binary or essentialist in character. There is a growing consensus among biologists that race and gender are more socially constructed categories than biological ones and more fluid than was once thought. But what about a person's sexual identity?

First and foremost, conventional definitions the world over suggest that there are only three broad categories of sexual identity—heterosexual, bisexual, and homosexual. Persons claiming one or more of these sexual categories exist in every part of the world. Thus, an interesting difference emerges between sexual identity and all other racial or ethnic identity politics, namely, that being gay (like being heterosexual) is transnational, transracial, transgender. People calling themselves gay, lesbian, bisexual, or heterosexual can rightly claim the flag of the whole planet as do other living species who resist categorization according to national, ethnic, racial, gender, or other boundaries. To some, the 1990s were also the "Gay Nineties" because of the strength and seeming durability, despite the scourge of AIDS, of the gay rights movement. To others, like the literary critic Margery Garber, author of the provocative book *Vice Versa,* we are now living in a bisexual moment. To others, all this talk about celebrating homosexuality or bisexuality is a premature declaration of victory in the face of considerable backlash. In a country like South Africa, confronting enormous social problems of violence and poverty, not to mention the AIDS pandemic, talk of gay rights frequently seems a luxury and irrelevant to the dire circumstances of the majority of the population.

Many ironies surrounded the 1994 International Gay Pride March, which celebrated the genuine gains in securing civil rights for gay men and lesbians over the previous quarter century. These gains included the opportunity to lead more open, less repressed lives in such anonymous urban centers as New York City, San Francisco, London, Sydney, and Rio. They also included possibilities for lesbians and gay men to hold jobs without fear of losing them, to raise children openly, to share in partners' legal benefits such as health insurance and child care, and to run for public office without hiding in the proverbial closet. A concrete example of this kind of progress is the fall 1995 decision of New York State's highest court, the Court of Appeals, that a heterosexual or homosexual couple does not have to be married to adopt a child. Gay rights advocates hailed the decision because it "offered a kind of recognition of the integrity of lesbian and gay households." While it was a split decision, the Chief Justice, Judith Kaye, writing for the majority, argued that the decision was consistent with recent changes in state law and fundamental changes in the nature of the American family. She concluded that the court should "encourage the adoption of as many children as possible, regardless of the sexual orientation . . . of the individuals seeking to adopt them."[26] With this ruling New York became the third state, after Vermont and Massachusetts, whose highest court has recognized the right of unmarried couples, including homosexual couples, to adopt children.

And yet, precisely because of these gains in securing basic civil rights, gay men and lesbians in the United States are also experiencing an unprecedented level of homophobic backlash. Conservative school boards have succeeded in establishing congressional hearings to explore prohibiting federal education programs from including curriculum materials that teach tolerance of homosexuality. And though the summer of 1994 is remembered as a high point of gay activism in New York City, it also had a more dubious distinction. There were more anti-gay attacks in New York City in June 1994 than in any other month in the fourteen years such records have been kept. This form of violence increased not only in New York but also in other American cities.[27]

Looking back, would it have made a difference if the gay rights march and the gay rights movement had had a charismatic gay spokesperson like Martin Luther King or, for that matter, Nelson Mandela? Why are there no charismatic gays or prominent lesbians in the leadership of the gay rights movement? What difference would it have made if the struggle for gay rights was more clearly linked in the minds of gay men, lesbians, and heterosexuals to other liberation struggles? And why is this linkage so difficult to achieve? Jesse Jackson tried to build a "rainbow coalition" that embraced lesbians and gay men in his 1984 presidential campaign. It was a valiant, yet all too fleeting attempt at the politics of inclusion.

What is so different and disturbing about celebrating sexual diversity along with biodiversity, racial diversity, and gender diversity? Why is there no easy correspondence between gay rights and the civil rights of blacks and women? These questions can be summed up in the sobering fact that both James Baldwin and Bayard Rustin, two of the most eloquent spokespersons for the black civil rights movement, were nevertheless prevented from speaking at the 1963 March on Washington out of fear that their homosexuality would cast a negative shadow on the "purity" and "high mindedness" of the civil rights movement. In 1997, Bill Clinton became the first U.S. president to address a gay civil rights group. It is telling that such a simple gesture should have carried such significance.

These shortcomings cast a shadow over the permanence of the gains gay men and lesbians have achieved during the last thirty years. For example, it is interesting to ponder whether American society would ever return to a time of the poll tax, where citizens had to pay to vote, or restrictive covenants in housing in which blacks were prevented from owning homes in certain neighborhoods. It is hard to imagine taking back the guarantees of basic human rights for blacks, and yet this is precisely the scenario state legislatures in Oregon and Colorado have created by rolling back urban and municipal ordinances that protect the rights of gays and lesbians to equal employment and fair housing. And, as these attempts to reinstate homophobic statutes continue, where are the contemporary equivalents to the prophetic voice of a James Baldwin, who embodied both the black protest and gay pride struggles in his writings and political commentaries? Why is there no gay or straight Rosa Parks or Susan B. Anthony to demonstrate the interconnectedness between all human rights? Two individuals who come closest to uniting these movements—the black intellectual and activist Cornel West and Gloria Steinem, the founder of *Ms.*, do not lead grass-roots organizations. These are some of the questions that emerge as we try to understand what sexual difference and diversity mean today. Is being a lesbian or a gay man a fixed category, to use a phrase that is currently in academic vogue? Is it more prevalent now than fifty years ago? Is it catching? Is it a choice? Is it a threat?

While there are many ways, especially biological ones, to answer such questions, it may be useful to start with a literary approach. When it was published in 1928, Virginia Woolf's novel *Orlando* was an immediate success. Woolf's account of her lover, Vita Sackville-West, in imaginary escapades through three hundred years of history as both man and woman was the turning point of Woolf's literary career. *Orlando* sold over twice as many copies in the first six months as *To the Lighthouse,* Woolf's previous best-seller. One London newspaper's favorable review began, "a fantastic biography: Mrs. H. Nicholson and Orlando, 300 years as Man and Woman."[28] Interestingly, *fantastic* was the word Woolf herself used in her journal to describe this work as it was taking shape: "Vita should be Orlando, a young nobleman . . . and it should be truthful, but fantastic."[29] What makes this remarkable novel so fantastic is, among other things, the way in which the protagonist moves easily not only across time but also across gender differences. Orlando is both male and female, and during the course of her/his extra-long life, goes from boy to mother.

What makes this book a useful foundation on which to build our understanding of sexual difference is that it contains an important message about fluidity and the indeterminate nature of gender and sexual desire. As scholars of human sexuality are learning, desire is not comprehensive in purely biological terms. Instead, according to Gayle Rubin, a pioneering gender theorist, sexuality is constituted in society and history, not biology.[30] In short, sexuality should be seen in much the same way as such socially constructed categories as race and gender. It is impossible to think with any clarity about the politics of sexuality, race, or gender as long as these are thought of as biological entities instead of as socially constructed, historicized, and, thus, changeable identities.

In a preface entitled "Reclaiming the Lesbian and Gay Past" to a biography series, Lives of Notable Gay Men and Lesbians, the distinguished historian Martin Duberman acknowledges, "Being different is always difficult."[31] In noting that to be a gay man or lesbian is to be different from a male or female heterosexual, Duberman is both stating the obvious and challenging recent gay studies scholarship. A new generation of scholars does not even accept Duberman's initial premise. Literary critics and philosophers question the use of the word *different* to describe gay men and lesbians because it presupposes a predefined heterosexual mainstream from which others divert. They argue, why give up the mainstream to a heterosexual category when it is not even clear what that term means?

These younger "queer" studies scholars, so named because they reject binary distinctions between gay and straight, argue that people do not live in oppositional categories such as heterosexual and homosexual and that there is great fluidity in sexual orientation. Thinking in the psychological community about sexuality has changed as well. For decades, psychological doctrine posited that being gay was an illness, but since 1974, when the American Psychiatric Association removed "homosexuality" from its category of disorders, most progressive therapists have accepted that homosexuality is a valid expression of feeling and behavior. As one historian of the gay rights movement wrote, "Early research supported the illness hypothesis because it was conducted on patients in prisons and mental hospitals. Homosexuality itself can only be studied through more representative samples, and, as soon as research used comparisons between heterosexuals and homosexuals, the myth of illness was exposed."[32]

In the more than seventy years since *Orlando* was written, scientific evidence has substantiated Woolf's splendid literary conceit. We now know that the human species does not divide into two neat categories of sexual behavior—gay and straight. Instead, advances in biology are demonstrating that a diversity of sexual responses are in part encoded in our genetic and physiological makeup. If this new science of sexuality is correct, then people can and do experience their sexuality as changing over time and, relatedly, changing according to the social and cultural context.

Simone de Beauvoir hinted at this fluidity in her pioneering 1949 study, *The Second Sex*. In it, she proclaimed that all women were bisexual. At the time, we knew only of Beauvoir's sexual liaisons with Jean-Paul Sartre. Now with the analytical frame of feminist scholarship, it seems that Beauvoir's sexuality was far more complex. Deidre Bair's 1990 biography of de Beauvoir devotes an entire chapter to her friendships with women and includes an interview in which de Beauvoir is asked, "Do you accept homosexuality on a theoretical level, for yourself?" Her straightforward answer was "Yes, completely and utterly. Women should not let themselves be conditioned exclusively to male desire any more. And, in any case, I think that . . . every woman is a bit homosexual. Quite simply, because women are more desirable than men."[33] De Beauvoir seems to believe that women can willingly change their sexual orientation.

Why does exposing and reframing the fluid sexual identity of de Beauvoir and other less celebrated women matter? At its best, feminist scholarship and analysis of human agency requires us to see the multidimensional nature of sexual identity in women as well as in men. An inclusive methodology does not leave out important clues to human behavior because they do not conform to a rigid, binary view of human sexuality. Further, it is important to remember that these are socially constructed categories of sorting and explaining behaviors and not necessarily proven scientific facts. Like the category "woman," the category "lesbian" needs to be understood in dynamic social and political terms. There is nothing biologically fated about being born homosexual or heterosexual, despite the ideology of fundamentalists or, for that matter, the orthodoxy of essentialist-oriented gay rights advocates. Feminist scholarship requires us to ask different questions about the lived histories of people, and thus we are bound to find new answers.

To argue the truth that sexuality is a fluid category does not diminish the demographic fact that the vast majority—perhaps more than 95 percent of all humans—call themselves heterosexual. But even these proclamations appear to be socially constructed. For example, a 1993 University of Chicago study provided a striking range of responses when interviewers asked over thirty-four hundred Americans about their sexual identities. The researchers themselves could not even agree on a definition of "homosexual"—was it a matter of self-identification, behavior, desire, or a combination of all three? The study found pronounced differences between the number of self-defined gay men and lesbians who live in cities and the number who live in smaller communities as well as statistically significant differences between the number of self-defined gay men and lesbians who had college educations and the number of those who did not.[34]

Even our language to define what we mean by homosexuality is not precise. While the word *homophobic* did not enter the language until the sixties, the word *heterosexual* appears to have been coined in 1862, according to the historian Jonathan Ned Katz. Ironically, this first definition of heterosexuality signified a desire for both sexes, hence the "hetero." This is a far cry from current usage in which a heterosexual is sexually interested in people of the opposite gender only. How "heterosexual" became a privileged category and not just another way to be sexual is an important question. Moreover, how this one form of sexual behavior came to be seen as not just moral but also superior requires theological, social, and historical research. And while scholars try to understand the privileging of this form of sexual behavior, gay activists are trying to secure for themselves the same individual rights as heterosexuals. As Katz puts it, "If homosexuals were to win society-wide equality with heterosexuals, there'd be no reason to distinguish them. . . . The hetero-homosexual distinction would be retired from use, just as it was once invented."[35] Unfortunately, we do not live in societies that easily abandon categories of difference, whether they pertain to race, ethnicity, or gender. In fact, it could be argued that difference without discrimination is the utopia gay rights activists should be seeking. At the very least, sexual difference should not be viewed as subordinate, immoral, deficient, and therefore disadvantageous.

Finally, to return to the questions that we posed earlier in this essay: What is lesbian and gay sexuality? The answer is not simple, but most would agree that it is a behavior in which an individual is erotically or deeply emotionally involved with a member of her/his own sex. This behavior could last for a lifetime or could come and go. Although homosexuality is probably no more prevalent now than it was fifty years ago—at least in the United States and South Africa— people are more willing to call themselves "gay" and live openly than ever before. Is it a choice? The jury is out on that one. Despite some provocative but largely discredited research that points to certain biological traits, an enlarged brain or a "gay" gene in men or more testosterone in lesbians, we do not understand what accounts for a predisposition to homosexuality. We know very little about the genetics of sexual orientation because the research is at such an embryonic stage. Perhaps it is like being born left-handed—it used to be stigmatized but no longer is. Is gay male or lesbian behavior a threat to heterosexual families, to monogamy, to core Judeo-Christian values? Clearly, millions of people around the world think it is, and we still do not have a good explanation for these fears apart from a literalist reading of biblical Scripture that is itself ambiguous. The historian George Chauncey has found that an economic motive made straight New Yorkers increase their efforts to segregate and persecute homosexuals in the thirties. Chauncey convincingly argues that men of the Great Depression, psychologically emasculated by unemployment, felt they could bolster their masculine self-image by demonizing others.[36] In other words, in rough times for men, do we stigmatize gayness to shore up our own embattled definitions of manhood? Could that be a possible explanation for what happened to German lesbians and gay men in the economic disaster that followed the fall of the Weimar Republic?

One supreme irony about the increasingly conservative face of gay rights is that the issue seems more threatening now that many gay men and lesbians want to be like everyone else. Gay men and lesbians have been experts in the politics of the possible, and advocates of assimilation seem to be enjoying center stage in the mainstream press. In securing individual rights for gay men and lesbians to be "just the same" as heterosexuals, large elements of the gay rights movement, like the women's movement, appear to have lost much of their revolutionary and transforming agenda. As the psychologist Carol Tavris explains, "Even as the media and the religious right wrongly emphasize biological differences between gays and straights, the evidence shows a convergence in life styles, sexual practices, consumer values, diverse family arrangements and endorsement of an ethic of sexual pleasure."[37]

That the prominent issues for lesbians and gay men in the nineties focused on the right to marriage, health benefits, child custody, and military service suggests that advocates have made pacts with leaders in the heterosexual establishment. As Tony Kushner pointedly comments, "It is entirely conceivable that we will one day live miserably in a thoroughly ravaged world in which lesbians and gay men can marry and serve openly in the Army and that's it." His worry is that "capitalism, after all, can absorb a lot. Poverty, war, alienation, environmental destruction, unequal development, the fetishization of violence—these things are key to the successful functioning of the free market. Homophobia is not; the system could certainly accommodate demands for equal rights for homosexuals without danger to itself."[38]

Equal rights thinking is a deeply flawed and counterrevolutionary impulse for this movement. Only false homogenization can result and no real attempt to understand how celebrating difference can eventually lead to a stronger and more democratic society will have been made. This failure to assert difference could inevitably affect the progress of all other actions designed to promote social justice and economic transformation. The struggle for sexual difference, therefore, encompasses more than an equal rights agenda for gay men and lesbians. It is not too late to reverse course in this thirty-year-old movement and proclaim solidarity with others fighting to sustain the inherent diversity of all living things. This will not be an easy or seamless solidarity since advocates of one cause may not see their commonality with lesbians and gays. But this should be the shared project going forward.

Finally, an inherent paradox lies in this demand for equality. Because gay men and lesbians are like everyone else except in their sexual behavior, they can and do participate fully in all forms of civic life as long as they repress or hide their sexuality. Other minorities and women face discrimination on the grounds of exclusion, but gay men and lesbians face discrimination on the grounds of repression. Because they act on a form of sexual desire that is labeled deviant or unnatural by large segments of the population, they expose themselves to a virulent form of prejudice. Indeed, a new study in the United States found that suburban Americans are surprisingly tolerant of everyone but gay men and lesbians. In this study, the sociologist Alan Wolfe found that "middle class Americans most hostile to homosexuality were most willing to see it as a conscious choice. . . . Make something a natural condition, and Americans are quick to empathize. Make it a choice and people feel that they have the similar choice in condemning it."[39] Too many gay rights activists are fighting to be treated the same as heterosexuals. Thus, the deeper challenge that ought to be posed by the gay rights movement is to fight for equal treatment while at the same time resisting any demand or inclination to proclaim that equality equals sameness.

5

Gender Differences:
The Struggles around
"Needs" and "Rights"

In 1991 in Durban, South Africa, at the first ever Women and Gender in Southern Africa conference, the muggy heat of a Natal summer was reflected in intense exchanges. Overall it was a controversial event: black women interrupted the dominant voices of white women to air their own concerns. Evident race and class differences mingled with ideological variances and the sometimes conflicting identities of activists and academics. The tears and anger of that occasion have colored our subsequent thinking, talking, and writing.

In composing this book years later, we focus on gender as one difference assumed to be biologically given and, in that sense, essentialist. Despite thinking to the contrary, the category "woman" is not monolithic but is rather the site of multiple, complex, and contradictory identities that are socially defined, not biologically fixed. It seems important to emphasize this truth at a time when sociobiology and evolutionary psychology threaten to reassert biological determinism. Similarly, "gender" is a relational identity through which historically men have been able to dominate and control women. But male domination of gender relations should not obscure racial, ethnic, and class structures, which also control relations of power and privilege. In social reality, race, class, and gender domination intersect. This has important implications. As the American historian Gerda Lerner has argued, "As long as we regard class, race and gender dominance as separate though overlapping systems, we fail to understand their actual integration. We also fail to see that they cannot be abolished sequentially, for like the many-headed hydra, they continuously spawn new heads."[1] Lerner spells out the implications of this analysis on practical politics: "Instead of engaging in the endless, fruitless and counter-productive activity of prioritizing discriminations and competing among targeted groups for scarce resources, it enables us to see the commonalities among them. New attempts at building coalitions between women separated by their differences can succeed if the differences are acknowledged and respected even as alliances are formed on partial goals on which there is a commonality of interest."[2] This surely characterizes the charter campaign of the Women's National Coalition (WNC) in South Africa between 1992 and 1994. It is an important illustration of a coalition arising from the negative politics of difference under apartheid. Moreover, the WNC stands in marked contrast to several failed attempts in the United States to build similar coalitions.

The WNC provided an inspirational and paradoxical example of women's unity and raises important questions regarding both the limits and the possibilities of feminist struggle. The exploitative nature of relations between South African white and black women presented a challenge to any notion of sisterhood. This exploitation was most visible in the space within which these women most frequently interacted—the institution of domestic service. Low wages, long hours, and demeaning treatment suggested a strong level of exploitation of black maids by their white female employers. In addition feminism was understood by many as a way women organized separately from and antagonistically to men, and thus was perceived as divisive, alien, and elitist. In contrast, it was also seen to obscure the very real differences between women. A pragmatic unity among women within the WNC was brought about not in the name of feminism but by a shared sense of women's exclusion from the negotiation process that marked South Africa's transition from authoritarian rule. That shared sense of exclusion was the generative force behind the formation of the coalition in 1992.

The Success of Coalition Politics in South Africa: The WNC, 1992–94

The WNC represents a watershed in the history of women's struggles in South Africa. Formed in April 1992 when some seventy women's organizations came together to identify women's needs, priorities, and aspirations through a dual process of campaigning and research, the WNC was created with a limited lifespan and a specific aim. Its goal was the Women's Charter, a clear statement of principles to be presented to Parliament: "This was a deliberately narrow mandate around which women could unite."[3] The WNC represented an extraordinary convergence of women across geographical, age, racial, class, religious, ideological, and political lines. The affiliated organizations represented the rich tradition of women's voluntary associations, from political parties to occupational and religious groups, service and special interest groups, and community organizations. They included women's *stokvels* (savings clubs), organizations of women hawkers, beauticians groups, coalitions of taxi drivers, political organizations such as the women's sections of the National party and the right-wing Transvaal Agricultural Union, the Pan Africanist Congress, the IFP, and the ANC. With representatives from all the major political parties, the WNC represented a broader grouping than the much heralded forum that negotiated South Africa's transition from apartheid to democracy. Such a show of political unity is still unprecedented in the history of South Africa. Furthermore, the Women's Charter, adopted in principle at a national convention convened by the WNC in February 1994 and presented to Parliament in August of that year, was uniquely successful. In all, delegates from ninety-two organizations from across the political and social spectrum approved the charter.

The focus of the WNC was on concrete issues and practical campaigns rather than theoretical debate. After lengthy and elaborate consultation, five issues were prioritized around which to campaign—women's legal status, women and land, women and violence, women and health, and women and work. Affirmative action and the political representation of women were identified as the main themes to run through these five focuses. In addition to grass-roots campaigning, the research process included strategies such as focus groups, questionnaires, chain letters, community report cards, tribunals, and in-depth interviews. Through all these efforts the research reached a total of approximately one million women.

The charter attempted to straddle a recognition of diversity and an appeal to unity. The authors recognized the diversity of their experience and also the commonalities of women's subordination. As a statement of women's aspirations, it is a very loose document, similar to the Bill of Rights in that it represents a broad vision of an alternative society. Its transformative tone is expressed in its comprehensive program: "We require society to be reorganised, and its institutions to be restructured to take cognisance of all women. . . . We hereby set out a programme for equality in all spheres of public and private life, including the law and the administration of justice, the economy, education and training, development infrastructure and the environment, social services, political and civil life, family life and partnerships, custom, culture and religion, violence against women, health and the media."

The range and unconventional nature of the "women's issues" identified in the campaign and the research activities reveal a clear acknowledgment of women's diversity. This is illustrated by the following comment documented during the research process: "Our main problems are no jobs and no houses. . . . I live in the squatter settlement. Our houses are very bad. They are made out of mud, sticks, zinc, tin, plastic and anything. There is only one tap per street and sometimes long queues. It used to be worse when the water was often only a trickle (Black woman from an Eastern Cape township)."[4]

Many women raised the prescriptions of customary law, which have historically regulated social relations and practices, and some (but not all) women asserted that practices such as *lobola* (brideprice) should be abolished. A participant from the northern Transvaal felt that the practice was degrading because "when a man marries you he pays lobola, and because of that he considers you his toy-thing."[5] At a focus group discussion in a remote rural area the priority issues were identified as polygamy, unemployment, the rights of unmarried mothers and widowed women to own land, electrification, health care, and telephone service.

The traditional Western understanding of "women's issues" as largely involving child care, maternity leave, and sexual harassment is far too narrow in the South African context. It leaves untouched too many institutions that structure access to power and resources in ways that penalize women and too many issues such as the arms trade and control of the military that affect women's safety. Furthermore, the notion of "women's issues" implies that it is possible to separate one's multiple identities and arrange them in an hierarchical order so that at different times one promotes the interests of women or the working class or traditional culture or citizens. As the British feminist scholar Denise Riley suggests, one reason for "the unwillingness of many to call themselves feminists" is the inadequacies of the label "woman" and that "it is neither possible nor desirable to live solidly inside any sexed designation."[6] By contrast a gender lens recognizes that gender is a significant social relation because it structures our social experience and shapes our social world. Women and men have distinctive and specific experiences and develop different understandings and aspirations. In other words, all experience is "gendered."

The WNC was the shared ground from which the categories of women's needs and experiences were constructed. The needs codified in the charter were not fixed or given at the outset but rather were generated, articulated, and circulated within a process of organizational development. The WNC—rather than the totalizing discourse of "feminism" or "woman"—provided the space to frame these needs. In the WNC women found a new collective identity. The coalition attempted to develop a political practice that incorporated and built supportive groups regardless of difference. This notion of coalition politics avoids political fragmentation or enforcement of a false universalism. Instead, it allows for both autonomous organization and actions as well as cooperation and coordinated programs.

It could be argued that the WNC is an unselfconscious expression of a feminist solidarity, that it illustrates what the Dutch feminist Rosi Braidotti has called a "post-modernist rainbow politics."[7] Despite an absence of feminist claims, the WNC, in analytical terms, provides a concrete expression of some poststructuralist feminist themes: the continual insistence on "difference," the refusal to naturalize the category of "woman" or to assume a common female oppression, the refusal to essentialize "culture" or "race," the recognition of the importance of "context" that frames identities that are multiple and fluid sites of contest and negotiation, and the refusal to naturalize social and economic processes. Overall, the WNC demonstrates an insistence on multiplicity that dissolves the tendency to absolutist and essentialist categorizations. In the South African context this means that white middle-class women can no longer insist that their experiences are universal. Instead, multiple ideologies, ages, religions, incomes, races, ethnicities, geographies, and sexual preferences among women have to be acknowledged. In doing this, the WNC represented a loosening of the notion that treating women en masse was the only viable strategy for change.

This is not to suggest, however that no tensions erupted within the WNC. The central challenge it faced was how to keep difference from degenerating into division. The WNC process involved deep animosities and antagonisms between personalities: "Tensions, anxiety, suspicion, uncertainty are common features of beginning phases in organisations. Members test each other and the organisation for acceptance as they locate themselves in the organisation. This was a feature of the coalition at the beginning, both within its leadership structure, . . . among the participating organisations and within regions."[8]

Managing diversity was particularly difficult: "The issues of race, class, organisational affiliation, and expertise had to be carefully managed in terms of who would be doing what. There were accusations and counter accusations from all quarters for excluding this or the other organisation, for being too middle class, being too black, or too white, for favouring one political party or the other."[9] A suspicion of ANC dominance led the National party representative to threaten to resign from the Steering Committee shortly before the February 1994 national conference at which the Women's Charter was to be presented. Some ANC women, in contrast, felt that the WNC was dominated by white middle-class women, particularly National party members.

Predictably, tensions developed along racial lines as well. At one point a convenor complained that black women were not being sufficiently involved in the research process. In light of such difficulties, the timeframe for the work's completion had to be extended several times; initially formed for a year, the WNC has been continued indefinitely. One force that sustained the charter campaign, however, was a commitment to inclusivity, which remained central when working with participating organizations and in setting up the infrastructure to run the campaign. Because of the WNC's heavy emphasis on national reconciliation and its commitment to nonracialism, the historical antagonisms were muted.

The WNC had another factor in its favor. The ANC, the majority party in government, had a tradition of support for women's rights. The ANC's most famous document, the Freedom Charter, clearly states the importance of equality for women. The outcome of struggles by women within the ANC itself is evident in the statement "On the Emancipation of Women in South Africa," released by the ANC's National Executive Committee in May 1990: "The experience of other societies has shown that the emancipation of women is not a by-product of a struggle for democracy. It has to be addressed in its own right within our organisation, the mass democratic movement and in society as a whole. . . . The prevalence of patriarchal attitudes in South African society permeates our own organisations, especially at decision-making levels, and the lack of a strong mass women's organisation has been to the detriment of our struggle." This statement provided the critical political base and ideological impetus to take the struggles for women's rights forward.

Another force that initiated and sustained the coherence of the charter campaign was the courage and commitment of a handful of quite remarkable women, including some who had been returned to South Africa from exile after the unbanning of opposition organizations in 1990. Their number included some who had been exposed to feminist ideologies in the Northern Hemisphere and had subsequently introduced feminist concepts into their political practice. The WNC, especially in its early stage, relied a good deal on these women. One in particular, Frene Ginwala, must be credited for strengthening a women's movement through the establishment of the WNC. Ginwala is an exceptionally forceful personality and her strong political credentials—she had been head of the political desk in the London ANC

Alison,

I went back to the women's coalition conference today despite my better judgment. I should have spent the time working on preparing for tomorrow's classes, but it feels like I shared in quite a historic moment.

It's really extraordinary that South African women, so marked by their diversity, have united to the extent of having produced quite a good charter of women's rights. I think the process has profoundly changed people. Yesterday I watched some of these white Afrikaner National party women listening and deferring to the authority of black women who were chairing sessions and talking with obvious expertise and confidence. Frene Ginwala can take a lot of the credit for this process. Everyone is vituperative in their criticism of her but, as they say, "tall trees catch the wind." She had the initial vision, energy, political stature, and interpersonal skills to hold it together. She's an amazing woman. In addition to being Indian, middle class, and an intellectual, she's from a rich family and Oxford educated. These social characteristics are very different from those of the majority

of ANC members and could be reasons for her having a marginal place within it. Instead, she seems to be politically quite powerful. Her commitment to the ANC goes back to the sixties when she was a journalist in Tanzania. Then she was appointed a key adviser to the head of the ANC, Oliver Tambo, in London and is now head of the ANC Research Department here. One remarkable thing about her is her capacity to reach up into elite decision-making circles as well as down into grass-roots communities. She's incredibly well-informed and passionate about politics. I like her enormously.

I lost out a couple of times in the plenary of the women's conference. For example, I tried to get the clause included that said "as the main managers of natural resources women demand the protection of those resources, particularly in relation to soil erosion, desertification, and air pollution." However, the drafting committee felt soil erosion is not a "women's issue." With women constituting the majority of agricultural workers it clearly is. Also, I was opposed to those members of the WNC steering committee who are also parliamentary candidates being forced to stand down from election. Doing so implies that the women's coalition and party political activity were mutually exclusive activities, and one of the great strengths of the coalition is that it has affirmed the opposite. But I lost out on that one too.

office for many years—her access to ANC leadership, and her position as head of the ANC's Research Department gave her added authority.

The final force that sustained the charter campaign was a genuine openness to the diverse social experiences of women of different classes, races, ages, and political loyalties. Organizers generally recognized at the outset that while all women may have a shared interest in issues such as sexual harassment, violence, and discrimination in employment, some issues are particularly important to black women, such as homelessness, polygamy, and customary law. For many rural women the demand "one husband one wife" appeared to have more relevance and mobilizing force than Western feminism's "one person one vote."

Consequently, the WNC did not attempt to frame "women's issues" in any a priori way. The energy was directed instead at locating the largest possible number of women and tapping their interests in an open, exploratory, and nondirective process. Although some "sisterhood rhetoric" developed, participants genuinely acknowledged women's diverse fears and needs. People unequivocally accepted women's multiple realities and the need to recognize and explore the concrete social realities of women from disparate cultures and ideologies, at all stages of the life cycle, and with contrasting sexual preferences.

Importantly, the WNC did not present itself as a feminist organization, though its leaders, including Ginwala, accepted the feminist label willingly. This decision illustrates what Denise Riley has named as a "strategic willingness to cap one's feminist hand over one's theoretical mouth and just get on with 'women' where necessary."[10] Riley suggests that we do not always need "the conviction of unifying experience to ground a rallying cry."[11]

For the WNC, success came because it did not explicitly claim to be a feminist organization. The political massing was a loose arrangement that allowed for each woman to assert her own understandings and aspirations. It incorporated women from many races, cultures, religions, classes, and ideologies. It did not attempt to create a new, shared definition of the women of South Africa but rather provided a platform for the formulation of gender-specific demands by the mass of women who generally do not accept the label of feminism even though they express its principles in their actions and commitments.

In Europe and North America, the acknowledgment of difference has sometimes been interpreted to imply subversion of any feminist project. Denise Riley's phrasing of a new Sojourner Truth plea, "Ain't I a fluctuating identity," should, in the South African context, read, "Ain't I a contested terrain," with an equally "catastrophic loss of grace in the wording."[12] Riley views feminism as the site of that contestation, but this notion is not appropriate in South Africa, where feminism is still considered contaminated by its Western origins.

This is not to say that the women of the WNC are unaware of gender inequalities. Their recognition is simply not framed theoretically or organizationally in terms of "feminism." Unlike other societies in transition, such as contemporary Poland, in South Africa gender inequalities do not have a low level of salience in social consciousness. South African women are acutely aware of their subordinate position as a secondary labor force and of their political underrepresentation. But in South Africa gender inequalities have been generally understood as epiphenomena—effects of the oppression created and maintained by the apartheid state. Because the apartheid state was all pervasive—extending even to prescriptions of legitimate sexual partners—its totalitarianism made the personal political. Thus, one of the pivotal insights of Western feminism had less impact for South African women because it was already apparent. Furthermore, the opposition to totalitarianism, whether to state socialism in Poland, as Peggy Watson shows, or to the apartheid state in South Africa, was a source of gender unity.[13]

Many social tensions that triggered a "feminist consciousness" in women of the North are absent in South Africa. The early debates of Western modernist feminism about how to free women from the kitchen sink have little meaning for women who lack a kitchen, access to clean water, and nutritious food for their households. For many South African women —especially the nine million living in rural areas—life is a daily struggle for physical survival. The strains experienced by South African women as mothers and workers were understood initially to derive from the apartheid state rather than from patriarchal relations within the household or the workplace. The racial character of the apartheid state has obscured its gendered nature. Whereas women in the North originally identified the family as a site of women's oppression, black women in South Africa have attempted to protect the family from the encroachments of capital and the state and point to the weakening of black family life as one of the most grievous crimes of apartheid.

The feminist issue of reproductive rights might appear easy to support in a society where until 1994 there were an estimated three hundred thousand illegal abortions a year. But the problem goes beyond traditional male resistance. Like in the United States, "population control" is widely considered an expression of white racism. A hostility to abortion among a sample of health workers in Soweto has been linked to a notion of motherhood as an affirmation of womanhood. No common experience of motherhood, however, can be invoked to form a bond among all women, though "motherhood" has been a central theme of women's political organization in South Africa throughout this century. Appeals to women from within both African and Afrikaner nationalist discourses were directed at women as "wives and mothers."

In South Africa there is no historical feminist tradition to which contemporary feminists can lay claim, no proud connection with feminist forebears whose efforts created important new points of access to power and resources. The suffrage movement in South Africa that achieved the vote for white women in 1930 was profoundly racist in that it largely (Olive Schreiner excepted) ignored the three-quarters of South African women who were black. Before 1990 the majority of those South African women with access to feminist literature and who claimed the political identity were living privileged lives financed by their husbands and serviced by the black women they employed as domestic servants. While there were important exceptions, such as Ruth First, these white educated women tended to generalize from their own experiences and prioritize their needs in a set of "feminist" demands. The "feminist voice" heard in South Africa until recently has been that of an elitist feminism, more concerned with extending the power and privilege of middle-class women than with transforming society to eliminate the source of that privilege.

Feminism was thus widely viewed as divisive, reactionary, or inappropriate; as a "poison," as Alexandra Kollontai would have it; as

Craddock is a dusty, brown little town framed by blue mountains. It feels very remote from much of the world and its association with Olive Schreiner will probably be overshadowed by the assassination of Matthew Goniwe by the apartheid police. But Schreiner does seem to have been a formative feminist influence on many women; it is extraordinary to think of the reach of her writing from this little cottage on the edge of the desert. For example, Vera Brittain read *Women and Labour* the year it was published—1911. Much later, when describing her evolution toward feminism, Brittain wrote that Schreiner's work "sounded with a note that had the authentic ring of a new gospel." I think for many women in the North in the 1960s feminism was a "new gospel" and did provide a new way of living and relating, but that revolutionary potential seems to have dissipated. There are lots of reasons why, but certainly the neo-liberal emphasis on individualism and competitiveness have contributed.

Schreiner remains a model of a strong feminist identity. Earlier this century she was one of the few white women involved in the struggle for the vote who wanted it extended to blacks as well. She argued for a more inclusive nonracial feminist politics and her notion of "female parasitism" captures the exploitative relations in which many black women domestic workers are still trapped.

Alison,

I was really affected by visiting Mondlane University and seeing where Ruth First was killed by a parcel bomb on August 17, 1982. She was then fifty-seven and her remains had to be scraped off the wall for burial. The person believed to be responsible for the parcel bomb, Craig Williamson, was seen at a restaurant in my neighborhood last night. He's reputed to be a bon vivant—a successful businessman living an easy, comfortable life. It makes a mockery of any notions of reconciliation and restitution.

I never met her but admired Ruth First enormously. Her writing is brilliant and her political commitment carried her through a lot, including five months in solitary confinement. One daughter described her as "bright, attractive, fiercely independent—she stood as a constant reminder that whites could choose to stand up and be counted." Also, she was not one-dimensional—she enjoyed fine clothes, cared about her appearance, had lovers, liked gourmet cheese. A strong feminist, she rejected the confines of motherhood and traveled widely. In 1954 she went on a four-month study visit to China even though her third daughter was only two months old. This was tough on her children and—to be fair—she had domestic workers to do the cooking, the cleaning, and much of the child care.

concerned with "exotic" and distant issues such as sexual preference.[14] For many, "feminist" remains a stigmatized identity, partly because of its association with lesbianism. For instance, the well-known author and activist Ellen Khuzwayo said in an interview that she did not see herself as a feminist "because there are connotations I don't agree with—like lesbianism."[15] The relationship between feminism and lesbianism has bedeviled women's struggles in many contexts, but in South Africa it took a particularly acrimonious tone, given the general understanding of political priorities. As an ANC woman told the 1985 Nairobi women's conference, "It would be suicide for us to adopt feminist ideas. Our enemy is the system and we cannot exhaust our energies on women's issues."[16] The feminist movement of the seventies and eighties was frequently dismissed by anti-apartheid activists as an "indulgence of bored, rich, white Americans."[17]

In the nineties, however, this attitude began to change in part because the WNC was one component in a wider political project whose aim was to transform all social relations of subordination. The WNC thus represented "the pursuit of feminist goals and aims within the context of a wider articulation of demands."[18] According to the theorist Chantelle Mouffe, "Those goals and aims should consist in the transformation of all the discourses, practices and social relations where the category 'woman' is constructed in a way that implies subordination."[19] In its objectives, its anti-essentialism, its refusal to conceptualize "woman" as a homogenous category confronting patriarchy as a monolithic structure, and its acknowledgment of the multiplicity of women's subordination, the WNC would appear to fit Mouffe's criteria for a feminist, democratic project.

The achievements of the WNC have been largely at the level of representation in two senses: the representation physically of women in the state; and a changed representation of women in the discourse on gender. Until 1994 South African women had been largely excluded from political decision making. Only 1 woman served in the National party cabinet and there were only 8 women among the 308 members of Parliament. The ANC had only 1 woman on its 26-person National Working Committee and 12 on its 90-person National Executive Committee.

South Africa has now moved from 141st place on the list of countries with women in Parliament to 7th.[20] South African women are now better represented than their British and American counterparts. In 1994, for example, 103 women served in Parliament, including a woman speaker (Frene Ginwala), 2 women were chosen as cabinet ministers (out of 30 posts), 3 women became deputy ministers, and 1 woman held the title of minister of security in the Johannesburg regional government. Of 90 senators, 16 are women. Many of these women, such as Dene Smuts (the only woman from the Democratic party, which had 7 seats), were active in the WNC. Ten women from the IFP served as members of Parliament (out of the party's total of 43 seats), 10 were from the National party (out of 82 seats), and 84 were elected from the ANC (out of 252).

The WNC also may claim to have raised the general level of awareness of gender inequality: As Frene Ginwala once expressed it, "We've created a climate in which sexism is unacceptable."[21] This altered discourse was illustrated by a public meeting in Cape Town on March 20, 1994, when Nelson Mandela appealed to men to do their share of domestic work—washing, cooking, and ironing—on alternate weeks. Furthermore, President Mandela's speech at the opening of Parliament that year expressed a strong statement about emancipation of women: "It is vitally important that all structures of government, including the President himself, should understand this fully: that freedom cannot be achieved unless women have been emancipated from all forms of oppression."

The South African Bill of Rights guarantees women equality before the law. This legal assurance for women is yet to be enshrined in the U.S. Constitution. Further, the Bill of Rights will override customary law. This means that millions of African women married under customary law may use the new constitutional framework to demand greater equality within their own households. During the negotiations that marked democratization there was a debate about whether customary law should be made exempt from this equality clause. The WNC deserves the credit for defeating the bid of the traditional male leaders for an arrangement whereby customary law should be made exempt from the equality clause. The traditional leaders stated strongly that customary law should be recognized in South Africa and maintained that the demand for the equality clause was "a western attack on an African way of life." One traditional leader asserted, "We respect western culture and we have respect for westernised people but they must respect our traditional African culture. We should promote our own cultures that were diluted by the system of apartheid."[22] A chief was overheard in the corridors describing the women speaking in the debate on the legal status of customary law as "prostitutes."[23]

Some draft versions of the Bill of Rights did make provisions for customary law to have equal status with clauses guaranteeing gender equality, but a WNC delegation petitioned against this. In a briefing paper the WNC argued that the effect of the recommendations of the traditional leaders "is that two states will be established in the new South Africa: the democratic South African state and an 'invisible' traditional state. The former will be subject to the Constitution and the Bill of Rights, and its citizens will have resort to the Bill of Rights to challenge discrimination. In the latter, rural communities (and particularly rural women) will be isolated in a traditional state with no resort to the full rights of citizenship. Like the apartheid state, we will be creating two classes of citizens."[24] An essentializing "culture" could be a substitution for "race" in a discourse of exclusion.

Thanks to the WNC, the equality clause prevailed, but women's struggles have only just begun. Improvements in the material conditions of the majority of African women in access to houses, land, jobs, and child care are limited at best. Others maintain that the achievements of the charter campaign are shallow, that still no widespread understanding of sexism exists, that recent gains are limited to middle-class women, that there is a wide gap between the rhetoric and what women experience in their day-to-day relationships with men.

Overall, the charter campaign involved a delicate calibration between the celebration of difference and the need for solidarity among women. The crucial question is how to sustain the momentum of revolutionary change of which it was a part. The danger is that this drive for democratic empowerment and socioeconomic transformation could easily be derailed and diluted. Theorists of political transitions have observed that authoritarians often opt for liberalization in the hope of averting the demand for democracy. Activists fear that the South African future will include only a limited "deracialization" rather than a true transformation. They similarly fear a limited "de-genderization," which would involve more blacks and more women within the prevailing political order. The fear is that the concept of black empowerment will be shriveled and reduced to the creation of a black business class, and that the concept of the empowerment of women will be reduced to the creation of a few women politicians and managers. It is in this context that an indigenous feminism with a transformative promise and potential is crucial.

During the transition period of 1990–94 women activists succeeded in creating the possibility for full citizenship and a gendered democracy in South Africa. This involved forming explicitly gendered institutions by ensuring the presence of women in the decision-making structures of the new democratic state, establishing mechanisms for promoting gender equality, and considering the impact of new policies on gender relations. These mechanisms are among the most comprehensive in the world. They include the Office on the Status of Women and the Commission on Gender Equality, which acts as an independent, statutory body to monitor, educate, and advocate policy. But now that a pluralist political system, a universal franchise, and a legitimate state have been achieved, the consolidation of democracy depends on the transformation of economic and social relations. This consolidation requires specific policies to redress contemporary patterns of gender inequality.

The Failure of Feminist Coalition Politics in the United States: The Struggle for the Equal Rights Amendment, 1972–82

The high tide of feminism as a political movement in the United States occurred in 1972 when Congress voted to submit the Equal Rights Amendment (ERA) to the states for ratification. President Richard Nixon supported the legislation, as did overwhelming numbers of Congressmen and women. For the pro-ERA activists of the late sixties and early seventies, as for women suffrage activists working more than fifty years before, the key to equality was entitlement: the belief that all citizens irrespective of sex, race, or other category of difference are entitled to certain basic rights and responsibilities. The second wave of the women's movement had thus begun politically where the first wave had ended—with a focus on equal rights feminism. In 1920, it was the vote; and in 1972, it was all other citizenship rights. Few in the nation's capital suspected that the ten-year drive to ratify the ERA would generate powerful opponents, many of them female, who would transform this simple guarantee of legal equality into a righteous struggle against what they saw as a feminist revolution to transform gender roles. Fewer still envisaged a decade-long struggle that would mobilize women politically as had no issue since suffrage. Yet by 1982, when the deadline for ratification expired, the battle had assumed epic proportions, especially in pivotal states like North Carolina, Florida, and Illinois, which were considered most likely to supply the remaining three votes of the thirty-eight required to secure ratification.

While national data on the socioeconomic characteristics of pro-ERA women are not available, several state studies at the time suggested that these women were predominantly white, well-educated, and middle class. They considered themselves "liberal" in political terms but belonged to both the Democratic and Republican parties. By the middle of the decade, however, the pro-ERA forces sided more frequently with the Democratic party, as the Republican mainstream became more conservative. Even though the pro-ERA movement was frequently led by self-styled "feminists" and, in particular, the National Organization for Women (NOW), which was founded in 1965, pro-ERA women were initially perceived by the press to be more diverse and behaved in a more inclusive manner. There was room at the top of the leadership chain for "nonfeminists." Traditional women's organizations, such as the League of Women Voters and the American Association of University Women, had large membership lists and media clout as the factual and dispassionate voices for legal equality for women. They helped form the backbone of this national pro-ERA coalition, though they did not claim to be "feminist" in their ideology.

This is an extremely critical point because as the decade moved along and ratification became a more elusive goal, the somewhat broad-based coalition of white women began to unravel. Even though surveys revealed that black women generally supported the ERA, women of color, with some rare exceptions like Aileen Hernandez and

Shirley Chisholm, did not find it easy to assume leadership positions in the movement. As the historian Jane Sherron De Hart has written, "Bridging differences of culture, class and race had always proved difficult for women's groups."[25] This failure to engage the energies, participation, and leadership of working-class women and women of color may well have contributed significantly to the defeat of the ERA. Certainly by the mid-seventies, certain feminist leaders, including Bella Abzug and Gloria Steinem, had begun to voice concern that the movement lacked a broad-based multiracial character.

In 1976 Abzug was named by President Jimmy Carter to head the national commission on the observance of 1977 as International Women's Year. She decided that the commission should convene a conference whose goal was to link women's issues, including the ratification of the ERA, to broader efforts to eliminate gender, race, and class discrimination and promote social justice in American society. Subsequently, Abzug convinced her feminist allies and a much broader coalition of women leaders to work on this conference, which was the first and is still the only federally funded, politically broad-based national women's conference in U.S. history.

The conference was a singular event for the women's movement. Over five thousand women from throughout the country went to Texas, a state that had not ratified the amendment. They represented various governmental and nongovernmental organizations, including voluntary women's associations, labor unions, church groups, the media, education, business, and, in a stunning reversal of traditional white-led feminist politics, women of color were visible and well represented in Houston.

Had the "Spirit of Houston" been sustained, perhaps the outcome of the ERA struggle would have been different. Instead, ratification stalled in part because pro-ERA forces could not sustain a genuine cross-racial, cross-class movement. By the late seventies white working-class women began to challenge what they saw as threats to their security posed by gender equality. The media began to give increasing coverage to the voices of such anti-ERA spokespersons as Phyllis Schlafly, a savvy public relations professional and head of the conservative Eagle Forum. Based in Illinois, the group provided a platform for women who opposed the ERA on the grounds that it challenged and demeaned the traditional roles of mother and homemaker and offered only a vague sense of what women could achieve in a non-gender-stereotyped world.

Clearly, the ERA was defeated because not enough male state legislators in key states supported it, but "there was no denying the divisiveness of the gender equality issue among women themselves."[26] As a by-product of the ratification struggle, the anti-ERA anti-feminist women's groups grew in political strength and quickly aligned themselves with the right wing of the Republican party. This enabled them to tackle the next big antifeminist issue, the 1972 *Roe v. Wade* Supreme Court decision that had legalized abortion.

Looking back over the ERA ratification struggle, two important conclusions stand out. As De Hart astutely observed, the failure "revealed the limits of feminist activism in an era of conservative ascendancy."[27] Also significant, however, is that the feminist politics of the period was profoundly narrow. Even though NOW's membership doubled between 1970 and 1972, no powerful and effective coalition of political groupings across gender, racial, and class lines could provide the grass-roots support to mobilize pressure in the three key states needed to ratify. Feminists in the United States remain committed to their goals, yet stymied by their seeming inability to draw women of all backgrounds together. This is in stark contrast to South Africa's WNC. Despite gains and losses, gender relations remain profoundly unequal in both societies, though in South Africa, gender equality was enshrined in the new Constitution, something the United States has still not accomplished.

Gender Inequality and Feminism in Post-Apartheid South Africa

The most dramatic change for women since 1994 is the establishment of a framework within the post-apartheid state to secure rights. Measures such as the Employment Equity Act and the Promotion of Equality and Prevention of Unfair Discrimination Bill empower South Africans to challenge inequality and discrimination on the basis of race, disability, and gender in areas including employment, education, health care, accommodation, land and property, insurance, pensions, and banking. A number of other legislative provisions have been designed to protect women in maternity issues and abusive relationships. Laws such as the Maintenance Act and the Domestic Violence Act are significant, but unfortunately lack infrastructure for effective implementation.

One of the most dramatic changes is the access of black women to the middle class. A number of black women serve in both private and public sectors as government ministers or managers. But the differences both between men and women and between women of various class, race, and ethnic groups remain particularly sharp in contemporary South Africa. For example, women generally, and women of color in particular, are remunerated less well than men. Average hourly earnings for women of color are around R7.50, compared with R17.50 for white women and R29 for white men. Unemployment is especially high among the African population, but whereas half of the African female population is unemployed, only 9 percent of white women are.[28]

Since 1994 the government has taken important steps toward gender equality, such as access to safe and legal abortions. In apartheid South Africa abortion was illegal except under special circumstances, such as severe deformity of the fetus or pregnancy due to rape or incest. For many women in impoverished rural areas, however, the gap between policy and reality makes the choice allowed by the Termination of Pregnancy Act virtually impossible to make. Many African women are still subject to exploitative employers—of all races—including farmers who demand long hours of work for wages as low as R40 a month supplemented by "rations" of mealie meal, rotten beans, and salt.

African women in rural areas are particularly powerless, voiceless, and dependent. Almost 65 percent cannot read or write.[29] Because African customary law still has support, these women are subjected to the patriarchal practices of chiefs and headmen, who treat them as legal minors entirely under the authority of men and with very limited economic rights. Customary law operates to deny women access to land. This denial is comprehensive because "access to land incorporates residential rights, rights to arable land, rights to communal grazing land and rights to use common resources like thatching grass, wood, water etc."[30] But the restrictions on access to resources such as land are not the only form of discrimination to which all South African women are subject.

Gender stereotypes that inferiorize women are still pervasive, and violence against women is increasing at an alarming rate. It is estimated that one out of every two South African women has suffered or will suffer the trauma of rape and that one out of every four South African girls will have been sexually abused by the age of sixteen.[31] Black women are most seriously affected and the increases in this behavior may be related to rising levels of social disintegration in South Africa's black townships. In a recent survey of three thousand residents of Soweto, 22 percent of the women interviewed reported that their husbands beat them. Many of these beatings were regular, severe, and accepted by men—and by many women—as part of "the natural order of things."[32]

This finding echoes those of the social anthropologist Adam Ashforth, who reports that in Soweto most men accept the legitimacy of the "right" of a man to inflict corporal punishment on "his" woman as a form of discipline: "The general right of a husband to punish, physically if necessary, is largely taken for granted."[33] According to several studies many young African men view their girlfriends as forms of property, and the institution of *lobola* (bridewealth), which is still widely practiced in urban townships such as Soweto and involves large cash payments, is often described as "buying a wife."

A growing number of women are challenging these practices in the name of feminism. Some of the most influential black South African women now describe themselves as "feminists," including Thenjiwe Mtintso, the deputy secretary-general of the ANC, a former member of Parliament, and a former guerrilla. Mamphela Ramphele, the former vice chancellor of the University of Cape Town, has written that after her banishment order, her "exposure to feminist literature" was one factor that "contributed to my growth into the person I am now."[34] Some even speak of an emerging "Black feminism" or "new feminism" in South Africa.

Unfortunately, in South Africa black feminism has some negative characteristics. According to Christine Hendricks and Deirdre Lewis,

Alison,

Went to an interesting conference on the advancement of women in the new army. It is an important topic, as at present women constitute less than 10 percent of the defense force and there are only two women (out of a total of forty-five) with the rank of major general. However, I was depressed at the narrowness of the focus, which was exclusively on the position of women in the army and issues relating to conditions of service, like access to pensions, medical aid, and housing. Obviously these are important, but no wider questions about the position of the military in our society were raised.

The best thing about the conference was sharing a platform with Thenjiwe Mtintso. She's an amazing and very likable woman whom I'd really like you to meet one day. She's forthright, warm, and funny and talks about her dieting as "the other struggle." She's been a guerrilla commander in Umkhonto we Sizwe (the military wing of the ANC), a diplomat, a member of Parliament, a student—did a degree in politics and sociology as well as a master's in public policy and management—a mother of three boys, and now is chair of the Commission on Gender Equality.

She left school at thirteen to work in a factory, studied privately, and then was expelled from Fort Hare University for her political activities. She was banned and detained in the seventies before going into exile in 1978.

She's a committed feminist (she calls herself "a Marxist/socialist feminist because I relate gender to class") and has been outspoken on gender issues within the ANC. For instance, she is critical of Mandela's reference in his inauguration speech to "women" as a separate category along with "youth." After the speech she was part of a delegation of ANC women parliamentarians who went to see him to argue for a gender lens to be applied to the transformation process. When she became a member of Parliament she argued that Parliament needed to be overhauled if it was to take the women's struggle seriously. Her theme in her first speech as a member was that the soon-to-be-established gender commission should audit "where women—particularly African women—are placed now in South African society, and again in five years' time." She's expressed a lot of anxiety about the future of women's liberation in South Africa. For example, she says that her "biggest fear and challenge is the loss of gender content in the transformation of our society."

black feminism "eloquently identifies its target as white or mainstream feminism, but tends to rely on an essentialist position, arguing that black women automatically have insight into their experiences by virtue of their socioeconomic, cultural and/or biological heritage."[35] This essentialism is close to the romanticism of "womanism," which celebrates the inherent spirituality and creativity of black women. Furthermore, it can be a perverse and hostile form of "feminism" that finds fault with other women. Postmodernist feminism can provide the necessary corrective to this focus on fixed identities that is characteristic of womanism and so-called African feminism.

It has been claimed that there is growing support for feminism in Africa. "Throughout the continent women are demanding to be heard, organising, questioning men's rights over them, throwing into doubt customary practices through which they are controlled, being 'difficult.'"[36] This is partly due to the internationalization of feminism through United Nations–sponsored conferences that have prioritized the empowerment of women. In the journey from Mexico City in 1975 to Beijing in 1995 a comprehensive approach has emerged and emphasized that society as a whole benefits from women's equality, that the empowerment of women is crucial to all forms of economic development. By contrast the feminist movement in the United States has been weakened since the mid-eighties by a right-wing backlash.

Gender Inequality and Feminism in the Post-Reagan Era

One argument with which feminism in both the United States and South Africa has had to contend is that gender struggles undermine racial solidarity. The U.S. black feminist scholar bell hooks laments the fact that "as we look at our contemporary past as Black people, the space between the sixties and the nineties, we see a weakening of political solidarity between black men and women. It is crucial for the future of Black liberation struggle that we remain ever mindful that ours is a shared struggle, that we are each other's fate."[37]

A genuinely feminist lens requires that this racial solidarity not come at the expense of black women. It is vital to reiterate this because black male movements like the 1995 Million Man March and the Nation of Islam seem to have touched a deep desire in men for change and spiritual renewal as well as anger toward the new roles of black women and changes in family patterns. The exclusion of women from the 1995 march provoked criticism, especially among black feminists. Some asserted that the rhetoric of protection and atonement during the march was just a mask for sexism. Angela Davis asserted that the Million Man March represented "retrograde politics," out-datedly casting men as the saviors of families and communities.[38] This was underlined by march organizer Louis Farrakhan's appeal to women to stay indoors and tend to the children.

The Million Man March brought together an estimated crowd of four hundred thousand—virtually all of them black men—exceeding by more than one hundred thousand the turnout in the 1963 civil rights March on Washington led by Martin Luther King Jr. On that occasion, King spoke of his great dream—a dream that appealed to the government to help build a color-blind society. But in 1995 the Million Man March's appeal was for racial solidarity; it was directed by blacks to blacks and, if not explicitly separatist, spelled out no clear role for whites, let alone the equality of black women. Ben Chavis argued that the march had "transcended all divisions in the black community."[39] Cornel West claimed that he marched "to promote black operational unity" in the tradition of King. Marching separated him from "color-blind neo-liberals and conservatives who cheaply invoke Dr. King's words even as they kill the substance and spirit of his radical message."[40]

This explicit exclusion of women is perhaps a second indicator of the strength of racial solidarity to override feminist appeals for gender solidarity. Many feminists in the United States were shocked to see black women cheering along with men at the acquittal of O. J. Simpson, also in 1995. Although in 1989 Simpson had pled no contest to charges that he had battered his wife, black women clearly were responding to a deeper hatred of the Los Angeles police force than to Simpson's treatment of women.

Just as feminists in the United States began to regroup after the defeat of the ERA, another major struggle—the fight to retain the right to a legal abortion—emerged in the eighties and nineties. As the Reagan era unfolded, reproductive rights became the centerpiece of the women's movement. Feminism, an already somewhat suspect ideology to the vast majority of American women—it has been claimed that only about one-third of voting American women identify themselves with the movement—became nearly synonymous with a kind of "female body politics." In the sixties and seventies the catch phrase of feminism had been "the personal is political" and it covered a range of gender equality issues from abortion rights to pay equity to political participation to new family roles. Two decades later, the phrase was inverted and thus narrowed to mean "politics is personal." While reproductive rights, domestic violence, and sexual harassment should all be important pillars of movement politics, it is troubling that the feminist project has had to become so narrowly focused on the private sphere instead of transforming the public arena. As the social theorist Constance Buchanan has suggested, perhaps "the most effective way to improve women's status in society may be to recognise their interest in more than a 'social feminist' agenda (reproductive freedom, childcare, parental leave). It may mean linking women's concern for their rights with their larger sense of social responsibility."[41]

How did the feminist project shrivel in the last twenty years in the United States? There are several obvious answers, though none is completely satisfying. The first and obvious one is that conservatives reacted powerfully to reverse the genuine gains made by feminists and women's rights leaders. Susan Faludi's important 1992 book, *Backlash,* chronicled in minute detail why the women's movement stalled in the Reagan and post-Reagan eras. And, sadly, both Clinton administrations have contributed to the further feminization of poverty in the United States, despite some gains for working women, such as child care leave and greater pay equality. But this was not a foregone conclusion. Indeed, one could have posited an alternative scenario that the threat of rolling back hard-won gains for women would have resulted in an even more powerful coalition to protect women's newly acquired rights. While one can never underestimate the power of the Right to reassert traditional values, it is dangerous to assume that feminists had no authority or power or agency of their own.

A second more surprising answer is that the feminist movement is finished because it has succeeded. Overly optimistic pundits cite a *Time*/CNN survey conducted in 1998 in which a "hefty 50 percent of those from ages 28–34 told the pollsters that they share 'feminist' values, by which they mean they want a world in which they can choose to be anything—the President or a mother, or both."[42] They also mention the changes the women's movement appears to have wrought in their lives and in expectations for girls. It sounds true, but little has actually changed in the structure of American society to support different choices. Further, these opportunities exist largely for those who are already economically and educationally privileged and many already had them before the women's rights advances. For most American women, and especially for women of color, the women's movement has not had much effect on their lives. The average female worker still earns only seventy-five cents for every dollar a man earns. There are few female CEOs of Fortune 500 companies. And, sadly, day care is not listed as a key issue on the NOW Web site.

A third answer, subtler and not always discussed, is that feminism has waned for complex and interwoven reasons: feminism was never as broad-based as it needed to be to sustain itself in conservative times; feminists picked up some early victories inside the Washington, D.C., beltway that were never fully embraced outside it; feminists became focused on fighting a rear-guard action against growing assaults on reproductive rights and thus gave scant attention to the economic inequalities devastating poor women; and feminism abandoned a transformative, radical ideology for a more mainstream role in conventional two-party politics. For example, more women held elective office after the 1992 elections than ever before in American history. Yet, looking back, few would argue that the nineties were marked by "feminist" critique in Washington. Perhaps the most positive feminist result of the 1992 election was Clinton's appointment of Ruth Bader Ginsburg, an advocate for women's equal rights, to the U.S. Supreme Court.

Lastly, feminism as a monolithic, "equal rights oriented" movement may have withered at the national level. Some might even say it has been silenced altogether except when a crisis involving a "women's issue"—such as the O. J. Simpson trial or the Monica Lewinsky revelations—incites action. Even in such cases, "feminist" spokespersons are demeaned or treated as though their concerns are trivial.

If we focus on and reconceptualize the battles that are being waged at local levels, however, the picture is not as bleak. For example, women are in the forefront of environmental justice struggles, movements for ethnic and cultural survival, anti-gun campaigns, and drives to rebuild inner-city communities. These women do not question whether they belong in the public arena. They assume it is their place. If these women do not constitute a "feminist" movement, they surely constitute the best hope for a new kind of feminist project.

Conclusion

Paradoxically, the transformative potential of feminism has not been fully realized in the society where the women's movement has been traditionally strongest—the United States. During the nineties, in both the United States and South Africa, two contradictory processes have been at work—a somewhat shallow feminization of power in the U.S. Congress (there are currently nine women senators, which is an all-time high) and the South African Parliament and an accelerated feminization of poverty in both societies. Both are a consequence of economic policies that have opened doors for some women while creating a widening gap between the rich and poor. Globalization and the growing digital divide appear to be making these contrasts between women's lives even starker. Addressing poverty will be the central challenge for feminists in the twenty-first century. One lesson we can draw from the experiences of the WNC and the ERA forces is that differences in women's lives need not be a barrier to coalition-building. The politics of difference must defer to needs of the disadvantaged if feminism is to regain its transformative potential.

6

A Feminist Perspective
on Understanding Difference
and Disadvantage

Leaning on the wooden balcony in Elizabeth Bishop's home in Ouro Preto, we had a wonderful view, framed by purple bougainvillea and emerald sunbirds, of the little town. The highlights of our visit to Brazil were seeing Bishop's studio in Petropolis with its soft, blue mountain views and her home in Ouro Preto, Casa Mariana. In Petropolis it was difficult not to be distracted by the current millionaire owner with her collections of poodles and orchids. But we tried to experience Ouro Preto as Bishop had done and even located the place under the window where "there used to be a fountain, where all the world still stops."[1] Bishop first visited the little town in 1953 and wrote, "It is a national monument—almost solid eighteenth century Portuguese baroque. Everyone talks of it but almost no one ever seems to get there. So we have cans of gasoline and extra automobile parts and Lota is insisting on a revolver."[2]

Elizabeth Bishop proved to be a wonderful guide in our efforts as feminists to understand difference and disadvantage. She had such a wide set of interests, ranging from the natural world to social practices to cultural expressions, and in her travels she really covered the globe. Reading and rereading her work helped us identify some building blocks that led us toward our feminist understanding of the relationship between difference and disadvantage and how they relate to equality and social justice.

In this chapter we argue in favor of "difference" both for strategic reasons (to achieve equality we have to take account of difference) and for empirical reasons (diversity is a reality). We conclude that a focus on the relationship between difference and disadvantage is essential to reconceptualize the feminist project. This focus is important in view of the tendency for the current preoccupation with understanding "difference" to displace the concern with addressing inequality and disadvantage. As the British theorist Anne Phillips explains, "Difference, in particular, seems to have displaced inequality as the central concern of political and social theory. We ask ourselves how we can achieve equality while still recognizing difference, rather than how we can eliminate inequality."[3]

In the United States, this displacement is most obvious in the concern among activists with "identity politics." At the same time, social scientists focusing on class and economic inequalities have tended to neglect cultural injustice and the right of groups to self-definition and self-determination. We are arguing that society needs a synthesis of both political traditions: the older one focused on class struggles around economic conditions and inequality and the newer one focused on struggles around cultural injustices.

None of the differences discussed in this book can be reduced to one of class, but all are affected by class dynamics. As the political economist David Harvey points out, a "concentration on class alone" is deficient because "it cannot and does not acknowledge explicitly the existence of heterogeneities and differences based on, for example, race, gender, sexuality, age, ability, culture, locality, ethnicity, religion, community, consumer preferences, group affiliation and the like."[4] As Phillips argues, however, "the shift from inequality to difference . . . often seems to divert attention away from economic aspects of inequality—and has remarkably little to say about specifically class inequality."[5]

Class is absent from the rainbow metaphor used to describe diversity in contemporary South Africa and the United States. So is gender. This metaphor, together with the discourse of reconciliation in

Our brief visit to Brazil has been framed by returning to some of Elizabeth Bishop's poems, letters, and paintings. One memento is a red-and-black-patterned leaf from the Tijuca Forest that we have pressed between her watercolor paintings reproduced in the book *Exchanging Hats.* Without knowing these paintings, I doubt we would have noticed the leaf. One reason Bishop is such a marvelous guide is that she was a great explorer. She traveled widely and many of her poems and letters were written while she looked out of windows en route to somewhere. Accepting an award, she once said that she was always "running along the edges of different countries, looking for something." Searching these "different countries" involved developing an acute understanding of cultural diversity. Bishop had a genuine and deep appreciation of different cultures and contexts and a distinctive voice; her poetry goes back and forth in time and space.

We reread her poem "Pink Dog" and remarked on the juxtaposition of the umbrellas coloring the beach while the naked dog trots across the street. This image captures the paradox of Rio. You first expect the poem to be about rich, naked beach people, but instead it's about beggars who rightly fear being thrown into tidal rivers by the generals who ruled Carnival and the country. She combines desperate images with a rage against cruelty and injustice.

There's plenty of that here despite all the claims about Brazil as a "racial democracy." Black Brazilians tend to live in harsh and violent circumstances in shanty towns known as *favelas* or *mocombos,* while whites tend to live in middle-class comfort. Brazilian blacks earn less than half as much as whites, their illiteracy rates are more than double whites', and their life expectancy is much shorter. Like South Africa, it seems like two nations existing alongside one another.

But I'm ashamed to say we had a great time despite all this poverty and violence. We danced the samba (clumsily), drank *cachaca* with limes and sugar, listened to *chorinho* music in Lapa (though the group only started playing at 11 P.M. and I struggled to stay awake, smiling), ate the national dish of *feijoada* (a meat stew with beans, rice, and orange slices), and swam in the ocean. We ate a picnic lunch in the Tijuca Forest and saw not only brightly colored tanagers and a star monkey but also the candles and bowls of food remaining from a *candomble* ceremony.

South Africa in which political and ideological differences are muted, is diverting attention from growing class inequalities around the world. Linking difference and disadvantage implies redistribution of power and resources.

Two Ships in the Night: The United States and South Africa

Linking difference and disadvantage is necessary in a feminist project for both political and theoretical reasons. While the United States is the wealthiest country in the world, among the advanced societies of the North it also has the highest proportion of people living in poverty, a meager system of welfare benefits, and a growing gap in income and wealth between the rich and the poor. In the United States the poor are disproportionately black, whereas in South Africa the poor are predominantly black. In South Africa one of the most dramatic changes since the fall of apartheid is the growing gap between rich and poor among the black population.

Today difference and diversity are framed in opposing ways in our respective countries. While the United States seems to be moving toward intolerance, South Africa is struggling to create a nation that celebrates difference. "One nation, many cultures" was the theme of President Mandela's 1994 inauguration. We also see practical expressions of this diversity in the recognition of eleven official South African languages and a Constitution asserting that no person shall be unfairly discriminated against directly or indirectly on the grounds of race, gender, sex, ethnic or social origin, color, sexual orientation, age, disability, religion, conscience, belief, culture, or language. "Equality" is not interpreted to mean sameness. Although the Constitution does not define the term, the Constitutional Court has agreed that equality must be given a substantive rather than a formal meaning so that one group or person will not always be treated in the same way as others, regardless of need. This notion will also be used to address structural patterns of disadvantage. The challenge is how to link diversity and national unity, how to promote a common South African national identity that is sensitive to difference and thus the country's diversity but committed to overcoming the disadvantage apartheid imposed on blacks.

While that challenge involves a strong policy commitment to social and economic rights in contemporary South Africa, by contrast, Americans today seem more willing to abandon a New Deal consensus on the state's responsibility to care for its neediest citizens than they have at any time during the last half century. Welfare reform seems likely to increase poverty and decrease income among poor families.

Railing against 1995 U.S. Supreme Court decisions limiting affirmative action for government contracts and desegregating education, the Reverend Jesse Jackson remarked that the United States and South Africa were passing each other in opposite directions like two ships in the night. He argued that South Africa is moving toward shared power, inclusive democracy, and bridge-building. Court rulings there are moving toward making South Africa whole. Court decisions in the United States, in contrast, are expanding gaps. Jackson went on to observe in 1991 that "this time three years ago we were the moral guardians of racist, apartheid South Africa. Today the light is coming from South Africa."[6] Anthony Lewis made a similar point in 1995 when he praised the South African Constitutional Court's ruling that the death penalty was unconstitutional. This judgment "made the rights of the individual the society's highest value." In the United States, "the culture of rights" was instead gradually giving way to public fear.[7] Since then New York State has reinstated the death penalty.

It is ironic that these disparate movements are happening in the world's oldest established democracy and in one of its youngest. The foundationalist documents on which these two democracies are structured are not that dissimilar, but they were constructed through very different processes—in closed negotiations among white men in Philadelphia in 1787 and openly among diverse black and white men and women in Johannesburg between 1990 and 1994. In the intervening two hundred years the concept of citizenship broadened beyond white propertied men. The American model is the source of many concepts and phrases in the South African Constitution, yet the divergent directions in which our two countries are moving give a particular twist to President Clinton's words of welcome to President Mandela at the White House on November 5, 1995: "You know and we know that progress and diversity CAN go hand in hand."

We try to link these two concepts of "progress" and "diversity"

Jackie,

Last night I had dinner with Johnnetta Cole, who is stepping down as president of Spelman College, and Beverly Guy Sheftall, a professor of English and head of the Women's Center at Spelman. It was one of these great events where the timing just worked. I had been planning to have dinner with Johnnetta—she was in town for a Rockefeller Foundation board meeting—and Bev, who was up from Atlanta giving lectures as part of a summer program for college teachers sponsored by New York University, called on the spur of the moment and we all connected at an Indian restaurant close to where Johnnetta was staying. For starters, we were a surprising bunch—three middle-aged but not badly preserved women drinking and laughing at the bar while we waited for a table. We were the only mixed-race group in the place. Indeed, Bev and Johnnetta were the only blacks, but the Indian restaurant felt like neutral space.

First, of course, we gossiped like schoolgirls. When the meal came, we began to talk about the future. Beverly admitted that it was hard to think of working at Spelman without Johnnetta—they had been such a team supporting one another. There might be rough times ahead for the Women's Center.

Johnnetta is going to be a professor at Emory and on leave next year, and the great news is that she and Beverly have decided to write a book together. It's still in the early stages of conceptualization but it's going to be a gentle rejoinder to Cornel West. West's book *Race Matters* was a best-seller, and while it did say a number of good things about sexism in the black community, it did not really have a feminist lens. Johnnetta and Bev are determined to write about such topics as the Clarence Thomas/Anita Hill controversy surrounding his nomination to the Supreme Court in 1991, the O. J. Simpson trial, and the Million Man March from the perspective of black women feminists.

It's a brave and absolutely critical project and I will do whatever I can to help it along. Johnnetta, the author of two widely used anthropology textbooks, turned Spelman into the college that all young bright black women want to attend. Beverly founded the first women's center on a historically black college campus and has written or edited some of the most important books recapturing black women's writing from the shadows of history. I've known both of them over a decade and consider them more than professional colleagues. I consider them friends. More than that—I admire them enormously.

more firmly for the future. In both South Africa and the United States class, race, and ethnicity are fault lines along which disadvantage runs. We try to understand the various ways in which racial, ethnic, and other differences between people have, both historically and in the contemporary world, been the grounds of social practices that have involved disadvantage and denial. As the black American scholar and former college president Johnnetta Cole has written, "Failure to acknowledge and respect diversity is the basis of racism, sexism and a host of other insidious 'isms.'"[8]

The central issue in both the United States and South Africa is how to address disadvantage and how to link diversity and unity. As James Joseph, the former American ambassador to South Africa, stated at his swearing-in ceremony on May 3, 1997: "The real challenge for both South Africa and the United States is to demonstrate that diversity need not divide, that the fear of difference is a fear of the future, that inclusiveness rightly understood and pluralism rightly practiced can be a benefit and not a burden."

The crucial point is that every citizen must first be equal under the law. Only then can difference be acknowledged. The new South African Constitution attempts to deal with both equality and difference. It protects diversity, through the prohibition of specific forms of discrimination, within a framework that promotes equality. Affirmative action is the constitutional means for linking diversity and equality: "To promote the achievement of equality, legislative and other measures designed to protect or advance persons or categories of persons disadvantaged by unfair discrimination may be taken." Paradoxically, at the same time South Africa is implementing affirmative action as a means of redress and collective empowerment, powerful forces in the United States are trying to dismantle it because it is considered discriminatory.

"Diversity" and "Equality" as Contested Concepts

Johnnetta Cole has written, "We're for difference, for respecting difference, for allowing difference, until difference does not make any difference."[9] This cannot happen simply by acknowledging and appreciating difference, even though this is a useful starting place. As Cole argues, "Accepting our diversity is not just humane, it is exhilarating. Championing and looking expectantly for diversity among us will not in and of itself make us free, but it is a step in the right direction."[10] The next step entails exploring the relationship between difference and disadvantage in various social and historical contexts.

In doing so it is necessary to steer a course between the Charybdis of naive pluralism and the Scylla of poststructuralist relativism. Naive pluralism ignores power relations involved in the social and historical processes whereby "difference" is the grounds of disadvantage and denial. From this perspective, as Christina Crosby has written of the modern university, "what is foreclosed is the possibility of thinking differently about differences, yet that is precisely what is to be done. Otherwise differences will remain as self-evident as identity once was, and just as women's studies once saw women everywhere, the academy will recognize differences everywhere, cheerfully acknowledging that since everyone is different, everyone is the same. Such is the beauty of pluralism."[11]

By contrast, poststructural analysis frequently elevates difference but often does so in abstract theoretical formulations that are inaccessible to those lacking epistemological training. Nevertheless, poststructuralism has much to teach us about how dualisms such as white/black and female/male sustain hierarchical worldviews and how the universalizing of bourgeois male Eurocentric voices excludes or silences those of the social categories we are most concerned with, such as women, blacks, and lesbians and gays. If we are to break free and truly "celebrate difference" we have to reject the assimilationist and homogenizing tendencies of the last two centuries.

Difference and equality, as we have been implying, are not polar opposites, although at first they might appear to be. As the historian Joan W. Scott has explained, "When equality and difference are paired dichotomously, they structure an impossible choice. If one opts for equality, one is forced to accept the notion that difference is antithetical to it. If one opts for difference, one admits that equality is unattainable."[12] Equality, however, means taking account of difference, not imposing neutrality; ignoring difference can only perpetuate inequality.

Because categories of difference are typically constructed by those in power, we cannot simply argue for diversity either. Without first challenging relations of dominance and subordination, if you argue for diversity you maintain the status quo. Only by focusing on the distribution of power in specific social and historical contexts can difference be fully recognized as a process. As Crosby reminds us, "difference is not a thing to be recognized but a process always underway." Understanding difference as "relational" "allows us to challenge the norm against which some people seem different and to see the ways in which institutions construct and utilize difference to justify and enforce exclusions."[13]

Equality, then, does not mean one group is the "same" as a dominant group. With that definition equality is a weak concept because all it implies is assimilation or incorporation into a preexisting and universalistic norm. Using this scheme, women are judged to be different in relation to an unstated male norm, as are blacks in relation to an unstated white norm and gays and lesbians in relation to a heterosexual norm.

For example, Cornel West points out that initial "Black efforts to combat racist cultural practices uncritically accepted non-Black conventions and standards in two ways. First they proceeded in an assimilationist manner that set out to show that Black people were really like White people—thereby eliding differences (in history, culture) between Whites and Blacks. Black specificity and particularity all are thus banished in order to gain White acceptance and approval"[14] West goes on to argue that these black responses rested upon a homogenizing impulse that assumed all black people were really alike—hence obliterating the differences (class, gender, region, sexual orientation) between them. Similarly, much of gay rights politics is flawed by these assimilationist and homogenizing impulses. Gender terms as well are usually defined with reference to a masculine standard. As Rosi Bradotti exhorts, "Difference must be freed from its negative meanings." It is time to assert "the positive value of being 'other than' the masculine, white, middle-class norm."[15]

Considering differences in an ahistorical sociopolitical vacuum lacks explanatory power and renders "diversity" an empty concept. So instead of blandly celebrating diversity as an end in itself, we need to emphasize the relational and contextual nature of differences that are socially and historically constructed. Without this focus comes falsity, "a make-believe world void of social memory where we all start on a clean slate."[16] The close connections between difference and disadvantage and the weakness of the concept of "equality" has led the American political scientist Jane Flax to prefer the notion of justice over equality. "In the contemporary West," she observes, "the recognition of differences seems inseparable from asymmetric dualisms and relations of domination. Within contemporary western culture, differences appear to generate and are certainly used to justify hierarchies and relations of domination."[17] This understanding has important social implications. It means that social justice does not require the erosion of differences, but rather the formation of institutions that nurture respect for group differences without oppression. Under the framework of justice, a new conception of diversity would incorporate inclusion, negotiation, compromise, and participation.

Wollstonecraft's Dilemma

The relationship between equality and difference has been the subject of a long-standing debate within feminism that dates back to the publication of Mary Wollstonecraft's *A Vindication of the Rights of Woman* in 1792. Wollstonecraft, the first feminist political theorist in England, argued simultaneously for equality and the recognition of difference, in what Carol Pateman has termed "Wollstonecraft's dilemma."[18] Wollstonecraft called for equal civil and political rights for women, but their service to the state and identity as citizens was to be expressed through their motherhood rather than through the military service then demanded from male citizens. She wrote, "I am not going to advise women to turn their distaff into a musket, though I sincerely wish to see the bayonet converted into a pruning hook."[19]

Historically, the struggle for women's rights has faltered over the fundamental question of whether women should be treated like men or differently. Unfortunately, the ideas of both "difference" and "equality" have been used to subordinate or erase women. All too often equality means having male-defined values and male-constructed institutions that are claimed to be universally valid. Any divergence is then regarded as a mark of deficiency or inferiority. In such a society women are either excluded (from knowledge, rights, or politics) or admitted but homologized. Liberation, however, does not mean making all women the same or making them like men.

The American legal theorist Deborah Rhode points out that "traditional approaches to gender difference have alternated between exaggeration and denial."[20] Both have worked against women. Gender differences, actual or perceived, such as the assumption of women's intellectual inferiority, were used historically to exclude women from the right to vote, to enter contracts, to hold property, and to run for political office. Yet the denial of dissimilarity has had similarly negative consequences because it has maintained the subordination of women and their vulnerability to sexual violence and economic dependence.

In response, some feminists have claimed, we think erroneously, that women's ability to bear children instills in them a distinct approach to resolving political conflict. For example, Olive Schreiner, the early South African feminist, asserted that "war violates a profound biological urge in women." In *Women and Labour* she argued that mothers have a special responsibility as well as a distinctive power to oppose war. She characterized a callousness toward life and death as "instinctual" in men of certain cultures: "'It is a fine day, let us go out and kill something,' cries the typical male of certain races, instinctively. 'There is a living thing, it will die if it is not cared for,' says the average woman, almost equally instinctively."[21]

Whether feminists ground the differences between men and women in "instinct" and biology, as Schreiner did, or in the construction of social identities, as contemporary feminist scholars prefer, they all vary in their approach to the link between difference and equality. Feminism has at times emphasized the right to be equal and at other times the right to be different. In fact, both rights are necessary and not mutually exclusive. Some feminists regard female difference as a starting point and equality as a goal to be achieved through special means, such as affirmative action. Others argue that women and men are entitled to equal access to academic positions even as they simultaneously practice a distinctive kind of feminist scholarship. In this instance, they treat equality as a means to an end, namely, asserting their difference as women. The most debilitating tendency for a feminist project

Jackie,

It's Martin Luther King Day in the United States, so the kids and I have an official holiday. I have dragged these two six-year-olds to an event more for me than for them, namely, a memorial service at the Cathedral of St. John the Divine. This seldom happens—church going and funerals are not my thing. Once I describe it to you, however, I think you will understand why I insisted that the kids and I spend this day, which officially honors one of the most beloved and respected men of the twentieth century, doing just this. We went because it is also honoring one of the least well known but to my mind equally important figures of our time—Audre Lorde.

Lorde, the black American poet and feminist activist, died last November at the age of fifty-eight. She had finally succumbed to cancer but she hadn't lost the battle in the traditional sense. She had fought her illness successfully for over a decade, defying all the odds and mystifying all the doctors. Ironically, she got to be more widely known after having cancer because she published several volumes chronicling her illness. I think that her writing on cancer

led in part to her being named poet laureate of New York State in 1991. Cancer was a theme everyone could relate to. By contrast, Lorde's passionate poetry about loving women was something else. What really hooked me on Lorde was her fierce inclusiveness. She would often introduce herself as a black feminist lesbian poet mother warrior long before some of these words were acceptable to use in daily conversation. She used words wonderfully as incisive weapons against prejudice, discrimination, and the fear of difference. Her poetry is not always pretty but it never ceases to unleash a power. One of my favorite lines that has now become a kind of epitaph is "poetry is not a luxury." Lorde was someone who saw the arts as supremely political and her lesbian black feminist politics were the stuff of her poetry. If critics complain that Adrienne Rich's poems are too political they haven't read Lorde! Yet it's precisely this directness—a talent for squeezing the passion of political engagement into intense poetic images—that sums up Lorde's gift.

I never met her, though I went to several conferences at which she spoke. She was a bit scary but had an impish smile that made you feel a lot of the swagger was, in part, an act. She took on an African name—Gamba Adisa (usually a turn-off for me because it sounds so phony and manufactured in its identity—imagine calling me by some Russian Jewish name)—and eventually left New York, where she was born and raised, to live out her life in St. Croix. She was the daughter of West Indian parents, so I guess this makes sense.

The memorial service was an odd mixture of an Upper West Side feminist rally and an African ritual. More than a thousand people jammed the pews. It began with a processional involving about forty black women who were dressed all in white and playing large African drums slung over their shoulders as they marched down the main aisle of the cathedral. It was a sight to see, and Emma and Julia seemed genuinely appreciative. They had never expected this from a church. Then there were a series of speakers—Kate Rushin, a brilliant young black women poet from Brown, Blanche Cook, who had known Lorde since college, and, most poignantly, Lorde's two children, Elizabeth and Jonathan. Lorde had been married to a white guy, so these two had been raised first as straight kids and then when Lorde left the marriage for a white woman, the children became among the first kids in this country to be raised by an openly lesbian couple.

Elizabeth and Jonathan's testimonials were not mushy. Quite the contrary. They were full of the pain and some of the pride of growing up different and having to learn to be strong in the face of conventional rejection. I am not sure whether my kids got much out of this part. They seemed antsy, but maybe they were just tired. Anyway, by this time, I knew I had been pushing my luck—they had sat quietly for over an hour and a half . . . so we left.

I am very glad I went. The memorial had a deeply interracial womanly character to it and I felt that this was my community. I fear that I've been so busy describing Lorde and this service that it only just occurred to me that you have probably never heard of her or read her poems. That will be rectified when I mail you a copy of *The Black Unicorn*. Read especially her poem "Woman." Until you get the book, consider this blessing, which Audre, who knew she was dying, wrote to be read at the service:

THE BLESSING

I leave you the will to fight, the desire to live; the right to anger, to love, to the erotic, to joy, to transform silence into language and action. I leave you a litany for survival.

is to see a forced choice in which equality (in the sense of identical treatment) and difference (in the sense of special consideration) stand for mutually exclusive approaches. In fact, both are necessary.

More recent feminist thinking has emphasized differences among women. It is arguable that "the preoccupation with women's differences from men obscured women's differences from each other, and deflected attention from the class, racial and ethnic bias of the early feminist agenda."[22] Poststructuralism has emphasized the multiplicity and fluidity of women's identities and the absence of any universal "women's experience." These accounts have drawn attention to the many forces that constitute women's identity—race, ethnicity, class, age, religion, and sexual orientation. Feminist practice must acknowledge these forces. As the poet and essayist Audre Lorde has noted, "It is not our differences which separate [us as] women but our reluctance to recognize those differences and deal effectively with the distances that have resulted."[23] Rhode argues instead that "no single categorical framework can adequately address the dynamics of difference. . . . The sameness dilemma cannot be resolved; it can only be reformulated. Our focus needs to shift from difference to disadvantage and to the social conditions that perpetuate it."[24]

Focusing on disadvantage implies challenging the prevailing concept of equal rights feminism. Equal rights feminism simply means advancing the position of women in society by gaining political, legal, economic, and social rights equal to those granted to men. Equal rights feminism is thus premised on sameness and no acknowledgment is made of cultural, social, economic, racial, or sexual variances among women; difference is not contextualized or related to disadvantage. In the United States, feminism's focus has primarily been on getting the vote and legal control over property and person. In other words, mainstream feminism has been about seeking unqualified access to male-dominated institutions of citizenship. This ideology does not provide critiques of those institutions or supply an alternative vision of transformation. In South Africa, this type of feminism has been viewed as contaminated and elitist because of the demands made in its name by white middle-class women concerned with extending their own privileges rather than with the equality of all women. But feminism still contains a transformative potential even in South Africa.

Despite arguments to the contrary, it *is* possible to be both different and equal. First, each group of people must be free. Second, the people and the government must commit to justice. In other words, to reconcile difference and equality requires social change: a new kind of society, new models of citizenship, and new forms of political struggle. Feminist initiatives, particularly in the form of transversal politics that step back from a universalism that denies difference and go beyond the fragmentation of identity politics, are our best hope of achieving justice.

Conclusion:
The Need for
Transformation

The second day of the conference on environmental racism held at the University of Colorado in September 1998 included a visit to Rocky Mountain National Park. In a meadow set among pine-covered hills, we broke up into small discussion groups. Listening to a young African American ranger from the National Park Service speak passionately about his admiration for John Muir, his enjoyment of the high whistling sound of elks "bugling," and the feel of the needles of the ponderosa pine made us both aware of how environmentalism has a unifying potential. The conference had demonstrated that many of the two hundred participants shared concerns with issues of social as well as environmental justice. The differences of race, class, gender, nation, and ethnicity among us in our small group faded in our shared appreciation of the views of distant snow-topped mountains, our growing discomfort as the soft autumn rain soaked our clothing, and our anxiety about the contents of our lunch boxes. Despite our pleasant afternoon, on the next day each of us returned to worlds of contrasting power, privilege, and opportunity.

This book is concerned with disparities. It differentiates between blacks and whites, men and women, humans and other animals, homosexuals and heterosexuals. It does *not* present an argument for the obliteration of diversity in the name of sameness or commonality. Each essay is the outcome of a conversation about an issue activists have focused on during the last decade. Although recognition of difference in the twentieth century seldom led to productive outcomes or social justice—and, quite the contrary, often provided the grounds for violent conflict and even mass extermination—activists still chant the mantra of diversity. In such political debates, however, particularly on the Left, one form of oppression keeps ousting another as the biggest evil, leading to a sense of displacement: "the cultural displacing the material; identity politics displacing class."[1] We instead try to link both cultural and economic forms of disadvantage in our discussion to encompass access to power, resources, and opportunity.

Despite debates over its value, diversity is an empirical fact, not a moral position. All forms of life come into being as diverse and wholly separate genetic entities. How we treat the diversity of our species, our behaviors, our cultures, our values, our sexual preferences, and our skin colors is the challenge of the millennium before us. What makes the notion of diversity so contested is that contradictory forces brought about by the increasing globalization of economic markets, changing population flows, proliferating mass communications, and environmental pressures threaten it. These changes are occurring at the same time that individuals are increasingly insecure and asserting their ethnic, religious, and cultural identities in a spirit of negative exclusivity.

This book is not a catalogue of the differences between blacks and whites, men and women, humans and other animals, homosexuals and heterosexuals. Nor does it try to present an argument for obliterating these differences in the name of sameness or commonality. Each essay is instead the outcome of a "North/South" conversation about a particular difference that points to how each issue is variously understood in the developed world of the North, as represented by the United States, and in the developing world of the South, as represented by South Africa.

The growing economic inequalities in both societies suggest that class is an important form of difference between people, but ethnic nationalism probably carries the most potential for violence today.

In this book, however, we have focused mainly on the differences that are assumed to be essentialist, that is, grounded in basic biology, and showed how these differences are instead socially constructed in different historical and social contexts.

Although we discuss them separately, these dimensions of difference—race, biology, culture, sexual orientation, and gender—are interconnected. Addressing them singly as we have done does risk objectifying and fragmenting social experience. Even so, conversations about these issues are generally fragmented—those concerned with biodiversity seldom talk to those who organize around gay rights, for example. One of our objectives in writing this book is to overcome such social and political fragmentation. We all must recognize that one's gender identity is not distinct from one's race or class and that all identities are fluid, multiple, and interrelated, even if class differences trigger the greatest economic inequalities or ethnic variances spur the most violence.

If difference is viewed as comparative and relational, it seems like a mistake to try to gain justice by constructing a hierarchy of difference. Michael Ignatieff points out that "it seems an error to suppose that some human differences, say race or gender, are intrinsically more important than others, like class or national identity. Gender and racial difference are certainly minor relative to the overwhelming genetic commonality that unites men and women and persons of different races but they become major when used as markers of power and status. Power is the vector that turns minor into major."[2] Because these power relations operate in hidden ways, Ignatieff urges us to "see beneath the skin."[3] Doing so is our project. This means emphasizing contrasts as well as similarities, because both can provide the basis for different groups to understand each other and form alliances. Because these related emphases require an experiential as well as an intellectual content, we have structured our book to include both personal observations and empirical information.

An appreciation of difference and diversity means creating a more just as well as a richer, more interesting, more varied, and more colorful world. Sexism, racism, and homophobia affect not only their victims but also their proponents. Those unable to accept the full humanity of other people are also damaged and deprived. But although we value diversity for its own sake, as other feminists do, we use it as a starting point on the path toward transformation.

Our concern is with difference in terms of fairness rather than sameness in treatment. Some oppressed groups, such as blacks and lesbians and gays, do not want to abandon their distinctiveness. Similarly, many feminists are not prepared to settle for access to the established male order. As feminists our goal is not equality and access to the existing system but transformation—not the abandonment of difference but rather a rethinking of the whole project.

This project requires first understanding the grounds on which gender, class, racial, and sexual diversities become categories of exclusion. In Western culture conceptions of "nature" and "the natural" are used to legitimize inequalities. Organized religion has often discriminated against gays and lesbians for their "unnatural" sexual practices. Similarly, the Judeo-Christian tradition that sets humans over nature has a special responsibility for Western civilization's exploitative attitude toward other species. Furthermore, biblical authority was cited to legitimize racial domination in apartheid South Africa, and in many countries race and ethnicity are understood as biologically constituted.

The choice, then, seems a stark one: either be enriched by variety or be embroiled in conflicts over differences; either adopt the politics of inclusion and engagement or promote those of exclusion and disregard. Joan W. Scott has pointed out that political developments such as decolonization and intellectual trends such as poststructuralism have changed the way we think about our world. From the South has come a decolonization movement that has challenged homogenizing forces and has led to "the emergence of national identities that positively value histories and cultural practices once obscured or demeaned by colonizers who equated European standards with civilization."[4] From the North has come poststructuralist critiques of universalism. A new school of intellectuals from these areas no longer claims Western values as universal standards.

This choice between inclusion and exclusion becomes especially poignant when we look back on a century marked by unparalleled violence and armed conflict. Nearly halfway through the twentieth century on the day the atomic bomb was dropped on Hiroshima and Nagasaki, Eleanor Roosevelt remarked that on this day "we came into a new world—a world in which we had to learn to live in friendship with our neighbors of every race and creed and color, or face the fact that we might be wiped off the face of the earth. Either we do have friendly relations, or we do away with civilization."[5] Earlier in the century another woman of compassion but with very different views, Rosa Luxemburg, conceptualized the choice of the future as "socialism or barbarism." While the possibility of socialism across the globe seems remote today, "the problems it purported to solve remain: the brazen use of social advantage and the inordinate power of money, which often directs the very course of events."[6]

These problems—particularly those of social and economic inequality—are increasing. If absolute poverty is defined as a situation in which people cannot regularly meet their most basic subsistence needs, over 20 percent of the world's population lives in such conditions.[7] This is happening despite United Nations social indicators that people worldwide are living longer than ever before and are receiving more education and health services. We are writing at a time of deepening global inequities: poverty, social disintegration, environmental degradation, and unemployment remain pervasive. But at the same time we also see new kinds of connections and alliances being constructed across nations, classes, regions, races, genders, ages, and sexual orientations.

This is the paradoxical impact of a globalization process that is both integrating and polarizing. An economically driven process, globalization encompasses the spread of industries and financial markets across state and national borders, the means of instantaneous communication across vast distances, mass transportation, promotion of market forces, competition, diffusion of standardized consumer goods, and cultural flows such as Sky News and CNN. In this sense it provides an impetus for cultural homogenization and threatens indigenous cultural and social forms. Its danger lies in a flat uniformity that fails to challenge or stimulate.

People, however, are not passive receptacles. Many creative responses to globalization involve local blends and appropriations rather than simple assertions of traditions or acceptance of consumerism.

After our Berkshire Conference panel on women and the military ended Saturday afternoon, I decided to drive Jackie up to Hyde Park, the hometown of President Franklin Roosevelt. I'd read that friends of Eleanor Roosevelt had recently restored her cottage, Val-Kill, which is two miles from Roosevelt's big Hyde Park house.

I'd always thought that the white columned mansion overlooking the Hudson in which Eleanor lived with Franklin, their children, and her dreaded mother-in-law was Eleanor's home. This was a mistake. Even though Eleanor's voice can be heard on the audiotape describing life at Hyde Park, this was not her real "home." That description belongs to Val-Kill, but the cottage had been ignored, largely by male historians. None had bothered to understand what Val-Kill meant to Eleanor Roosevelt until Blanche Wiesen Cook revealed it in her wonderful new biography. As Cook wrote, "Val-Kill had touches of romance that fully justified FDR's sobriquet: 'The Honeymoon Cottage.' ER was free for the first time to invite her own guests to a home where she felt in control." Eleanor embroidered towels, dressing table cloths, and

linens "E" (for Eleanor), "M" (for Marion Dickerman), and "N" (for Nancy Cook). These women were her dearest friends and they often came to Val-Kill when they weren't in their house in Greenwich Village.

At Val-Kill, the middle-aged Eleanor had a kind of freedom and autonomy she had never known before . . . all this from a plain brick and wood house. As we wandered through the small, dark, conventionally furnished rooms (we saw the somewhat kitsch embroidered towels)—with a sullen and not terribly knowledgeable guide from the National Park Service, I kept thinking that Eleanor, though privileged in virtually all respects— money, social class, the wife of one president, and the niece of another—had previously been denied a crucial quality. Val-Kill gave her precious space to be herself.

By contrast to the cottage, the grounds of the private space she created here are lovely. We walked along the stream, had a picnic lunch of beer, cheese, and summer sausage on the grass, and—to Jackie's great delight—briefly glimpsed three otters swimming through the reeds. Then rushed back to Vassar for the dance to mark the end of the Berkshire Conference.

Globalization does not have to equal homogenization. Instead, it can imply a relativization in what the British sociologist Anthony Giddens has identified as a "post-traditional social order." In this world established traditions—particularly those relating to religion, gender, the nation, and the family—are typically loosened and questioned.[8] In such a context, globalization becomes a complex interweaving of homogenizing and differentiating trends.

At the same time, globalization has the potential to subvert an appreciation of difference. The global restructuring driven by what Manuel Castells has termed "informational capitalism" provides an impetus to conflict, violence, and war by widening the gulfs between the rich and the poor.[9] Global changes are creating increasing levels of poverty and marginalization. As James Mittelman contends, "The foremost contradiction of our time is the conflict between the zones of humanity integrated in the global division of labor and the ones which are excluded from it."[10]

This gap between the excluded and the excluders exists both between and within nations and is often linked to the other paradoxical effect of globalization—the explosion of fundamentalist movements and particularistic identities, often of an ethnic or religious kind, that are antagonistically defined. As Judith Butler, Joan W. Scott, Stuart Hall, and Max Jacquees have emphasized, "difference" defines the boundaries of identities and thus all identities operate through exclusion.[11] The social dislocations of our time seem to be thrusting increasing numbers of people into exclusive and antagonistic identities in which, as Castells expresses it, we "see the other as a stranger, eventually as a threat."[12] Such divisiveness is at the core of identity politics. As the scholar Eric Hobsbawm observes, we "are living through a gigantic 'cultural revolution,' an extraordinary dissolution of traditional social norms, textures and values. In this context men and women look for groups to which they can belong, certainly and forever, in a world in which all else is moving and shifting, in which nothing else is certain. And they find it in an identity group."[13] In this sense identity politics can threaten an appreciation of difference because of its emphasis on exclusivity. However, as Audre Lorde reminds us, identity politics can also mean a recognition that difference is the starting point toward true reconciliation, unity, and solidarity.[14]

Although globalization is reaching into virtually all corners of the world, its effects on the United States and South Africa vary dramatically. While the United States is driving globalization, South Africa is facing a reduction in state autonomy. State actors are constrained by impersonal and nonaccountable forces beyond their control. This consequence is the "South African paradox": that the post-apartheid state is beginning to formulate progressive social policies at a time when its power is being eroded by globalization. Because poverty, violence, AIDS, and homelessness remain massive problems in South Africa, it is hard to see how neo-liberal economic policies, with their reliance on the power of the market, could deliver the social and economic goods to solve them. South Africa instead needs a strong state, not the hollowed-out one neo-liberal economists exhort. Despite its difficulties, this nevertheless is South Africa's most hopeful moment. By contrast, Blanche W. Cook has described the American present as "arguably the meanest moment in United States history since slavery, marked by rancor, and a politics of spite and cruelty."[15] In both societies, however, communal traditions of service and sacrifice central to the struggle for democracy and human rights remain strong.

It is within these traditions, and within a renewed feminism, that we continue our search for models. For, as Cornel West puts it, "persons from all countries, cultures, genders, sexual orientations, ages and regions with protean identities who avoid ethnic chauvinism and faceless universalism; intellectual and political freedom-fighters with partisan passion, international perspectives, and, thank God, a sense of humor."[16] As part of our feminist project, we also need to discover models of strong adventurous women. In our conversations and travels we have searched for women who lived differently, who defied the scripts of their time, and who moved outside of both social and geographical boundaries. Some of the most compelling of these were travelers such as Alexandra David-Neel and Marianne North.

In this book we have challenged the dualisms, boundaries, and hierarchies of conventional modernist thinking. We have shown that these boundaries are profoundly political in the sense that they maintain relations of power and domination. They are political at

A magical day—after meeting Alison at Heathrow we took a boat to Kew Gardens. I needed a whiskey mac and a ploughman's lunch to unfreeze from the river trip. But Kew was magical—especially a purple beech tree, the giant water lilies in the palm house, and the Marianne North gallery. We especially liked her painting of the Taj Mahal and some of the Kowie River, which capture the orange of the aloes, the coral tree flowers, and the ocher blankets of the Xhosa.

I felt a new appreciation for Marianne North as another one of the adventurous women who lived differently and wrote their own scripts. In her case the adventure started late—at the age of thirty-nine—and involved setting off alone in 1871 to visit every continent and make a pictorial record of the tropical and exotic plants of the world. Her eight hundred paintings are a glorious celebration of color and biological diversity—she portrayed some one thousand different species.

I identify with her liking of both solitude and sociability and both travel and stillness. The biographical note in *A Vision of Eden: The Life and Work of Marianne North* talks about how "though she often yearned for solitude, no-one was more ready to enjoy the company of unpretentious people of all races and classes."

Her autobiography, marvelously entitled *Recollections of a Happy Life,* clearly shows an appreciation of food (e.g., of chowder tasted when staying in Massachusetts, "a most glorious compound of codfish, soup and crackers") as well as of female friendships. In a long conversation she agreed with a Mrs. Agassiz "that the greatest pleasure we knew was to see new and wonderful countries and the only rival to that pleasure was the one of staying quietly at home. Only ignorant fools think because one likes sugar one cannot like salt; these people are only capable of one idea, and never try experiments."

Much of her life was an experiment and an adventure and depended on her contradictory relationship to the power of men—her travels would not have been possible without an income from her father, and as Anthony Huxley once remarked, if she had married, "her works might still be largely unknown or even undone."

Alison,

Alexandra David-Neel is another feminist pioneer who sought out what was different from her childhood world and deserves to be remembered for her courage and curiosity. She set out in 1923 at the age of fifty-five to travel to Lhasa and was the first European woman to enter the Forbidden City. She had to disguise herself as a pilgrim by dyeing her hair black with Chinese ink, lengthening it with yak's hair, and smearing her face with a mixture of cocoa and crushed charcoal. The journey took two years on foot, she ate mostly *tsampa* (barley flour) and buttered tea and had to endure up to six days without any food at all and nights without shelter. She used to restore her energy with a granule of strychnine. She learned to will heat into her body by practicing *thumo reskiang,* and it is possible that she witnessed the art of flying, *lunggom,* which the Tibetans maintain humans are capable of. On one occasion she focused her binoculars on a man moving at high speed in a series of spectacular leaps. "The man did not run," she wrote. "He seemed to lift himself from the ground, proceeding by leaps."

Much more than Marianne North, I think David-Neel is a model of a courageous, observant, nonjudgmental, and responsive traveler. She always had the urge to travel and explore: "Ever since I was five years old, a tiny precocious child of Paris, I wished to move out of the narrow limits in which, like all children of my age, I was then kept. I craved to go beyond the garden gate, to follow the road that passed it by, and to set out for the Unknown." She doesn't talk explicitly about how these "narrow limits" were class and gender based, but part of what inspired her was a feminist drive. She writes, "I took an oath that in spite of all obstacles I would reach Lhasa and show what the will of a woman could achieve." I think much of what she writes is inspirational, e.g., in a lonely place surrounded with the dangers of attacks from wild animals or hostile locals, she describes barricading her hut and going to sleep: "That was all that we could do; and in whatever case, when one has done one's best, worries of any kind are superfluous and unwise." But she also writes, "I profoundly despise everything that is connected with politics, and carefully avoid mixing in such matters." Disappointing.

I'm fascinated by how many women used travel to escape the constraints of their gender. They often did so in their middle age, venturing into unknown places, and were wonderfully observant and appreciative. I think my favorite is Isabella Bird, whom Simon Winchester describes as "the redoubtable, imperturbable, amazing, thick-tweed-skirted and courageous matron venturer." Visiting Indonesia, she once had a formal dinner with three orangutans who were seated at the table.

Part of the appeal is that many of these women travelers were concerned with the small and distinctive rather than the large tapestries of conquest and combat. That's not true, however, of one of my favorite writers—Martha Gelhorn. For her "travelling is the best answer," the antidote to boredom and depression. In 1986 she wrote, "Now I am alive again. . . . I have only to go to a different country, sky, language, scenery, to feel it [life] is worth living." A marvelous woman—for example she went swimming naked at midnight when she was age eighty. But it also seems that she was somewhat homophobic.

such a deep level that many people accept them as "normal" and biologically created. In the last twenty years their socially constructed nature has been revealed. Our next political challenge is to harness this new way of thinking and promote alliances based on similarity rather than sameness. We have to identify the similarities that can provide the bases for different groups to understand each other and act together. The next step is to imagine an ecological community that recognizes our multiple, blurred, and changing identities, a community that does not depend on visible ties or shared values, customs, or languages. This sense of community means, as Giddens has emphasized, that we must repair solidarities that have been damaged by the self-seeking individualism of the marketplace. Enhancing solidarity depends on "active trust, coupled with a renewal of personal and social responsibility for others."[17]

Feminism may be the one remaining ideology still asserting this sense of community. We need to recreate, strengthen, and widen networks of support and sharing among women. The writer bell hooks stressed the transformative potential of feminism when she described it as the political movement that most radically addresses the person—the personal—by citing the need for transformation of self and of relationships. This would enable us, hooks believes, to act in a revolutionary manner, to challenge and resist domination, to transform the world outside the self.[18] Given the increasing fragmentation of the labor movement and the collapse of state socialism, few ideologies connect people to a shared project. In this book we describe how an inclusive feminism focused on gender relations more broadly could reassert the traditions of solidarity and friendship among different women.

Feminism is one contemporary set of initiatives with the capacity to confront difference and disadvantage simultaneously. Thus, the key challenge for feminism at the beginning of the new millennium is to address power relations between and among women that involve dominance and exploitation. Until now feminism has been preoccupied with differences between men and women and with demonstrating a commonality summed up in the title of Robin Morgan's 1970 pioneering collection, *Sisterhood Is Powerful.* The feminist goal at that time was to get women to recognize their common oppression. More than thirty years later, we are somewhat closer to achieving that goal, not in the sense of a redistribution of power and resources to achieve equality between men and women, but in the sense that even in the most impoverished and oppressive societies, such as South Africa, movements for gender equality have erupted.These movements do not necessarily call themselves "feminist" but are nevertheless deeply committed to gender equality.

It seems to us that at the beginning of the twenty-first century, the feminist challenge is not only to address the differences between men and women but also to confront the differences between women of different nations, races, cultures, classes, ages, and sexual orientations. Once this reassessment of difference and diversity occurs, women all over the world will be in a better position to unite to challenge male power and privilege. Deep-seated social transformation is necessary for such a project. Because women are not a homogeneous category, feminism has to confront their difference in a new, appreciative, and affirming way. Because in virtually all societies women make up the poorest social category, feminism also has to confront disadvantage more powerfully than it has in the past. This is an urgent task because the impact of globalization on women has been particularly harsh. There has been a feminization of the lowest-paid labor, and women have been hit disproportionately with reductions in state expenditures on health care, education, and welfare that have been part of the dismantling of the welfare state in Europe and the Structural Adjustment Programs in Africa.

We can take from the divergent experiences of the WNC and NOW at least one lesson about tackling this challenge. In addition to focusing on the relationship between difference and disadvantage, "we must pay close attention to the similarities that can provide the basis for differing groups to understand each other and form alliances."[19] Recognizing these similarities often involves acknowledging their interdependence. As Lorde stressed, tolerance of difference is not enough: "Advocating mere tolerance of difference is the grossest reform. . . . Difference must be not merely tolerated, but seen as a fund of necessary polarities between which our creativity can spark like a dialectic. . . . Difference is that raw and powerful connection from which our personal power is forged."[20]

This transformative potential lies in several values of modern feminism: it is multidimensional; it links the need for change at both the personal and the societal level; and it links the need for change at both the material and the ideological level. The notion of "gender equality" implies changes in material conditions of life for the most disadvantaged social category—women—as well as challenging current notions of violence and power. These changes in material conditions imply a redistribution of power and resources. Feminism challenges the contemporary ideologies of gender, particularly the linkages between ideologies of masculinity, violence, and power. It has a comprehensive holistic agenda linking justice and peace to social development, disarmament, and environmental protection. Given that much of the violence and armed conflict in the contemporary world is caused by material disadvantage and "differences" of various kinds, all these linkages are crucial. Feminism has to confront "difference" in a new, appreciative, and affirmative way.

A central paradox to feminism's mission is that in the contemporary world both power and poverty have been feminized. In many different societies, the increased representation of women in politics is one of the most remarkable developments of our time. In most of the world, women have gained the right to vote in only the last fifty years. The political scientist Jane Jaquette points as well to significant worldwide increases in female representation beginning in 1975. Of the thirty-two women who have served as presidents or prime ministers during the twentieth century, twenty-four were in power during the nineties. Jaquette points to three reasons for this increase in the last ten years: the rise of the women's movement worldwide; a new willingness by political actors to support women's access to politics and adopt mechanisms such as quotas, which require a certain percentage of women to be nominated or elected; and the emergence of social issues that supplant security concerns in the post–cold war political environment.[21]

This pattern of increasing women's political power and participation, however, parallels an increase in the number of women living in poverty. Indeed, in global terms the gap between men and women in income is increasing. According to the feminist Chilean scholar Myra Buvinic, in 1965–70, women made up 57 percent of the rural poor in developing countries, and by 1988 they accounted for 60 percent. According to UNIFEM, women currently constitute 70 percent of the world's 1.3 billion people living in absolute poverty. Thus the advances in power made by some women are overshadowed by the increasing poverty of others.[22]

Given these realities, the feminist project is clearly in trouble. Twenty years ago commentators had already begun speaking of "postfeminism," as though gender equality had been achieved and change was no longer needed. Even feminist activists are speaking of the end of the movement. For example, Sheila Tobias has remarked, "The feminist movement is losing its center and its power to convert because for some years now feminism has been engaged in a self-destroying, casting-off process, distancing itself first from one set of constituents and then another. The risk is 'remarginalization,' and the tragedy is that this is occurring just when mainstreaming is in view."[23] Tobias maintains that this sliding away is occurring under the impact of "identity politics." This leads to "inhibition" in the name of "political correctness" and "exclusionary politics," excluding first men, then married women, then white women, and so on "until the great diversity that had characterized the movement in its early stages seemed a problem rather than a source of strength."[24]

We see the issue differently. First, the later stages of feminism were less diverse than Tobias suggests. In a universalizing discourse, white middle-class women asserted claims for all women. Second, "mainstreaming" implies accommodation within the existing order, rather than its transformation. Third, feminism confronts at once a hopeful and a troubling moment in history. Feminism does seem threatened on a number of different fronts. In the North there is the issue of "backlash" and the "burnout" of some of our peers who see feminism as tired, dated, and passé. In many rich, industrialized countries feminism has overemphasized women's ambition and achievement until the search for purely personal fulfillment has replaced the effort to contribute to the common good. Too many younger women dismiss feminism as irrelevant or dated as they pursue their careers and goals in public spaces to which they have access only because of the struggles of their feminist forebears. Even as women gain greater access to power, male dominance is asserting itself in new ways. For example, Peggy Watson has pointed to a "rise in masculinism" as "the primary characteristic of gender relations in Eastern Europe today."[25] In the political zone of cyberspace, dominant forms of masculinity are being reinscribed. In post-apartheid South Africa, violence against women is increasing.

But it is also a hopeful moment in that the widespread notion that feminism was irrelevant, "Western," and divisive is changing. Carolyn Baylies and Janet Bujra point out that throughout the African continent, "women are demanding to be heard, organizing, questioning men's rights over them, throwing into doubt customary practices through which they are controlled."[26] In post-communist Russia, energy is resurging around "women's issues," despite what Nanette Funk and Magda Mueller have termed "a fully elaborated and sometimes hegemonic antifeminist ideology."[27] As recently as the mideighties Soviet women were unable to form independent organizations, but now "women may develop a common consciousness and come to articulate and advance a uniquely Russian feminism."[28] The emerging "global civil society" can strengthen such burgeoning feminism.

In this book we have used feminism as a lens, a type of framework to understand the world. As feminists we have struggled to understand difference and to find models of how to live. But to adapt the title chosen by Joan W. Scott—*Only Paradoxes to Offer*—we end this record of our search with a paradox of our own. Our central concern is with the relationship between difference and disadvantage. The globalization process is threatening the survival of difference, deepening disadvantage, and exacerbating inequalities in the world. The paradox is that it is this same process of globalization, with its technological advances in the form of cyberspace, e-mail, computer networks, and cheap, fast international air travel, that has made it possible for us to maintain our relationship. It has made our conversations across the boundaries of time and space possible.

This relationship has sustained us in our personal experiences of being different. Indeed, part of the impetus for this project comes from the sense we both have of being different from the majority of our colleagues in the mainstream institutions in which we work. Both institutions—a university and a philanthropic organization—

are committed to a liberal, pluralist ideology. Both provide the kind of space from which one can advance a new, transformative feminist agenda. However, within the university the bridge between women's studies courses and the women's movement seems to have been fractured; feminist theorizing threatens to become increasingly abstract and divorced from the philanthropic efforts, policy debates, and political struggles outside the academy. Within both, the challenge is to give a fresh and contemporary meaning to feminism, to create new knowledge about women, and to locate that knowledge in a way that advances the feminist project.

In our modest efforts to do this we have searched for route maps and role models of feminist and nonfeminist women. We found women who wrote their own scripts, like Johnnetta Cole, Marianne North, Ruth First, Frene Ginwala, Thenjiwe Mtintso, Audre Lorde, Rachel Carson, and Alexandra David-Neel. We wrote this book to share some of the insights they have passed along to us. In the process we are "breaking silence," as Lorde called on all feminists to do.

A beautiful green-blue day and we decided to paddle our canoe, *Sanibel,* across the harbor for a clam lunch at the yacht club. Even going against the wind and an outgoing tide, we synchronized our paddling and achieved a good speed with a foamy wake. To avoid capsizing we concentrated on avoiding the wake of the large yachts moving to their berths. We paused often to watch the terns diving just in front of us, a giant egret with its feathery plumes, and the cormorants taking off from their perches on the various buoys we passed. We made plans to come back to the creek that evening, as with a high tide and a full moon, the horseshoe crabs should be coming into the shallow water to lay their eggs. But more often we stopped the rhythm of our paddling to exchange comments on the yachts moored in the harbor— each one costing hundreds of thousands of dollars—while people in sub-Saharan Africa live in the deepening poverty that an average income of one dollar a day allows. We argued fiercely about the meaning of class, about the impact of globalization on living standards in our countries, about President Mbeki's response to the AIDS crisis in South Africa, about whether politicians are grappling (we agreed they are not) with the crucial issues of homelessness, gun violence, racism, and the corporatization of the university that is happening in both our societies. Spurred on by what Cynthia Enloe has termed a "feminist curiosity," we know that these conversations will surely continue.

Notes

Introduction

1. Heilbrun, *Writing a Woman's Life*, 138.
2. Ibid., 171.
3. Castells, *The Power of Identity*, 61.

Chapter 1: Race, Difference, and Disadvantage

1. Du Bois, *The Souls of Black Folk*, 3.
2. Clinton quoted Richard L. Berke, "Clinton Calls for Task Force on Race," *New York Times*, Mar. 15, 1997, 5.
3. West, *Race Matters*, 153.
4. Pollack, *Signs of Life*, 162.
5. Scott, *Gender and the Politics of History*, 52.
6. Jefferson quoted in Wilkins, "Racism Has Its Privileges," 409.
7. Foster, "Difference and Equality," 135.
8. Lerner, *Why History Matters*, 157.
9. Ibid., 28.
10. Castells, *The Power of Identity*, 59.
11. Lani Guinier, "Who's Afraid of Lani Guinier?" *New York Times*, Feb. 27, 1994, 18.
12. Cose, "Dialogue of Dishonesty," 32.
13. Hugh Price, "Keynote Address," Commonwealth Club, San Francisco, Calif., Feb. 10, 1995.
14. Sparks, *Tomorrow Is Another Country*, 189.
15. Gordimer, "Separate," 46.

16. Unsigned editorial, *New Republic,* June 30, 1997, 43.
17. Cose, *Colorblind,* 26.
18. Makgoba, *The Makgoba Affair,* 2.
19. Casper, "Affirmative Action," 1.
20. Patterson, *The Ordeal of Integration,* 147.
21. See ibid., 73–75.
22. Nettles, "The Role of Affirmative Action," 6.
23. Sandel, "Picking Winners," 123.
24. Ibid.
25. Carmel Richard, "The Affirmative Action Dilemma," *Johannesburg Sunday Times,* Mar. 9, 1997, 25.
26. Ramphele, "Affirmative Action," 5.
27. Ibid.
28. Terry Oakley-Smith, "Makgoba—South Africa's 'OJ Simpson Case,'" *Port Elizabeth Eastern Province Herald,* Dec. 13, 1995, 6.
29. Mbeki quoted in James Tomkins, "South Africa Needs Reconciliation," *Johannesburg Star,* Aug. 5, 1997, 5.
30. African National Congress, "The National Democratic Revolution," discussion document, July 1997, Cock's possession.
31. Mbeki quoted in "Thabo Mbeki Lays It on the Line to Complacent Whites," *Johannesburg Sunday Independent,* Nov. 2, 1997, 6.
32. Filatova, "The Rainbow," 48.
33. Cronin, "The African Renaissance," 8.
34. Greenstein, "Identity, Race, History," 11.
35. Wilson and Ramphele, *Uprooting Poverty,* 17.
36. Ibid., 18.
37. Mbeki quoted in Estelle Randal, "Plea for a New South Africa," *Johannesburg Saturday Star,* May 30, 1998, 2.
38. Budlender, *The Women's Budget,* 22.
39. Ibid.
40. Patterson, *Ordeal of Integration,* 155.

Chapter 2: Biodiversity

1. Wilson, "Is Humanity Suicidal?" 32.
2. Leopold, *A Sand County Almanac,* 12.
3. Devall, *Deep Ecology,* 320.
4. "A Case for Biodiversity," 14.
5. Budlender, *The Women's Budget,* 55.
6. Hynes, *The Recurring Silent Spring,* 15.
7. Carson, *Silent Spring,* 75, 205.
8. Theodore Roszak, "Green Guilt and Ecological Overload," *New York Times,* June 9, 1992, 7.
9. Reisman quoted in Terrance Roska, "Green Guilty and Ecological Overload, *New York Times,* June 9, 1992, 7.

10. Hynes, *The Recurring Silent Spring*, 6.

11. Seager, *Earth Follies*, 20.

12. Dickson, "Endangered Species," 5.

13. Ledger, "Biodiversity," 230.

14. Wilson, "Is Humanity Suicidal?" 32.

15. Lawson, *Sustainable Development for Beginners*, 11.

16. Dickson, "Endangered Species," 4.

17. Kahn, "Involvement of the Masses," 39.

18. Derek Hannekom as cited in "Our Protected Areas," *Johannesburg Star*, Sept. 11, 1994, 7.

19. Beinart and Coates, *Environment and History*, 75.

20. Ibid., 90.

21. Bullard, *Confronting Environmental Racism*, 11.

22. *Environmental Justice Networker*, no. 8 (Summer 1995): 1.

23. Ledger, "Biodiversity," 235.

24. Kahn, "Involvement of the Masses," 36.

25. Ibid., 38.

26. Weiner, *The Beak of the Finch*, 134.

27. Ibid., 202.

28. Ibid., 281.

29. Leakey quoted in Will Self, "The Dissent of Man," *London Observer Review*, Feb. 18, 1996, 4.

30. Rolston, *Environmental Ethics*, 175.

31. Darwin quoted in Weiner, *The Beak of the Finch*, 281.

32. Freud quoted in Galdikas, *Reflections of Eden*, 19.

33. van den Berghe, "Why Most Sociologists Don't," 4.

34. Rasa, *Mongoose Watch*, 13.

35. De Waal and Lanting, *Bonobo*, 35.

36. Masson and McCarthy, *When Elephants Weep*, 27.

37. Walker, "Interview," 22.

38. Snyder, *A Place in Space*, 35.

39. Beinart and Coates, *Environment and History*, 108.

40. International Fund for Animal Welfare quoted in Dickson, "Endangered Species," 3.

Chapter 3: Cultural Diversity

1. Johnson, *Major Rock Paintings*, 8.

2. Quoted in Volkman, "The Hunter-Gatherer Myth," 29.

3. Minister quoted in Volkman, "The Hunter-Gatherer Myth," 27.

4. Gusinde, "Primitive Races," 291.

5. "Endangered Bushmen Find Refuge in a Game Park," *New York Times*, Jan. 18, 1996, 3.

6. Appiah, "Why Africa? Why Art?" 6.

7. Ibid.

8. Ibid., 7.
9. Thybony, "Rock Art," 35.
10. Maybury-Lewis, *Indigenous Peoples,* 15.
11. Thornton, *American Indian Holocaust,* 11.
12. Gordon, *The Bushman Myth,* 16.
13. Ibid., 54.
14. Ibid., 43.
15. Ibid., 45.
16. Ibid., 46.
17. Ibid., 46.
18. Volkman, "The Hunter-Gatherer Myth," 28.
19. Norval, "SADF's Bushmen Battalion," 71.
20. Ibid.
21. See Bernstein, *American Indians and World War Two.*
22. Mead, *The Changing Culture,* xi.
23. Gump, *The Dust Rose like Smoke,* 3.
24. Gordon, *The Bushman Myth,* 157.
25. Pharaoh quoted in Anne Wallach, "Montauks Reclaim Culture," *Earth Times,* Jan. 15–30, 1996, 18.
26. Deloria, *Custer Died for Your Sins,* 135.
27. N. Scott Momaday, "Disturbing the Spirits," *New York Times,* Nov. 2, 1996, 23.
28. W. Richard West, "New Smithsonian American Indian Museum," *New York Times,* Oct. 4, 1994, 51.
29. Momaday, "Disturbing the Spirits," 23.
30. Ibid.

Chapter 4: Differences in Sexual Orientation

1. Duberman, *Stonewall,* 5.
2. Nava and Dawidoff, *Created Equal,* xvii.
3. Plant, *The Pink Triangle,* 43.
4. See Cammermeyer, *Serving in Silence.*
5. Scalia quoted in Linda Greenhouse, "Gay Rights Laws Can't Be Banned, High Court Rules," *New York Times,* May 26, 1996, 20.
6. See Kaplan, *Sexual Justice,* chap. 2.
7. Linda Greenhouse, "Supreme Court Backs Boy Scouts in Ban of Gays from Membership," *New York Times,* June 29, 2000, 28.
8. African Christian Democratic party, "Submission."
9. Mompati quoted in Tatchell, "Gays in South Africa," 12.
10. Thabo Mbeki to Peter Tatchell, Nov. 24, 1987, Peter Tatchell Papers, Gay and Lesbian Archives, William Cullen Library, University of the Witwatersrand, Johannesburg.
11. Peter Tatchell to Graham Read, Feb. 12, 1999, Tatchell Papers.

12. LAGO to ECC, June 25, 1987, Tatchell Papers.
13. Edwin Cameron to Ivan Toms, Feb. 10, 1989, Tatchell Papers.
14. Nkoli, "Gay Rights," 8.
15. Castle, *The Apparitional Lesbian,* 4.
16. Costello, Miles, and Stone, *The American Woman,* 301.
17. Bawer, "Editorial," 12.
18. Kushner, "A Socialism of the Skin," 9.
19. Duberman, "Reclaiming the Lesbian and Gay Past," 8.
20. See Clark and Clark, "Racial Identification."
21. For a discussion of demographics and homosexuality, see Rubin, "Thinking Sex."
22. See Brooten, *Love between Women.*
23. See ibid., 1–71.
24. Christiansen, "Ending the Apartheid of the Closet."
25. Rich, "Compulsory Heterosexuality," 228.
26. Kaye quoted in James Dao, "New York's Highest Court Rules Unmarried Couples Can Adopt," *New York Times,* Nov. 3, 1955, 1.
27. David W. Dunlap, "June 94 Produced a Record for Antigay Attacks," *New York Times,* Mar. 8, 1995, 21.
28. Glendinning, *Vita,* 205.
29. Woolf quoted in ibid.
30. Rubin, "Thinking Sex," 43.
31. Duberman, "Reclaiming the Lesbian and Gay Past," 7.
32. Cruikshank, *The Gay and Lesbian Liberation Movement,* 105.
33. Bair, *Simone de Beauvoir,* 435.
34. David W. Dunlap, "Gay Survey Raises New Questions," *New York Times,* Oct. 18, 1994, 8.
35. See Katz, *The Invention of Heterosexuality,* 19–32.
36. See Chauncey, *Gay New York,* 223–30.
37. Tavris, "Straight Talk," 34.
38. Kushner, "A Socialism of the Skin," 10.
39. Wolfe, *One Nation, after All,* 10.

Chapter 5: Gender Differences

1. Lerner, *Why History Matters,* 197.
2. Ibid., 198.
3. Letsebe and Ginwala, "Convenors' Report," 4.
4. Unpublished research report on the WNC, 11, Cock's possession.
5. Ibid.
6. Riley, *Am I That Name?* 112.
7. Braidotti, *Women,* 30.
8. Letsebe and Ginwala, "Convenors' Report," 3.
9. Ibid.

10. Riley, *Am I That Name?* 113.

11. Ibid., 100.

12. Ibid., 30.

13. Watson, "Gender Relations."

14. Kollontai, *Selected Writings,* 51.

15. Ellen Khuzwayo, "Feminism," *Johannesburg Star,* Dec. 13, 1990, 3.

16. Ramphele, "Dynamics of Gender," 185.

17. Ramphele, "Affirmative Action," 5.

18. Mouffe, "Feminism and Radical Politics," 382.

19. Ibid.

20. Jacquette, "Women in Power," 25.

21. Personal communication with Cock.

22. Chiefe Nonkonyana quoted in Finnemore, "Negotiating Power," 18.

23. Ibid., 19.

24. WNC briefing paper, 5.

25. De Hart, "Rights and Representation," 219.

26. Ibid., 223.

27. Ibid., 224.

28. Budlender, *The Women's Budget,* 56.

29. Small, "Women's Land Rights," 45.

30. Ibid., 46.

31. Morris, *Change and Continuity,* 47.

32. Ibid., 32.

33. Ashforth, "Weighing Manhood in Soweto," 55.

34. Ramphele, "Dynamics of Gender," 182.

35. Hendricks and Lewis, "Voices from the Margins," 66.

36. Baylies and Bujra, "Challenging Gender Inequalities," 5.

37. hooks, *Talking Back,* 72.

38. Davis quoted in Robert E. Pierre, "Assessing the Million Man March, *Washington Post,* Oct. 11, 1996, D5.

39. Chavis quoted in ibid.

40. West quoted in ibid.

41. Buchanan, *Choosing to Lead,* 20.

42. Locayo, "The New Gay Struggle," 33.

Chapter 6: A Feminist Perspective on Understanding Difference and Disadvantage

1. Bishop, *One Art,* 256.

2. Ibid., 259.

3. Phillips, "From Inequality to Difference," 143.

4. Harvey, *Justice,* 345.

5. Phillips, "From Inequality to Difference," 144.

6. Jackson quoted in Peter Fabricus, "True Test of Democracy Still Awaits South Africa's Rulers," *Johannesburg Star,* June 22, 1998, 4.

7. Lewis quoted in ibid.

8. Cole, *Conversations*, 117.

9. Ibid.

10. Ibid.

11. Crosby, "Dealing with Difference," 14.

12. Scott, "Deconstructing Equality," 172.

13. Crosby, "Dealing with Difference," 14.

14. West, "The New Cultural Politics of Difference," 27.

15. Braidotti, "On the Female/Feminist Subject," 181.

16. Foster, "Difference and Equality," 134.

17. Flax, "Beyond Equality." 193.

18. Pateman, "Equality, Difference, Subordination," 17.

19. Wollstonecraft, *A Vindication of the Rights of Woman*, 219.

20. Rhode, "The Politics of Paradigms," 149.

21. Schreiner, *Women and Labour*, 176.

22. Rhode, "The Politics of Paradigms," 151.

23. Lorde, *Sister Outsider*, 116.

24. Rhode, "The Politics of Paradigms," 158.

Conclusion

1. Phillips, "From Inequality to Difference," 143.

2. Ignatieff, *The Warrior's Honor*, 71.

3. Ibid., 56.

4. Scott, "The Campaign against Political Correctness," 32.

5. Roosevelt quoted in Blanche W. Cook, "Eleanor Roosevelt and the Struggle for Human Rights," unpublished ms., 7, Cock's possession.

6. Luxemburg quoted in Aleksandr Solzhenitsyn, "To Tame Savage Capitalism," *New York Times*, Nov. 28, 1993, 11.

7. Giddens, *Beyond Left and Right*, 10.

8. Ibid., 98.

9. Castells, *The Rise of the Network Society*, 3.

10. Mittelman, "The Globalization of Social Conflict," 334.

11. See Butler and Scott, *Feminists Theorize the Political*, and Hall and Jacquees, *New Times*.

12. Castells, *The Rise of the Network Society*, 3.

13. Hobsbawm, *The Age of Extremes*, 40.

14. Lorde, *Sister Outsider*, 116.

15. Cook, "Eleanor Roosevelt and the Struggle," 7.

16. West, "The New Cultural Politics of Difference," 33.

17. Giddens, *Beyond Left and Right*, 14.

18. hooks, *Talking Back*, 22.

19. Lorde, *Sister Outsider*, 112.

20. Ibid., 111.

21. Jacquette, "Women in Power."

22. Buvinic, "Women in Poverty," 42; for UNIFEM statistics see Khadija Magardie, "Women Still the Second Sex," *Johannesburg Mail and Guardian,* Dec. 23, 1999, 39.

23. Tobias, *Faces of Feminism,* 253.

24. Ibid., 257.

25. Watson, "The Rise of Masculinism in Eastern Europe," 71.

26. Baylies and Bujra, "Challenging Gender Inequalities," 4.

27. Funk and Mueller, *Gender Politics in Post Communism,* 2.

28. Racioppi and See, "Organizing Women before and after the Fall," 351.

Bibliography

Adams, Jonathan, and Thomas McShane. *The Myth of Wild Africa.* Berkeley: University of California Press, 1996.

African Christian Democratic party. "Submission to the Theme Committee on Fundamental Rights of the Constitutional Assembly." Peter Tatchell Papers. Gay and Lesbian Archives. William Cullen Library. University of the Witwatersrand. Johannesburg.

Appiah, Anthony. "Why Africa? Why Art?" In *Africa: The Art of a Continent.* New York: Guggenheim Musuem, 1996. 6–14.

Arendt, Hannah. *Eichmann in Jerusalem: A Report on the Banality of Evil.* Harmondsworth: Penguin, 1994.

Ashforth, Adam. "Weighing Manhood in Soweto." *Codesria Bulletin,* nos. 3–4 (1999): 51–58.

Bair, Deirdre. *Simone de Beauvoir: A Biography.* New York: Summit Books, 1990.

Barrett, Paul, ed. *Charles Darwin's Notebooks.* Ithaca: Cornell University Press, 1987.

Bawer, Bruce. "Editorial." *New Republic,* June 13, 1994, 12.

———. *A Place at the Table.* New York: Simon and Schuster, 1994.

Baylies, Carolyn, and Janet Bujra. "Challenging Gender Inequalities." *Review of African Political Economy* 20 (Summer 1993): 3–10.

Beinart, William, and Peter Coates. *Environment and History: The Taming of Nature in the USA and South Africa.* London: Routledge, 1995.

Bernstein, Alison R. *American Indians and World War Two: Toward a New Era in Indian Affairs.* Norman: University of Oklahoma Press, 1991.

Bishop, Elizabeth. *Exchanging Hats: Paintings.* New York: Farrar, Straus, and Giroux, 1996.

——. *One Art: Letters.* New York: Noonday Press, 1994.

Bock, Giselle, and Susan James, eds. *Beyond Equality and Difference: Citizenship, Feminist Politics, and Female Subjectivity.* New York: Routledge, 1992.

Bowen, William G., and Derek Bok. *The Shape of the River: Long-Term Consequences of Considering Race in College and University Admissions.* Princeton: Princeton University Press, 1998.

Braidotti, Rosi. "On the Female/Feminist Subject." In *Beyond Equality and Difference: Citizenship, Feminist Politics, and Female Subjectivity.* Ed. Giselle Bock and Susan James. New York: Routledge, 1992. 177–92.

——. *Women, the Environment, and Sustainable Development.* London: Zed Books, 1994.

Brooten, Bernadette J. *Love between Women: Early Christian Responses to Female Homoeroticism.* Chicago: University of Chicago Press, 1996.

Buchanan, Constance. *Choosing to Lead: Women and the Crisis of American Values.* Boston: Beacon Press, 1996.

Budlender, Debbie. *The Women's Budget.* Pretoria: Idasa, 1996.

Bullard, Robert, ed. *Confronting Environmental Racism.* Boston: South End Press, 1997.

Butler, Judith, and Joan W. Scott, eds. *Feminists Theorize the Political.* New York: Routledge, 1992.

Buvinic, Mayra. "Women in Poverty: A New Global Underclass." *Foreign Policy* 108 (Fall 1997): 38–53.

Cammermeyer, Margarethe. *Serving in Silence: The Story of Margarethe Cammermeyer.* New York: Viking, 1994.

Carson, Rachel. *Silent Spring.* Greenwich, Conn.: Fawcett, 1962.

"A Case for Biodiversity." *On Tract,* Summer 1994, 14.

Casper, Gerhard. "Affirmative Action." *Stanford University Alumni Magazine.* 1997. 1–5.

Castells, Manuel. *The Power of Identity.* London: Blackwells, 1997.

——. *The Rise of the Network Society.* Oxford: Blackwells, 1996.

Castle, Terry. *The Apparitional Lesbian: Female Homosexuality and Modern Culture.* New York: Columbia University Press, 1993.

Chauncey, George. *Gay New York: Gender, Urban Culture, and the Making of the Gay Male World, 1890–1940.* New York: Basic Books, 1994.

Christiansen, Eric C. "Ending the Apartheid of the Closet: Sexual Orientation in the South African Constitutional Process." *Journal of International Law and Politics* 32 (Summer 2000): 997–1058.

Clark, Kenneth B., and Mamie Clark. "Racial Identification and Preference in Negro Children." In *Readings in Social Psychology.* Ed. Eleanor Maccoby. Boston: Beacon, 1955. 602–11.

Cock, Jacklyn. *Maids and Madams.* Johannesburg: Ravan Press, 1980; reprint, London: Women's Press, 1989.

Cock, Jacklyn, and Eddie Koch, eds. *Going Green: People, Politics, and the Environment in South Africa.* Cape Town: Oxford University Press, 1991.

Cole, Johnnetta. *Conversations: Straight Talk from America's Sister President.* New York: Doubleday, 1993.

Cose, Ellis. *Colorblind: Seeing beyond Race in a Race-Obsessed World.* New York: HarperCollins, 1997.

———. "Dialogue of Dishonesty," *Newsweek,* June 30, 1997, 39.

Costello, Cynthia B., Shari Miles, and Anne Stone, eds. *The American Woman, 1899–2000: A Century of Change—What's Next?* New York: Norton, 1998.

Cronin, Jeremy. "The African Renaissance." *Global Dialogue,* Oct. 1997, 8.

Crosby, Christina. "Dealing with Difference." In *Feminists Theorize the Political.* Ed. Judith Butler and Joan W. Scott. New York: Routledge, 1992. 14–43.

Cruikshank, Margaret. *The Gay and Lesbian Liberation Movement.* New York: Routledge, 1992.

Dankelman, Irene, and Joan Davidson. *Women and Environment in the Third World.* London: Earthscan, 1988.

de Beauvoir, Simone. *The Second Sex.* 1949. Trans. and ed. H. M. Parshley. New York: Alfred A. Knopf, 1953.

De Hart, Jane Sherron. "Rights and Representation: Women, Politics, and Power in the Contemporary United States." In *U.S. History as Women's History: New Feminist Essays.* Ed. Linda K. Kerber, Alice Kessler-Harris, and Kathryn Kish Sklar. Chapel Hill: University of North Carolina Press, 1995. 214–45.

Deloria, Vine. *Custer Died for Your Sins: An Indian Manifesto.* New York: Delacorte Press, 1969.

Devall, Bill. *Deep Ecology.* Salt Lake City: Gibbs M. Smith, 1980.

De Waal, Francis, and Frans Lanting. *Bonobo: The Forgotten Ape.* Berkeley: University of California Press, 1997.

Dickson, Barney. "Endangered Species." *Zimbabwean* 4.1 (Jan. 1998): 3–5.

Douglas, Marjory Stoneman. *The Everglades: River of Grass.* New York: Rinehart, 1947.

Duberman, Martin. "Reclaiming the Lesbian and Gay Past." Preface to *James Baldwin* by Randall Kenan. New York: Chelsea House Press, 1994. 7–9.

———. *Stonewall.* New York: Dutton, 1993.

Du Bois, W. E. B. *The Souls of Black Folk.* New York: Modern Library, 1996.

Durning, Alan. *Apartheid's Environmental Toll.* Washington, D.C.: Worldwatch Institute, 1990.

Enloe, Cynthia. *Maneuvers: The International Politics of Militarizing Women's Lives.* Berkeley: University of California Press, 2000.

Faderman, Lilian. *Odd Girls and Twilight Lovers: A History of Lesbian Life in Twentieth-Century America.* New York: Penguin, 1992.

Faludi, Susan. *Backlash: The Undeclared War against American Women.* New York: Anchor Books, 1992.

Filatova, Irina. "The Rainbow against the African Sky." *Transformation,* no. 34 (Apr. 1977): 47–56.

Finnemore, Marianne. "Negotiating Power." *Agenda,* no. 20 (1994): 16–20.

Flax, Jane. "Beyond Equality: Gender, Justice and Difference." In *Beyond Equality and Difference: Citizenship, Feminist Politics, and Female Subjectivity.* Ed. Giselle Bock and Susan James. New York: Routledge, 1992. 193–210.

Foster, Patricia. "Difference and Equality: A Critical Assessment of the Concept of Diversity." *Wisconsin Law Review,* no. 89 (Summer 1993): 105–61.

Freeman, Martha, ed. *Always, Rachel: The Letters of Rachel Carson and Dorothy Freeman, 1952–1964.* Boston: Beacon Press, 1995.

Funk, Nanette, and Magda Mueller. *Gender Politics in Post Communism: Reflections from Eastern Europe and the Former Soviet Union.* New York: Routledge, 1993.

Galdikas, Biruté. *Reflections of Eden: My Life with the Orangutans of Borneo.* London: Indigo, 1996.

Garb, Yacob. "Change and Continuity in Environmental World-view: The Politics of Nature in Rachel Carsons's *Silent Spring.*" In *Minding Nature: The Philosophers of Ecology.* Ed. David Macauley. New York: Guilford Press, 1996. 229–56.

Garber, Margery. *Vice Versa: Bisexuality and the Eroticism of Everyday Life.* New York: Simon and Schuster, 1995.

Giddens, Anthony. *Beyond Left and Right.* Stanford: Stanford University Press, 1995.

Glendinning, Victoria. *Vita: A Biography of Vita Sackville-West.* New York: Quill, 1983.

Gordimer, Nadine. "Separate." *New York Times Magazine,* June 8, 1997, 46.

Gordon, Robert J. *The Bushman Myth: The Making of the Namibian Underclass.* Boulder: Westview Press, 1992.

Greenstein, Ran. "Identity, Race, History: South Africa and the Pan-African Context." Institute for Advanced Social Research seminar paper. Aug. 1996.

Gump, James O. *The Dust Rose like Smoke: The Subjugation of the Zulu and the Sioux.* Lincoln: University of Nebraska Press, 1994.

Gusinde, Martin. "Primitive Races Now Dying Out." *International Social Science Bulletin* 9 (1957): 291–98.

Hacker, Andrew. *Two Nations: Black and White, Separate, Hostile, Unequal.* New York: Ballantine Books, 1995.

Hall, Stuart, and Max Jacquees. *New Times: The Changing Face of Politics in the 1990's.* London: Lawrence and Wishart, 1989.

Harvey, David. *Justice, Nature, and the Geography of Difference.* Oxford: Blackwells, 1996.

Heilbrun, Carolyn G. *Writing a Woman's Life.* New York: Ballantine Books, 1989.

Hendricks, Christine, and Deidre Lewis. "Voices from the Margins." *Agenda,* no. 20 (1994): 61–75.

Hobsbawm, Eric. *The Age of Extremes.* Harmondsworth: Penguin, 1994.

hooks, bell. *Talking Back: Thinking Feminist, Thinking Black.* Boston: South End Press, 1989.

Hynes, Patricia. *The Recurring Silent Spring.* New York: Pergamon Press, 1989.

Ignatieff, Michael. *The Warrior's Honor: Ethnic War and the Modern Conscience.* New York: Metropolitan Books, 1997.

Jacquette, Jane. "Women in Power: From Tokenism to Critical Mass." *Foreign Policy,* no. 108 (Fall 1997): 23–37.

Johnson, R. Townley. *Major Rock Paintings of Southern Africa: Facsimile Reproductions.* Cape Town: David Philip, 1986.

Kahn, Farieda. "Involvement of the Masses in Environmental Politics." *Veld and Flora* 12 (June 1990): 36–39.

Kaiser, Charles. *The Gay Metropolis: 1940–1996.* Boston: Houghton Mifflin, 1997.

Kaplan, Morris B. *Sexual Justice: Democratic Citizenship and the Politics of Desire.* New York: Routledge, 1997.

Katz, Jonathan Ned. *The Invention of Heterosexuality.* New York: E. P. Dutton, 1995.

Kollontai, Alexandra. *Selected Writings.* London: Allison and Busby, 1992.

Kushner, Tony. "A Socialism of the Skin." *Nation,* July 4, 1994, 9–12.

Lamar, Howard, and Leonard Thompson. *The Frontier in History: North America and South Africa Compared.* New Haven: Yale University Press, 1981.

Lawson, Leslie. *Sustainable Development for Beginners.* Johannesburg: Group for Environmental Monitoring, 1991.

———. *Working Women.* Johannesburg: Ravan Press, 1984.

Ledger, John. "Biodiversity: The Basis of Life." In *Going Green: People, Politics, and the Environment.* Ed. Jacklyn Cock and Eddie Koch. Cape Town: Oxford University Press, 1991. 230–41.

Leopold, Aldo. *A Sand County Almanac, with Essays on Conversation from Round River.* New York: Ballantine Books, 1996.

Lerner, Gerda. *Why History Matters: Life and Thought.* New York: Oxford University Press, 1997.

Letsebe, Anne, and Frene Ginwala. "Convenors' Report to the National Conference of the Women's National Coalition." 25–27 Feb. 1994.

Locayo, Richard. "The New Gay Struggle." *Time,* Oct. 26, 1998, 32–36.

Lorde, Audre. *The Black Unicorn: Poems.* New York: Norton, 1978.

———. *Sister Outsider: Essays and Speeches.* Trumansberg, N.Y.: Crossing Press, 1984.

Lowton, Rachel. *Mary Anning: Family and Friends.* Dorset: Creeds, 1997.

Makgoba, William. *The Makgoba Affair: A Reflection on Transformation.* Johannesburg: Vivlia, 1997.

Masson, Jeffrey Moussaieff, and Susan McCarthy. *When Elephants Weep: The Emotional Lives of Animals.* New York: Delacorte Press, 1995.

Maybury-Lewis, David. *Indigenous Peoples, Ethnic Groups, and the State.* Boston: Allyn and Bacon, 1997.

Mead, Margaret. *The Changing Culture of an Indian Tribe.* New York: Putnam, 1966.

Mittelman, James. "The Globalization of Social Conflict." *Conflict and New Departures in World Society.* Ed. Bornschier Volker and Peter Lengyel. New Brunswick, N.J.: Transaction Publishers, 1994. 3:317–55.

Moon, Brenda. *A Vision of Eden: The Life and Work of Marianne North.* Exeter: Webb and Bower, 1980.

Morgan, Robin, ed. *Sisterhood Is Powerful: An Anthology of Writings from the Women's Liberation Movement.* New York: Vintage Books, 1970.

Morris, Alan, ed. *Change and Continuity: A Survey of Soweto in the Late 1990s.* Johannesburg: Department of Sociology, University of the Witwatersrand, 1999.

Mouffe, Chantelle. "Feminism and Radical Politics." In *Feminists Theorize the Political.* Ed. Judith Butler and Joan W. Scott. New York: Routledge, 1992. 369–84.

Myrdal, Gunnar. *An American Dilemma: The Negro Problem and Modern Democracy.* New York: Harper and Brothers, 1944.

Nava, Michael, and Robert Dawidoff. *Created Equal: Why Gay Rights Matter to America.* New York: St. Martin's Press, 1994.

Nettles, Michael T. "The Role of Affirmative Action in Expanding Student Access at Selective Colleges and Universities." Report for the Frederick D. Patterson Research Institute of the United Negro College Fund. Oct. 1997.

Nkoli, Simon. "Gay Rights." *Equality* 1 (Mar. 1995): 5–8.

North, Marianne. *Recollections of a Happy Life.* Exeter: Webb and Bower, 1980.

Norval, Martin. "SADF's Bushmen Battalion: Primitive Trackers Fight Twentieth Century War." *Soldier of Fortune,* Mar. 1981, 71.

Pateman, Carol. "Equality, Difference, Subordination: The Politics of Motherhood and Women's Citizenship." In *Beyond Equality and Difference: Citizenship, Feminist Politics, and Female Subjectivity.* Ed. Giselle Bock and Susan James. New York: Routledge, 1992. 17–31.

Patterson, Orlando. *The Ordeal of Integration: Progress and Resentment in America's "Racial" Crisis.* Washington, D.C.: Civitas, 1997.

Pemberton, Gail. *The Hottest Water in Chicago: On Family, Race, Time, and American Culture.* Boston: Faber and Faber, 1992.

Phillips, Anne. "From Inequality to Difference: A Severe Case of Displacement." *New Left Review* 224 (Summer 1997): 143–53.

Plant, Richard. *The Pink Triangle: The Nazi War against Homosexuals.* New York: Henry Holt, 1988.

Pollack, Robert. *Signs of Life: The Language and Meaning of DNA.* Boston: Houghton Mifflin, 1994.

Racioppi, Linda, and Katherine O'Sullivan See. "Organizing Women before and after the Fall: Women's Politics in the Soviet Union and Post Soviet Russia." *Signs: Journal of Women in Culture and Society* 20.41 (1995): 340–53.

Ramphele, Mamphela. *Across Boundaries: The Journey of a South African Woman Leader.* New York: Feminist Press, 1996.

———. "Affirmative Action." *Democracy in Action* 9.2 (Apr. 1995): 4–6.

———. "Dynamics of Gender within Black Consciousness Organizations." In *Bounds of Possibility: The Legacy of Steve Biko and Black Consciousness.* Ed. Barney Pityana. Cape Town: David Phillip, 1992. 180–92.

Rasa, Anna. *Mongoose Watch: A Family Observed.* London: John Murray, 1984.

Rhode, Deborah. "The Politics of Paradigms: Gender Difference and Gender Disadvantage." In *Beyond Equality and Difference: Citizenship, Feminist Politics, and Female Subjectivity.* Ed. Giselle Bock and Susan James. New York: Routledge, 1992. 149–63.

Rich, Adrienne. "Compulsory Heterosexuality and Lesbian Existence." In *The Lesbian and Gay Studies Reader.* Ed. Henry Abelove, Michele Aina Barele, and David Halpern. New York: Routledge, 1993. 227–54.

Riley, Denise. *"Am I That Name?": Feminism and the Category of "Women" in History.* Minneapolis: University of Minnesota Press, 1988.

Rolston, Holmes. *Environmental Ethics.* Philadelphia: Temple University Press, 1988.

Rubin, Gayle S. "Thinking Sex: Notes for a Radical Theory of the Politics of Sexuality." In *The Lesbian and Gay Studies Reader.* Ed. Henry Abelove, Michele Aina Barele, and David Halpern. New York: Routledge, 1993. 3–45.

Sandel, Michael. "Picking Winners." *Atlantic Monthly,* Feb. 1996, 121–27.

Schreiner, Olive. *Women and Labour.* London: Unwin, 1911.

Schullery, Paul. *Searching for Yellowstone: Ecology and Wonder in the Last Wilderness.* Boston: Houghton Mifflin, 1997.

Scott, Joan W. "The Campaign against Political Correctness: What's Really at Stake." *Change* 17 (Nov. 1991): 30–43.

———. "Deconstructing Equality versus Difference; or, The Uses of Poststructuralist Theory for Feminism." *Feminist Studies* 14.1 (1988): 33–50.

———. *Gender and the Politics of History.* New York: Columbia University Press, 1988.

———. *Only Paradoxes to Offer: French Feminists and the Rights of Man.* Cambridge, Mass.: Harvard University Press, 1996.

Seager, Joni. *Earth Follies: Coming to Feminist Terms with the Global Environmental Crisis.* New York: Routledge, 1993.

Skotnes, Pippa, ed. *Miscast: Negotiating the Present of the Bushmen.* Cape Town: University of Cape Town Press, 1996.

Sleeper, Jim. *Liberal Racism.* New York: Viking, 1997.

Small, Janet. "Women's Land Rights." In *Women, Land, and Authority.* Ed. Shamin Meer. Cape Town: David Phillip, 1997. 45–54.

Snyder, Gary. *A Place in Space.* Washington, D.C.: Counterpoint, 1995.

Sparks, Alister. *Tomorrow Is Another Country: The Inside Story of South Africa's Negotiated Revolution.* Pretoria: Struik Books, 1994.

Stein, Gertrude. *The Autobiography of Alice B. Toklas.* New York: Vintage Books, 1990.

———. *Everybody's Autobiography.* Cambridge: Exact Change, 1993.

———. *Wars I Have Seen.* New York: Random House, 1945.

Stendhal, Renate. *Gertrude Stein in Words and Pictures: A Photobiography.* Chapel Hill: Algonquin Books, 1994.

Sullivan, Andrew. *Virtually Normal: An Argument about Homosexuality.* New York: Alfred A. Knopf, 1995.

Tatchell, Peter. "Gays in South Africa." *Labour Briefing,* no. 49 (Oct. 1987): 12–27.

Tavris, Carol. "Straight Talk." *New York Times Book Review,* Apr. 16, 1995, 34.

Thernstrom, Stephen, and Abigail Thernstrom. *America in Black and White.* New York: Simon and Schuster, 1997.

Thornton, Russell. *American Indian Holocaust and Resurgence: A Population History since 1492.* Norman: University of Oklahoma Press, 1995.

Thybony, Scott. "Rock Art." *Native Peoples* (Fall–Winter 1995): 35.

Tobias, Sheila. *Faces of Feminism: An Activist's Reflections on the Women's Movement.* Boulder: Westview Press, 1997.

van den Berghe, Pierre. "Why Most Sociologists Don't (and Won't) Think Evolutionarily." Paper presented at the annual meeting of the Association for Sociology in South Africa. University of the Witwatersrand. Johannesburg. July 1989.

van der Post, Laurens. *The Lost World of the Kalahari.* 1958. London: Chatto and Windus, 1988.

Volkman, Toby. "The Hunter-Gatherer Myth." *Cultural Survival Quarterly* 10.2 (1991): 26–30.

Walker, Alice. "Interview." *Animal Rights* 3 (Aug. 1984): 21–23.

Watson, Peggy. "Gender Relations, Education, and Social Change in Poland." *Gender and Education* 4.1–2 (1992): 127–47.

———. "The Rise of Masculinism in Eastern Europe." *New Left Review,* no. 198 (Mar.–Apr. 1993): 71–82.

Weiner, Jonathan. *The Beak of the Finch.* New York: Vintage Books, 1995.

West, Cornel. "The New Cultural Politics of Difference." In *Breaking Bread: Insurgent Black Intellectual Life* by bell hooks and Cornel West. Boston: South End Press, 1991. 19–36.

——. *Race Matters.* New York: Vintage Books, 1994.

Wilkins, Roger. "Racism Has Its Privileges: The Case for Affirmative Action." *The Nation,* Mar. 27, 1995, 409–12.

Wilmsen, Edwin N. *Land Filled with Flies: A Political Economy of the Kalahari.* Chicago: University of Chicago Press, 1989.

Wilson, Edward. "Is Humanity Suicidal?" *New York Times Magazine,* May 30, 1993, 30–32.

Wilson, Francis, and Mamphela Ramphele. *Uprooting Poverty: The South African Challenge.* Cape Town: David Phillip, 1989.

Wolfe, Alan. *One Nation, after All: What Middle-Class Americans Really Think about God, Country, Family, Racism, Welfare, Immigration, Homosexuality, Work, the Right, the Left, and Each Other.* New York: Viking, 1998.

Wollstonecraft, Mary. *A Vindication of the Rights of Woman.* Harmondsworth: Penguin, 1975.b

Woolf, Virginia. *Orlando.* Oxford: Blackwell, 1998.

——. *A Room of One's Own.* New York: Harcourt Brace Jovanovich, 1991.

——. *To the Lighthouse.* New York: Routledge, 1994.

Index

American Indians, 102–6, 108–9;
and archeological research, 104,
108; creationism of, 104, 108;
cultural identities of, 103–4, 108;
federal recognition of, 102–3;
gambling casinos of, 106; holocaust of, 93; military service of,
100; repatriation to, 104; rock art
of, 91–93; and tribal sovereignty,
93, 95, 101, 104, 108. *See also*
specific tribes
ANC. *See* African National Congress
Ancestral names: retention of, 23
Animals: and animal rights movement, 65, 67–68, 81; evolution of,
76–77, 82; fur trade, 65; and human exceptionalism, 77; ivory
trade, 67–68, 81–82; people compared to, 14; vivisection of, 80.
See also Biodiversity
Anthony, Susan B., 140
Anthropocentrism, 77, 81
Anthropomorphism, 80
Apartheid: as affirmative action
program, 28; disclosures about,
15–16; and environmental racism,
73–74; and family life, 62; homeland system of, 62; legacy of, 37;
national liberation movement
vs., 116; pass system of, 105; per-
vasiveness of, 157; politics of difference under, 148; racial exclusions in, 21; racial focus of, 19;
racial oppression in, 12, 14; reparation for, 53; transition to democracy from, 149, 164
Appiah, Anthony, 90
Arendt, Hannah, 8–9
Ashforth, Adam, 169
Auschwitz concentration camp, 8

Backlash (Faludi), 173
Bair, Deidre, 142
Baldwin, James, 117, 140

Bali: cultural diversity in, 87–88
Barnard, Ferdi, 15
Basson, Wouter, 16
Bawer, Bruce, 133
Baylies, Carolyn, 208
Beahr v. Levin, 125
Beauvoir, Simone de, 142–43
Bering Strait: land bridge of, 104,
108
Bernstein, Hilda, 112
Bernstein, Rusty, 112
Biodiversity, 54–83; and animal
rights, 65, 67–68, 81; complexity
in, 56; consumerism vs., 65, 67–
69; defined, 55–56; economic
value of, 56, 61; and ecotourism,
56, 59–60, 70, 75; elite male dominance in, 65; environmental
degradation vs., 54–55, 62–64,
68–69, 72–75; and environmental
justice, 73; and environmental
racism, 72–74; extinction vs., 55,
68–69, 84; feminist lens applied
to, 61–65; and global warming,
55; and green movements, 64–65,
66; and habitat destruction, 55,
63, 68, 69, 74; and human rights,
65, 71–72, 74; and new environmentalism, 75; and "Noah Principle," 55; and overpopulation, 74;
politics of, 66–69, 71, 75; protected areas of, 69, 71–72; in rich vs.
poor nations, 66–69, 71; and sustainable utilization, 66–67, 72;
and wilderness, 66, 75. *See also*
Environment, dangers to
Bird, Isabella, 203
Bisexuality, 111, 138. *See also* Heterosexuality; Homosexuality
Bishop, Elizabeth, 2, 121, 176, 178
"Blessing, The" (Lorde), 189
Bok, Derek, 43–44
Bopape, Stanza, 15
"Boston marriages," 116

102; in Venice ghetto, 94; and women's rights, 108–9

Culture: defined, 92–93; and language, 23, 92–93, 179

Daly, Mary, 61

Darwin, Charles, 76, 77

David-Neel, Alexandra, 200, 202

Davis, Angela, 172

Dawidoff, Robert, 113

Death penalty: abolishment of, 112; reinstatement of, 180

Debt for Nature, 60

Defense of Marriage Act (1996; United States), 125

DeGeneres, Ellen, 122

De Hart, Jane Sherron, 166, 167

"Delmas" treason trial (South Africa), 128

Deloria, Vine, 103

Democracy: and nationalism, 21; transition from apartheid to, 149, 164

Devall, Bill, 56

De Waal, Francis, 80

Diallo, Amadou, 19, 52

Dickerman, Marion, 198

Difference: categories of, 144; celebration of, 146, 163, 179; defined, 141, 177; dimensions of, 195; and disadvantage, 2, 3, 7, 176–91, 205, 208; and diversity, 3, 179, 183, 185–86, 195–96; and equality, 184, 186, 187, 190–91; and exclusion, 199; insistence on, 151; politics of, 19–28, 148; poststructural analysis of, 184; power relations of, 195; social justice in, 196; solidarity vs., 163–64, 171–72. *See also* Gender differences; Homosexuality; Race

Disadvantage: in class, race, or ethnicity, 177, 179, 183, 195; and difference, 2, 3, 7, 176–91, 205, 208; in diversity, 183, 185–86; and equal rights feminism, 190–91; and native pluralism, 184; of poverty, 179–80; in traditional gender roles, 186–87; wealth gap, 47, 50, 179, 199, 210

Diversity: as aim of affirmative action, 33–34; as contested concept, 183–86; and difference, 3, 179, 183, 185–86, 195–96; disadvantage in, 183, 185–86; excellence enhanced by, 41; fight to sustain, 146; genocide as attack on, 8–9; management of, 152; and national identity, 47, 196; and progress, 180, 183; as reality, 177, 194; and sense of community, 204–5; and social class, 177, 179; support for, 38–39; among women, 108–9, 150, 156. *See also* Biodiversity; Cultural diversity; Race

Domestic violence, 169, 187

Douglas, Marjory Stoneman, 63

Duberman, Martin, 141

Du Bois, W. E. B., 11–12

Eagle Forum (United States), 166–67

Earth Summit, Rio (1992), 66–67

Ecofeminism, 61–62

Ecosystems. *See* Biodiversity

Ecotourism, 56, 59–60, 70, 75

Educational system: affirmative action in, 29, 32–34, 35–36, 39, 41–42, 43; cultural capital lacking in, 40; desegregation of, 180; homophobic backlash in, 139; illiteracy in, 168

Eichmann, Adolph, 8

End Conscription Campaign (ECC; South Africa), 129

Enloe, Cynthia, 136–37, 210

Entitlement, 164

Environment, dangers to: chemical and biological weapons, 15–16; global warming, 55; habitat destruction, 55, 63, 68, 69, 74; lead, 72; multinational corporations, 75; overpopulation, 74; pesticides, 64, 69; pharmaceuticals, 56; pollution, 63, 68, 69, 72, 73, 75; soil erosion, 68; toxic waste, 63, 72, 73, 75; urbanization, 75. *See also* Biodiversity

Environmental Justice Networking Forum (South Africa), 73

Equal rights: and affirmative action, 29, 33, 38–39; and gender issues, 164–67, 172, 190–91; and sexual orientation, 146

Equal Rights Amendment, 164–67, 172

Ethnicity: disadvantage in, 177, 183; as process, 18; as social construct, 18–19

Ethnonationalist movements, 18–19, 85

Ethology, 76, 77

Everglades: destruction of, 63

Evert, Chris, 117

Evolution, 76–77, 82

Extinction of species, 55, 68–69, 84

Faderman, Lilian, 115

Faludi, Susan, 173

Family, changing nature of, 139, 172, 173

Farrakhan, Louis, 20, 172

Female genital mutilation, 108

Feminism, 4–6; backlash against, 173, 207–8; breaking silence in, 209; contamination of term, 157, 158, 161; ecofeminism, 61–62; elitist, 40, 158; equal rights, 190–91; and Equal Rights Amendment, 164–67, 172; focus on biodiversity, 61–65; focus on gender differences, 169, 171–72; focus on race, 31–32, 40, 169, 171–72; in global terms, 5–6; in historic mo-

ments, 6, 116; later stages of, 207; leadership sought for, 200; and lesbianism, 161; narrow focus of, 167; in personal terms, 6; and political activity, 162, 164–67, 173, 174, 175, 206; in post-apartheid South Africa, 167–69, 171; postmodernist, 171; in post-Reagan era, 171–75; power of, 6; right-wing, 40; and sense of community, 204–5; successes of, 173–74; and traditional gender roles, 165

Fields, Annie, 58

Filatova, Irina, 48

Fires in the Mirror (Smith), 25

First, Ruth, 112, 158, 160

Flax, Jane, 186

Fossey, Dian, 78, 80, 83

Foster, Patricia, 17

Franklin, Benjamin, 76

Freeman, Dorothy, 57–58

Freud, Sigmund, 77

Frontier in History, The (Lamar and Thompson), 101

Funk, Nanette, 208

Fur trade, 65

Galdikas, Biruté, 78, 80, 83

Garber, Margery, 138

Gay and Lesbian Organization of the Witwatersrand (GLOW), 129

Gay Association of South Africa (GASA), 128–29

Gay Liberation Front (United States), 111

Gay Pride March (New York City), 111, 113, 138

Gays and lesbians. *See* Homosexuality

Gelhorn, Martha, 203

Gender: coining of term, 13; as process, 18; and racial profiling, 52; as relational identity, 147–48; sex vs., 13

Gender differences, 147–75; celebration of, 163–64; and Equal Rights Amendment, 164–67, 172; feminism and, 157, 158, 161; inequality in, 153, 162–63, 167–69, 171–75; solidarity vs., 163–64, 171–72; traditional roles and, 165, 167, 186–87; in wages, 168, 173, 174; and women's coalition, 148–53, 154–55, 156, 162; and women's issues, 151, 156, 158, 161, 164–67, 168, 172–75

Genital mutilation, 108

Genocide: in Holocaust, 8–9, 114–15; of "surplus people," 16

Giddens, Anthony, 199, 204

Ginsburg, Ruth Bader, 174

Ginwala, Frene, 40, 153, 154, 156, 162

Glass Ceiling Commission (United States), 50

Globalization: changing politics in, 48; era of, 4; and feminism, 5–6; fundamentalist movements in, 199; impact on women, 205; market forces in, 200; paradox of, 197, 199, 208; as post-traditional social order, 199; state autonomy reduced by, 200

Global warming, 55

Gomes, Peter, 136

Goniwe, Matthew, 159

Goodall, Jane, 78–79, 80, 83

Gordimer, Nadine, 11, 23

Gordon, Robert J., 95, 102

Greenhouse, Linda, 125

Green movements, 64–65, 66

Greenstein, Ran, 49

Griffin, Susan, 61

Grumbach, Doris, 118

Guinier, Lani, 19

Gulf War (1991), 122

Gwala, Harry, 16

Habitat destruction, 55, 63, 68, 69, 74

Hacker, Andrew, 50

Hague Appeal for Peace (1999), 126

Hall, Stuart, 199

Han culture (China), 86

Hani, Chris, 21

Harvey, David, 177

Heilbrun, Carolyn G., 5, 6

Hendricks, Christine, 169, 171

Hernandez, Aileen, 165–66

Heterosexuality: defined, 143–44. *See also* Bisexuality; Homosexuality

Heye, George Gustave, 104

Hickok, Lorna, 58

Hill, Anita, 181

Hinduism, 87

Hobsbawm, Eric, 199

Holocaust, 8–9, 114–15; defined, 93

Homer, Winslow, 102

Homophobia: roots of word, 114, 143

Homosexuality, 110–46; and adopting a child, 138–39; advocates of assimilation of, 145–46; backlash against, 138, 139, 144–45; and the Bible, 130, 135–36; as condition vs. construction, 132, 135–46, 143; defined, 143; and feminism, 161; gay rights movement, 111, 113, 115, 116, 128–29, 133–34, 138–40, 142, 143; hate and bias crimes, 137; historical roots of, 114–17, 122; and homophobia, 114, 143; in legal context, 115, 123–25, 127–29, 131–35; in military, 117, 122, 136–37; and Nazi party, 114–15; as progressive phenomenon, 133; same-sex marriages, 116, 125, 131; and social justice, 134; and suicide, 134; tolerance for, 114

hooks, bell, 171, 204

Yanomani Indians (Brazil), 85
Yellowstone National Park (United
  States), 71–72
Yosemite National Park (United
  States), 71

Zimbabwe University, 22
Zulu (South African tribe): ethnic
  violence of, 48; interviews of, 35;
  nationalism of, 19, 21; tribal powers of, 95, 101

Jacklyn Cock is a professor of
sociology at the University of the
Witwatersrand in South Africa.

Alison Bernstein is the vice
president of the Education,
Media, Arts, and Culture Program
with the Ford Foundation in
New York City.

The University of Illinois Press
is a founding member of the
Association of American
University Presses.

———————————————

Composed in 9/13 Stone Serif
with Stone Sans display
by Jim Proefrock
at the University of Illinois Press
Designed by Copenhaver Cumpston
Manufactured by Thomson-Shore, Inc.

University of Illinois Press
1325 South Oak Street
Champaign, IL 61820-6903
www.press.uillinois.edu